Highland Journal

1. The making of a hillwalker

Jack P Harland

Matador
9 Priory Business Park,
Wistow Road, Kibworth Beauchamp,
Leicestershire. LE8 0RX
Tel: 0116 279 2299
Email: books@troubador.co.uk
Web: www.troubador.co.uk/matador
Twitter: @matadorbooks

ISBN 978 1789013 252

British Library Cataloguing in Publication Data.
A catalogue record for this book is available from the British Library.

Printed and bound by CPI Group (UK) Ltd, Croydon, CR0 4YY
Typeset in 12pt Minion Pro by Troubador Publishing Ltd, Leicester, UK

Matador is an imprint of Troubador Publishing Ltd

To Bogle

Contents

Contents

Foreword

The sketch maps illustrating the walks in this journal should not be used for navigation, an Ordnance Survey map (or similar) should always be taken.

I have shared many happy days in the mountains with the best of friends and, with a few exceptions, have changed their names to protect their privacy.

Introduction

I had never seen a landscape like that on either side of the long, twisting single track road. Strange rock towers rose from a hundred sparkling lochs in a frozen sea of ancient rock. The light and colour shifted, chameleon-like, on the mountains.

We stopped on the crest of the hill overlooking the crofting village of Polbain. Jim Muir was at work restoring his lovely old boat. At the low cottage, we sat in the sun on the lawn drinking tea made by Jim's wife, Jean, enjoying one of the finest views in the country. We told her that we would be sad to leave. She pointed to a little white cottage by the shore that looked out over this panorama of mountains, islands and sea and said that Jim rented it out. Half an hour later we were drinking more tea in the Muir's kitchen and had booked the first of our many happy holidays there.

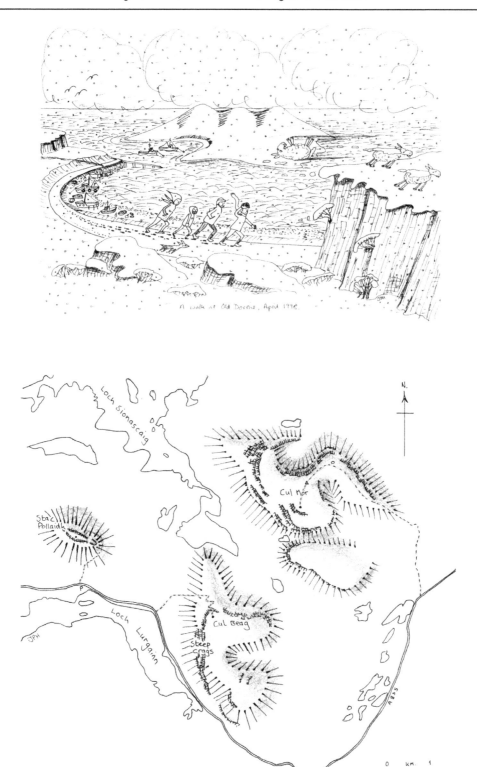

A walk at Old Dornie, April 1998.

Cul Mor, Cul Beag and Stac Pollaidh.

Once, at Easter, we got cruel weather. The wind was in the north and snow fell. Once, we got a fortnight of sun and drought. The spring that provided our water dried up and we spent lazy days swimming in the sea and sunbathing on the hot rocks. Mostly, though, the days had that peculiar mix of simultaneous sunshine and rain so characteristic of the North-west Highlands.

Those strange towers of rock we had seen from the road on that very first day called to my son Tom and me and exploring them began a passion for Scotland's mountains that has lasted to this day. The first we climbed were Stac Pollaidh, Cul Beag and Cul Mor.

Stac Pollaidh

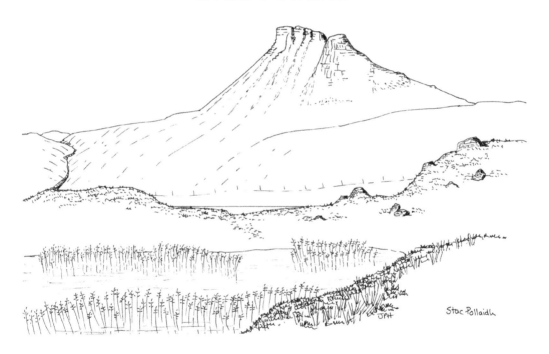

Stac Pollaidh

From the car park it looks impregnable. Sheer walls of Torridonian sandstone soar upwards to end in a skyline of pinnacles like a flesh-eating dinosaur's jaw. The path that winds around the east side of the mountain to deliver walkers to the summit from the north had not been made so Tom and I went straight up from the south. It was hard work but worth it as the views moved us to silence. A scatter of extraordinary, almost vertically-sided mountains made of the same rock as Stac Pollaidh rise from a bare floor of ancient Lewisian gneiss. They used to be protected by hard caps of Cambrian quartzite but this only remains on Canisp, with fragments on Cul Mor and Quinag. It has long gone from Stac Pollaidh, allowing weathering and erosion to create this fantastic mountain with its broken and spiky top.

Tom at 15 was in his youthful prime and he scaled the dizzy pinnacles like a circus acrobat, providing photographs that I was nervous about his mother seeing. We worked our way west to what seemed the highest point and I stopped on the brink of a deep, narrow chasm with a large rounded boulder beyond. To get round and over the boulder meant leaning back as there is an overhang. The drop beneath took my breath away. Tom edged round without a thought, I hesitated. The grizzled faces of two septuagenarians appeared over the top of the boulder and I was advised, in a broad Glasgow accent that, "If we can dae it, son, so can you!"

Five years later we met a team of climbers on Suilven who had come up the east wall of the ridge. They said that they had been disappointed not to get past the overhang on Stac Pollaidh to get to its west summit. Two years after that Tom returned with his girlfriend and found, to his horror, that he'd lost his nerve for that same overhang.

I have returned to Stac Pollaidh but will not go up again. This honeypot of a mountain is literally being worn away by the feet of those who come to climb it. Jim Muir knew it many years ago as a young man and he told me of the bright green lawn that used to cap the summit, now, thanks to the number of visitors, no more than a distant memory.

Cul Beag

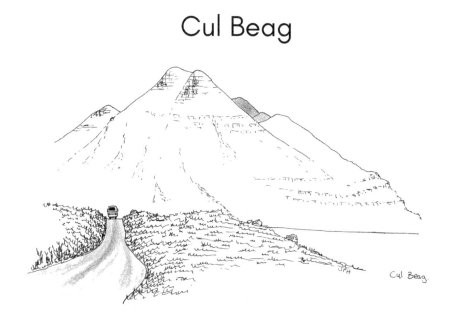

Cul Beag.

Stac Pollaidh's name is from the Norse and easy to understand, meaning the stack (as in a sea stack) by the pool. Cul Beag means little back, while Cul Mor means big back. Back of what? Gaelic is often obscure.

Tom and I had determined to climb Cul Beag next. We worked out where to park the car (not easy as it is a cardinal sin to leave a car in a passing place) and set off. The mountain is a sharp-pointed, steep-sided pyramid of rock from the west, with no obvious route to the top. We picked our way through heather and boulders, soon reaching bare rock. Although numbers climbing Cul Beag are tiny when compared to its neighbour, Stac Pollaidh, enough had made the climb to create a narrow path that zig zagged to the summit. This is very steep indeed, not a place to stumble or slip.

Breathless and with heart hammering against my ribcage I reached the top to be surprised by a perfect little bright green lawn. Tom was lying flat on his back enjoying the sun and waiting patiently. He sprang up when I arrived, declared this little lawn on one of Sutherland's most stunning mountains as heaven and did some cartwheels to show how he felt. We went to the south-west edge of the lawn and sat with our legs dangling over the cliff that falls dramatically to the road with its tiny vehicles far below. The views over Loch Lurgainn, Ben Mor Coigach and the sea beyond were wonderful and we lingered over our lunch to soak in all this beauty.

All good things must end, however, and we decided to go down. Neither of us liked the idea of descending that precipitous little path on the north-west side, so we decided to go down the relatively gentler south-east side and work our way south-west down to the road, where we could easily walk back to our starting point. Happy and chatting, we explored the wild country on that side of the mountain, never consulting our map nor considering that there could be problems ahead. We kept glancing at the sun as there was to be an eclipse that afternoon. Had we looked at the map, we would have seen the line of crags marked and remembered looking up at them as we had driven past.

Down we went over the first low crag and dropped onto the wide, grassy ledge below. Then down the next, rather larger crag and onto a rather narrower ledge.

I had not read Samuel Taylor Coleridge's account of his descent of Scafell Pike by Broad Stand or I might have decided at that point that we should stop, look at the map and go back to find a safer route down. Coleridge had found each giant rock step steeper than the last as he descended. He hung by his arms from the lip of a crag before dropping dangerously onto a very narrow ledge. That was the point of no return, he was committed to going down this rock wall. He dropped down onto more narrow ledges, each drop now turning his legs to jelly, until he was stuck. There was nothing more to drop down onto. Some would not have lived to tell the tale, but Coleridge calmed his mind, gained control of his fear and carefully examined the ledge. He noticed a narrow chimney in the rock, took off his rucksack and squeezed himself into this crack. It was the move that got him safely off the mountain.

Tom and I dropped down progressively bigger rock steps onto ledges that were narrowing, exactly as Coleridge had done all those years before. At one point I stopped and suggested it might be safer to return before we could not. Tom, with all the confidence of youth, could not entertain this suggestion. I should, of course, have insisted.

We dropped again and then again and at that point the descent became something we had not expected. We could not go back up and it looked scary indeed below our tiny grassy ledge. It was a climb down the vertical rock face or sit where we were. Our pride overcame our fear and we knew what we must do.

Tom decided that his rucksack would be a burden and dropped it over the edge. This, of course, is not to be recommended. Those who set off with the idea of surviving a day in the mountains generally hold onto their rucksacks. Tom's decision, however, did not help my agitated state of mind because I watched the rucksack fall for what seemed a very long time. It became a small speck before it crashed onto a rock outcrop, jumped in the air, crashed again, jumped again and then disappeared from sight. We both stared in silence, there was no need to say what we felt about a slip that would allow gravity to do its thing and ensure that we had the same unpleasant descent as the rucksack.

Although this was an early moment in my mountain climbing career, it was a turning point. I became aware that I needed to focus exclusively on my task. I must switch off everything else to gain the necessary control. The jelly-like feeling in my legs began to fade away to be replaced with a new strength. I looked over the edge and could see a number of good holds. Over I went and slowly, steadily, began to climb down.

At the foot of each pitch of two or three metres I talked Tom down from hold to hold. It was oddly warm, I was wet with sweat. The air was still and there was a strange feeling to it. The midges found us and began to bite. It was uncomfortable and exhausting, but I was climbing calmly and with growing confidence.

Down at last at the place where Tom's rucksack had ended up, we were out of danger. I looked back up in awe at the cliff we had descended. A marvellous feeling of satisfaction and wellbeing flooded over me. The sun was shining, the sky was blue, the birds were calling and the breeze brought the sharp smell of the sea. All my senses were heightened.

We walked and scrambled down the remaining crags to the road and when we got there paused to look back at our line of descent. We could not have chosen a more difficult route. I wondered whether the element of danger in climbing mountains is part of the attraction. From that day I have worked hard to minimise risk but however well prepared a walker is, the mountains are hazardous.

Tom and I walked happily along the road to the car. He stopped suddenly and asked me to look at my watch. We had missed the eclipse. It had happened when we were climbing down the cliff, completely involved and shutting out everything not essential to our survival.

I have experienced this same dislocation many times since that day on Cul Beag. When faced with a situation demanding total concentration, my mind relinquishes its firm hold on time. The lurch from the secure to the potentially dangerous seems to plunge me into another dimension where the normal rhythms of life do not apply.

Mountains are not my wife's thing. If she reads this she will be surprised. Some details are best forgotten when home again and telling the tale.

Cul Mor

Cul Mor

Viewed from Stac Pollaidh, Cul Mor, beloved by poet Norman MacCaig, is an impressive mountain. It rises in perpendicular fashion on all sides from the ancient floor of the strange country of Assynt. This area is regarded by many as the best landscape to be found in the British Isles. It is a marvellously wild place of cnocs and lochans, with the Lewisian gneiss outcropping through the blanket of peat that covers much of it. Rising abruptly from this outlandish landscape of water and thousands of small knobbly hills are the breathtakingly odd mountains. They stand like lighthouses, each separate from its neighbour, with views of Stac Pollaidh, Suilven and their kin among the most photographed of the Highlands. Cul Mor lies at the heart of it all.

Tom and I planned to climb Cul Mor on first seeing it from Stac Pollaidh. From that direction, the mountain resembles an impregnable giant's fortress, with three sharp peaks rising from its walls. We parked just past the visitor centre for the Knockan Cliff, went through the little gate and followed a well-made path that goes north and then west to access the massive shoulder of Meallan Diomhain. We had picked a fine day of blue sky with a few white cumulus clouds racing on a strong north-westerly wind. In the lee of the mountain, the wind was no problem.

The top of Meallan Diomhain is a great place to explore. The exposed Torridonian sandstone has been weathered over long ages so that drifts of sand lie around the bases of distinctive tors. The strong winds of the North-west have picked up these hard grains and sand blasted the tors so that they resemble giant stacks of soda bread.

There is a little lochan with a perfect beach but it was a bit too breezy to lie and sunbathe.

The highest point is 849 metres but seems loftier than many a Munro. We made our way up a very steep slope, commenting on the change to the hard Cambrian quartzite, the cap rock of Cul Mor's impressive peaks. With the top in sight, a sketchy path led upwards.

We were aware that the gentle rise to our right ended abruptly on the lip of what must be the massive headwalls of the Coire Gorm on the north side of the mountain.

I was a little ahead of Tom and could see that I was at the top, just two more steps upward. I took the two steps, turned around to shout back to Tom and was blown flat on my face.

Tom hurried towards me and I shouted and waved to warn him not to make the same mistake. He dropped onto his knees and together we crawled to the top and peered over the edge. The cliffs plunge in a sheer fall of 300 metres, an impressive wall of rock. I took photographs in the shelter of some outcrops and we considered the consequences of a gust of wind like that coming from a more southerly direction. I would have been blown over the edge of this cliff. Falling swiftly past the horizontal beds of sandstone, I think it unlikely that I would be reflecting on the millennia represented by each.

We spent the rest of the day exploring each peak in turn and were surprised again and again by the contrast in mountainscape and vista. My favourite view was from the top of the Creag nan Calman on the south side of the complex. It was also relatively sheltered by the taller peak to the north. We sat and ate our lunch, soaking in the views of Stac Pollaidh, Cul Beag and the mountains of Coigach beyond. It was a day that nourished the soul; Coleridge would have used the term sublime.

My children grew up and I had other mountains to climb so the holidays in the little white cottage came to an end. Those years were very special and have left me with many dear memories.

Tom showing Faye Suilven (left), Cul Mor, Stac Pollaidh and Cul Beag before going to fish in Loch na Béiste.

Carn Dearg, my first Munro

The Jolly Boys and gear

June

A few weeks into my new job I was signed up for The Jolly Boys. I was told that this was a hillwalking weekend.

Colleagues had given me a generous cheque on leaving my previous job and I had spent this on items of equipment for walking on the hills. The most expensive item was new boots, the first quality boots I had ever owned. I felt ready to go with proper hillwalkers.

The Jolly Boys was an institution. The weekend was the penultimate of the session and the exclusively male participants had chalked up some exploits that had become legends. Most of these concerned alcohol rather than mountains.

I was exhausted by the time that Friday afternoon arrived. One of the Jolly Boys, Victor, an ex para, invited me to change at his house and then the minibus arrived. Victor loaded me and the rucksacks with military efficiency and we were off on our adventure. Fionn opened a large container of bottled beers. There were examples from many of the world's brewing countries, including China, India, Japan and Mexico. Each was passed around and sampled, some surprisingly good, some disgusting.

At one point where the traffic was going slowly, Victor jumped out to walk beside the bus and smoke a cigarette. The driver playfully accelerated away at the first opportunity, much to the enjoyment of his passengers. We stopped a number of times to alleviate the discomfort of drinking so much exotic beer and again for fish and chips but eventually arrived at the little hostel in Glen Feshie on the western flank of the Cairngorms. The sign that read "free porridge" promised a warm welcome.

It was indeed a warm welcome we were given by Jean, our hostess. The old stove radiated heat and the sitting room was full of comfy old sofas and an ample table, large enough to sit all the guests.

The evening that followed was typical of Jolly Boys evenings. Crates of beer, bottles of wine and spirits were unloaded and no time was wasted in filling the glasses. Table football and a knockout film quiz were relatively tame. The drinking games that followed were frenzied.

Victor went outside to smoke. Fionn crept upstairs and out onto a little balcony above Victor's head. Silence fell, we froze with anticipation and everyone fell helpless with laughter as Victor re-entered the room to announce that he felt a little rain coming on.

The Jolly Boys were much less so the next morning. Some ate the free porridge from the large black cast iron pot on the stove. Most ate Jean's delicious mixed grain bread with salty butter. Some ate all that and a massive fried breakfast. Some groaned quietly and sipped tea.

Most were at the stage of packing rucksacks for the day when Fionn woke. He had not made it to his bed and was lying flat out on one of the sofas. He ate a massive cooked breakfast, then all the leavings from all the plates, then announced that he'd give a shower and change of clothes a miss.

Meanwhile, a debate was gathering heat. One of the time-served Jolly Boys was arguing the case for the Cairngorms while Struan argued for the Monadhliath mountains to the west. He argued with an energy that I found remarkable considering his alcohol consumption of the previous evening. He talked of the plant and animal life being far superior to that of the Cairngorms. A cynic then pointed out that this was a load of rubbish as all Struan wanted was to add another Munro to his tally. "What is a Munro?" I asked, and by this stopped all argument. Out of the stunned silence, someone kindly explained that it is a mountain of over 3,000 feet in height and there are 284 of them in Scotland. They were listed by Sir Hugh Munro in 1891, except there were not so many of them then. I was informed that most hillwalkers collected Munros. It occurred to me that the magical mountains of Coigach and Assynt that had stolen my heart were not Munros. I said, "Surely one should climb a mountain because of its character and the challenge it presents rather than whether it is over 3,000 feet or not?" I declared that I, for one, would not collect Munros, nor would it ever influence my choice of hill or mountain to climb. The others gave me a knowing look and said nothing.

I hardly need to record that I was soon keeping a tally of Munros climbed. At first I went through a phase when I pretended that I was not actually collecting them, it just so happened that this particular mountain was a Munro that I had not climbed before. Soon, however, I was openly discussing Munros with fellow hillwalkers.

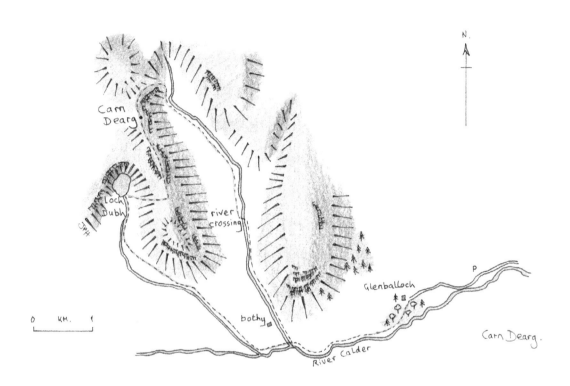

Final preparations were made for an expedition to the Monadhliath range, (Struan and the lust for new Munros had won) and the walkers began to talk gear. This again was a new experience for me. Words like Goretex, Vibram soles, gaiters, Leckie poles and Buffalo shirts began to swim around the room. I realised that I was out of my depth and quietly pushed my waterproof jacket (non-breathable) into my rucksack (cheapest in the shop). I looked at the soles of my new boots and was pleased to see Vibram written there, one thing was right at least. I had no gaiters but pulled my walking socks over my heavy cotton trousers to look more like a proper hillwalker. Then we were off.

The minibus was parked at the road end and we walked up the River Calder. It was a splendid summer day and I liberally applied sunblock cream to my face and bald patch. By the time the party was toiling up into the big corrie that has been carved into the west side of Carn Dearg, the cream had combined with sweat and was running down my forehead and stinging my eyes. One learns from such mistakes and now I wear my old cotton sun hat, a relic of my Boy Scout days.

As we approached Loch Dubh which sits in the corrie floor, I was ready to strip off and swim in the dark blue water to cool my overheated body. The fickle Highland weather, however, had one of its characteristic changes of mood. The moment the rucksacks were lowered to the loch shore, with our minds on rest, tea or cooling off, dark cloud covered the sun and the first spits of rain spotted the surface of the warm grey rock. Fionn quickly removed his trousers to reveal underpants decorated with the union flag. "It's a pity to get the trousers wet," he declared and the trousers were not worn again until the rain stopped in the late afternoon.

By the time we had drunk our tea the rain was coming down hard. Most of the party set off for a high bealach while Fionn led gullible Eric, (a first timer) up a steep and rocky route that he insisted was a good shortcut. It was a hard pull up onto the ridge and I was wet inside my waterproof with the exertion. The others explained about breathable mountain jackets and I decided that I should really have one.

We trudged along the ridge and waited in the rain for Fionn and Eric to appear at the top of their shortcut route. My legs were cold and my knees rubbed against the saturated cotton of my trousers. The others explained about lightweight walking trousers and breathable waterproof trousers and I decided that I should really have a pair of each.

Fionn and Eric eventually appeared, Eric staggering and unable to speak for a while. When he did speak, it was to inform us that death would be preferable to his present condition.

We squelched on through the rain to a cairn on the ridge. When we had gathered around it Victor soberly announced, "This is a Munro."

Rucksacks were opened for flasks and chocolate and I noted that the heavy rain had soaked the contents of mine. The others explained about plastic liners for rucksacks and I decided that I should really have one.

It was time to go down. I had been fine on the ascent but my lack of hill fitness began to become apparent on the steep descent. My knees in particular were wobbly and sore. I noticed the veterans employing various walking poles at this stage and they explained about them easing the strain. I decided that I should really have one or two of these.

We came to the Allt Fionndrigh, swollen with the heavy rain and the Jolly Boys declared that we had to cross this torrent. After some scouting up and downstream, a wide section that did not look as dangerous as the rest was chosen as our crossing place. Eric, already near despair, let it be known that he was not happy at the prospect.

Fionn was born for adventures such as this. He cast about the bank and found a long, heavy old fence post. He then waded into the deepest and fastest channel and used the fence post to keep himself upright. Struan did likewise and the Jolly Boys began to make their way across, using Fionn and Struan as anchor points, holding on to the less confident.

27/6/98
The Jolly Boys
Crossing the river

After this adventurous crossing, I sat on the bank and poured the water out of my new boots. I had taken much pleasure in having dry feet up to that point, the new leather and careful waxing having kept out the deluge. The Highlands have the knack of bringing the cocky walker down to earth.

As I wrung out my socks I noticed that Fionn was pulling his boots from his bare feet. His socks had been stowed in his sack before he plunged into the river. I made a mental note, keep your socks dry.

We were soon off again, a bedraggled bunch. Around the next spur in the valley I was first to catch sight of the bridge. I made another mental note, always have a map, look at it regularly, spot the bridge, (yes, it was marked), and thereby avoid crossing rivers in spate.[1]

I was soon in the minibus, steaming off the moisture and noticed that those with quick-dry walking trousers were a lot more comfortable than I was.

Back at Glen Feshie, most of us showered and changed and we all sat down to a

---

1   Recent 1:50,000 editions of Sheet 35 no longer mark this bridge.

splendid dinner cooked by Jean. She told me that she had cooked in her St Andrews restaurant before heading north for a quieter life.

The next day dawned grey and misty, with a steady drizzle. Those who had come up on their motorbikes decided to go home. The rest were soon embroiled in a heated debate, would they climb another Munro in the unfavourable weather or not? Despite the hardships of the previous day, I very much wanted to join the more adventurous lobby. In the end, however, those depending on the minibus had to content themselves with a walk up Gleann Einich to the loch. As I gazed at the impressive cliffs surrounding Loch Einich, wishing I was up on Sgor Gaoith which towered above, I thought of the others climbing Beinn a' Ghlo to the east of Blair Atholl. I determined to take my own car in future to give me freedom to make the most of such precious weekends.

On the walk back along the glen I fell back a little from the others and found myself thinking about my first Jolly Boys trip. Those with considerable experience had taught me a lot, (and were to teach me more in the years to come). I pictured a list of kit that I would build up for future trips and it looked like this.

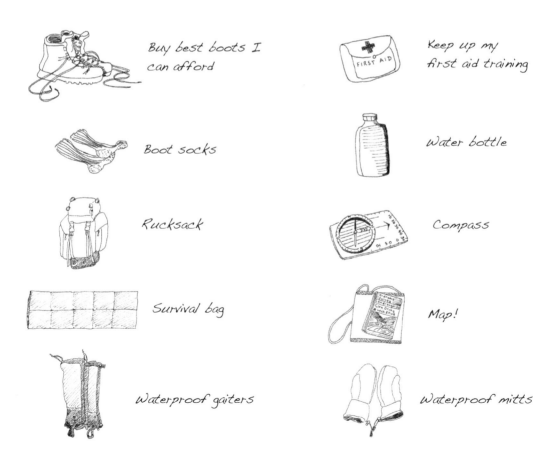

Buy best boots I can afford

Keep up my first aid training

Boot socks

Water bottle

Rucksack

Compass

Survival bag

Map!

Waterproof gaiters

Waterproof mitts

 Walking trousers in quick-dry fabric

 Moisture wicking shirt

 Take gloves even in summer

 Warm layer

 Hat

 Waterproof and breathable mountain jacket

 Waterproof, breathable trousers

 Whistle

 Torch

 Plenty of food!

Carn Sgulain, A' Chailleach

Back to the Monadhliath range with the Jolly Boys

June

It was good to be back in Glen Feshie at Jean's charming hostel again. Friday evening was much as the previous year, being filled with alcohol and laughter. Most were not asleep until the small hours and Fionn again failed to get out of his clothes or find a bed.

I listened to the moans and groans coming from some of the not very jolly boys as I ate a breakfast of free porridge, creamy milk, Jean's warm home-made bread and butter. Maps were spread on the breakfast table as plans were made for the day. There was the same debate as last year, with a lobby for the Cairngorms but there were still two Munros to be climbed in the Monadhliath mountains that no one had bagged and this won the day.

As I prepared for the expedition I remembered the last time and was pleased that I now had some gear that should make the day more comfortable. In particular, I was grateful for my Gortex-lined mountain jacket, expensive yes, but making such a difference. I set off feeling a little less of a novice at this great game.

We parked at the same spot on the River Calder and set off on our long ramble, following a good track that ran on the east side of the Allt a' Chaorainn and then a path

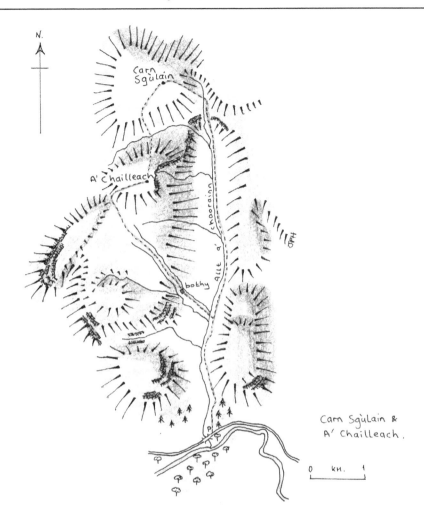

N.

Carn
Sgulain

A' Chailleach

allt a' chaorainn

JPH

bothy

P

Carn Sgùlain &
A' Chailleach.

0   KM.   1

going north-west to an old bothy. The bothy had a rusty pink roof and rickety wooden walls but was clean and dry inside. From there we climbed up onto the high Monadhliath plateau and turned north-east along a broad ridge to A' Chailleach, the first of the day's two Munros.

The weather stayed warm and clear and I began to appreciate the charms of this high rolling country with its wide skies. The peat was dry and crispy and I walked with an easy stride. These mountains are made of vast thicknesses of schists and the sun caught the mica in the rock, making it glint and sparkle. Larks sang their song of joy and the mood of the walkers was buoyant.

When dropping down from A' Chailleach I felt the strain on my knees, the first time my body had complained all day. We descended into a narrow valley, crossing the stream at a point where large rocks made stepping stones. It was a good place to stop and, sprawled among the rocks and heather, we ate lunch. Frogs were discovered and orange-bellied palmate newts. Giant dragonflies shone in the sun like sapphires and emeralds and we were mercifully free of midges.

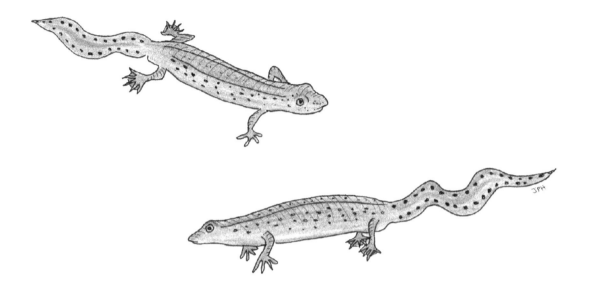

Red-faced, hot and sticky, Fionn asked Eric if his pack seemed heavier today. Those who had known Fionn for some time looked over and grinned. Eric became suspicious and threw out the contents of his rucksack, coming at last to the tins of beer hidden there in the morning by Fionn. "Thanks very much, Eric," he said, "I would love one," and, helping himself, added, "Good, still cool from the fridge."

I tucked into my sandwiches and banana and noticed that my basic picnic was outclassed by those of my companions. There were fancy breads, pork pies, spreading cream cheeses, oatcakes, fruitcake and chocolate. Here was another interesting side to hillwalking, it was an excuse for a special lunch. I still, however, had much to learn about the importance of food and drink when in the mountains.

We were soon toiling up the north side of this quiet valley and it did not take long to reach Carn Sgulain. The exertions had sweated out the hangovers and there were high spirits and good banter as photos were taken.

The climb down to the Allt a' Chaorainn was sore on my knees but I was fine once we were on the track that runs beside the stream. The Boys were on best form on the walk back.

14/10/99

Carn Liath and Braigh Coire Chruinn-bhalgain

Beinn a' Ghlo

October

had enjoyed a fantastic summer in Polbain. It was one of those rare times in the North-west when the sun shines day after day and transforms this hard-edged wilderness to a sub-tropical paradise. We had sunbathed on the rocks below the cottage and dived down into crystal-clear water, exploring the kelp forest.

It had really been too hot to climb but we had a new member of the family staying with us and we made the effort to show off our rather special mountains. Fabrice had grown up in the cultivated and populated landscapes of southern France and he was left speechless by the views from local hills like Stac Pollaidh. It was hot work, however, and we were easily persuaded to spend days on Achnahaird Beach instead, swimming in the bay at intervals to cool off.

So it was a brown skinned and healthy party on that October day standing at the foot of Carn Liath, the most westerly mountain of the group collectively known as Beinn a' Ghlo. With me were my son, Tom, my friend from work, Kenny and my boss, Allan. Kenny had been here in June with some of the Jolly Boys, climbing Carn Liath on a day of low cloud, rain and very poor visibility. The group had been in a hurry and had stormed up the unforgiving slope to the summit cairn and promptly turned back again. His memory was of sore legs and he had vowed never to return.

We parked at Loch Moraig and walked up the track, the mountains growing more impressive as we approached. There was low cloud like a blanket across the tops but a hill-walker has to be an optimist and I cheerily assured the others that it was likely to lift as the autumn sun warmed the air.

The track up the steep side of Carn Liath was every bit as arduous as Kenny had vividly described and I recognised many of the same swear words as he slogged up this second time. Tom was in his peak of fitness and kept running ahead then scrambling back to report on distances still to be climbed.

The cloud had thinned by the time we got to the top but still obscured any possible views. Kenny vowed again never to return and had to be coaxed to walk north along the sinuous ridge that connects Carn Liath to Braigh Coire Chruinn-bhalgain, its neighbour in this mountain complex. As we walked I explained that Beinn a' Ghlo means hill of the veil or mist, the others retorting that this was a statement of the obvious.

The ridge drops to a bealach where we were low enough to see tantalising glimpses of the glens and mountains to the north and west. We were soon toiling upwards again,

however, into the cold water droplets of the enveloping cloud. The clear path ended on stony ground and I used my compass to make sure of the route to the second summit of the day.

At the cairn we stopped for tea and decided to return the way we had come, this was not a day to push on to Beinn a' Ghlo's third Munro and turn a strenuous day into a major undertaking.

Decision made, we set off to retrace our steps, Kenny expanding on his conviction that there is no point in climbing a mountain unless one has clear views. Visibility was certainly poor and it was not until we were well down the SSE ridge that I realised we should have been on the south-west ridge. There was no obvious track on the stony surface and coming off on the wrong ridge was easy to do. Maybe my tally of three Munros had not properly qualified me to lead a party into the mountains.

I consulted the map and gave two alternatives, we retrace our steps or continue around the east-facing slopes of Carn Liath to regain the track at its foot. No one was prepared to climb back up, so down we went.

There were the inevitable comments about my map reading, use of compass and leadership, all of which I deserved. Kenny expanded further on his theme of a wasted day.

At this point we heard the first stag roaring and looking about, (we were well under the cloud base), we could see hundreds of red deer. The stags roared and clashed antlers and groups of hinds scurried out of the way of these battles. We walked nearer, sure that they would melt away up the mountainside, but they did not. So preoccupied were they

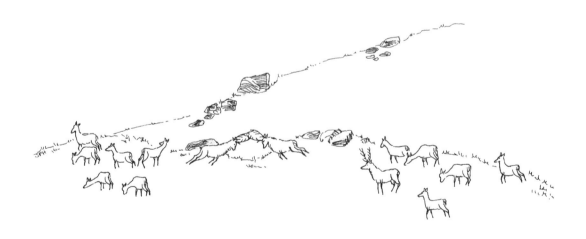

The rut on Beinn á Ghlo
14/10/99.

with the titanic struggles of the great stags that they ignored this little party of walkers. We were in the front stalls and stood still to watch the spectacle. Roaring, booming and the occasional percussion of antlers filled the air. Harems of hinds were shepherded to one side or another by wide-eyed and steaming stags.

The short October day was coming to its close, however, and we had to turn for home in the gloaming. As we walked in companionable silence I reflected on a great day on the hills, for me anything but wasted.

Schiehallion

A day on the fairy mountain marks an auspicious start to the new millennium

April

had missed the mountains badly over the winter and drove north with Kenny and Allan full of anticipation and optimism for the year ahead. We passed Weem, followed the narrow road north that leads to Glen Lyon and parked at the car park just short of Braes of Foss.

The sun shone and there was little more than a gentle breeze as we set off up the well-marked track to climb the east ridge of the mountain.

We talked about the level of fitness needed to climb Munros. Kenny the rugby player kept in shape with a daily run and press-ups. Allan had joined the local gym and I took a brisk half hour walk every evening, rain, sleet, or snow. We thought that we were doing well for middle-aged men before we noticed two walkers gaining on us on the track below. They soon caught up and we exchanged pleasantries. The two women were in their late seventies. Each wore a tweed jacket and tweed breeches with long woollen stockings. They were slim and tough-looking, with well-cut, lined faces framed by short grey hair. With a cheery wave they were off, leaving us in no doubt that their level of hill fitness left us well behind.

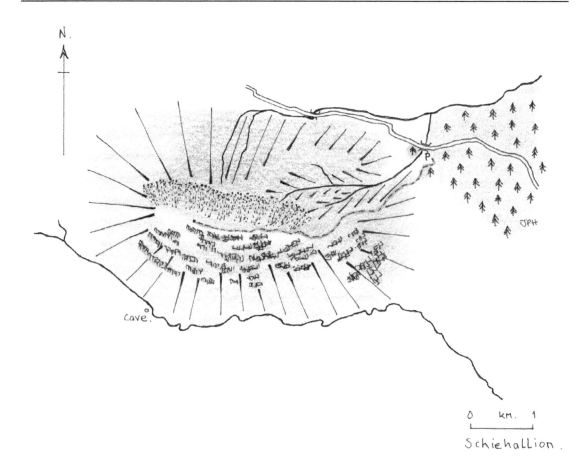

Schiehallion.

On we trudged, our egos bruised ever so slightly. The heavily eroded track through the peat gave way to stony ground as we reached the higher slopes and we were soon trudging through the snow which capped the mountain top. The very top has rock outcrops and these had been dried by the warm spring sun, providing an ideal spot to have lunch.

The views were impressive in the clear spring air and my companions were soon bombarding me with questions. I could easily identify Loch Tummel and Loch Rannoch to the north. Looking due west I pointed out the great watery wilderness of Rannoch Moor and Glen Coe beyond, bordered on each side with dark mountains. To the north-west, Ben Nevis reared above the surrounding Mamores and Grey Corries, a distinctive shape that I have learned to pick out from numerous mountain tops. To the south was an interesting landscape with many mountains I was unable to identify, so I took out my map and spread it onto a flat rock. As I did so I realised that we had been so lucky with the weather and guessed that opportunities to spread out a map on a Highland summit would be few and far between on future expeditions.

Using the map, I picked out the rounded summits of the Glen Lyon hills to the south with the more rugged profiles of the Ben Lawers range beyond and began to plan walks on them. I asked Kenny if he would like a look, "You'd be as well showing me a jam sandwich as a map," he replied, a phrase he was to use again under very different circumstances but he accepted the map out of politeness. Allan took Kenny's photograph, commenting that it would have rarity value. I laughed and explained that it would also have comedy value to those who knew enough to see that he was attempting to read the map upside down.

Map reading
on Schiehallion
14/4/00.

While I had been making the most of this opportunity to survey the southern and central Highlands, Kenny, being the fastest eater I have ever known, had consumed his lunch, packed his rucksack and was standing ready to go. I explained that I had no intention of leaving until I had eaten and downed a cup of tea or two while enjoying this wonderful panorama. I also reminded him that he was miserable if he did not get the views and should linger while he had the chance. He replied that I could have eaten my lunch in the time I took to say all that.

I explained that Schiehallion is the fairy mountain of the Caledonians and that the door to the fairy kingdom is in a cave in the south face, suggesting that we could come off the mountain on the west ridge and work round its base to explore this legendary entrance. Kenny, however, expressed the opinion that I was "losing my marbles" with all this talk of fairies and Allan said that it sounded too strenuous.

So, all too soon for me, we were returning the way we had come. Allan fell on the rocky section just below the summit. I realised that his legs were a bit wobbly and his balance was not all that good. It had been the right decision to return the easiest way to the car. He was bruised but otherwise undamaged and we made our way back in high spirits, Allan determining to step up his exercise regime, me planning walks on the mountains we had seen on this great day.

On the way home I quietly wondered why the mountain had been given that strange name. What stories lay behind it? I decided, not for the last time, to return to explore the mountain I had just climbed.

Carn Liath, Stob Poite Coire Ardair and Creag Meagaidh; Geal Charn and Creag Pitridh

With the Jolly Boys at Tulloch Station

drove alone to Tulloch Station late on Friday night, heavy with emotion as I had just said farewell to Tom who was to start his summer holiday job in Aviemore and then go on to university. We were a close father and son and I knew that I would miss him.

Arrival at the station was the best thing in the circumstances. The Jolly Boys were already in the swing of things, all packed into the snug sitting room with its open fire. I stayed up for a nightcap but was soon in my bunk, falling asleep to the muffled shouts and laughter of the die-hards.

The next morning was one of blue sky and the early sun held promise of a grand day. Over breakfast, I listened to plans, content to go anywhere. Struan made a pitch to walk a high level counter-clockwise circuit around Coire Ardair, the spectacular corrie carved deeply into the north-east side of Creag Meagaidh. Fionn was at his most persuasive over his alternative route, climbing the long ridge which runs from Creag Meagaidh to the

19

south. I think it had something to do with Fionn's unpredictable, Peter Pan like qualities that engenders doubt in his leadership potential. Anyway, we decided to go with Struan and Fionn, always a free spirit, decided to go his own way and meet us on the top.

We parked by Loch Laggan and followed a well-made path through an open deciduous woodland, alive with birdsong.

Carn Liath,
Stob Poite Coire Ardair,
Creag Meagaidh.

The trees gave way to grass and heather as we left the main path up the glen and plodded up the south ridge of Carn Liath, our first Munro of the day. It was heavy work in full sun and I was glad that I had remembered to pack my old sun hat. The hillside was carpeted with flowers. Some were easy to name, like blaeberry and cloudberry, the latter with its red berries. I could recognise yellow flowering bog asphodel by its long spiky leaves and purple flowering thyme by the unmistakeable smell when I crushed the small leaves between my fingers. There were patches of creeping tormentil with its pretty yellow flowers and the ubiquitous cotton grass and heathers. Many others grew, red, blue, yellow, white and I determined to learn their names.

Once at the top there was the glorious prospect of a high ridge walk ahead. The views were magnificent and could be savoured as we were no longer toiling up steep slopes. We walked along the northern rim of the deep glacial valley and could see ahead the huge corrie where the ice had gathered. The walls were steep cliffs and the deep blue corrie lochan reflected the July sky.

A sharp-eyed member of the group spotted a person far ahead on Stob Poite Coire Ardair, our next Munro, on a summit that perched on the very rim of the corrie. The person sat in the sun, watching us get slowly nearer and soon we saw that it was Fionn waiting for us to join him.

"Hello all," he greeted us, "a nice beer would go down well."

"Oh no!" said more than one of the Jolly Boys as we rummaged in our packs to find the cans he had hidden earlier. The same old trick had worked yet again.

"Far too hot to lug all of this up," he added, swigging beer, "tastes all the better knowing you carried it for me."

Refreshed, fortified and forgiving, of course, we set off around the rim of the deep corrie, enjoying the views down the cliff-lined glen. Soon we turned west, walking through the snowfields that still covered the high plateau from which Creag Meagaidh rises. The day was at its hottest and Eric shouted to Fionn that more of the same was needed, but iced this time please. We were trudging through a snowfield at the time and Fionn replied, "Well, we might be in luck, have a look at this." We gathered round to see the necks of bottles sticking out of the snow. They turned out to be cider, ice-cold and delicious. "I wonder who buried them in the snow and left them?" said Fionn.

The walk back was spectacular, the path twisting among the rock pinnacles at the head of the corrie and then following the cliff tops along the south side of the glen. The sun was low and began to cast long shadows in front of us as we reached the final ridge and began to descend.

I had managed this long walk without discomfort but now began to feel the strain on my knees. It must have been obvious to the others because Struan asked if I would like to use his walking poles. He told me that they would have reduced some of the stress on my knees had I used them on the walk. They certainly helped me to get down and back to the cars. I decided that a pair of poles would be the next addition to my gear.

Back at the hostel the pleasant couple who ran the place made us a much needed hot dinner and then we settled for the evening in the little sitting room. I looked out of a window and saw a lithe and athletic animal slip down the side of the far platform and cross the railway tracks, heading towards us. It was a pine marten, something I had only seen in the wild twice before. Most of the Jolly Boys who crowded to the window had never seen this shy creature. We found out later that the pine marten knew when scraps of food would be put out and happily overcame its shyness for a free meal.

We warmed bottles of red wine in front of the coal fire and talked well into the night. The next day dawned bright and sunny and we decided to tackle the hills on the south side of Glen Spean.

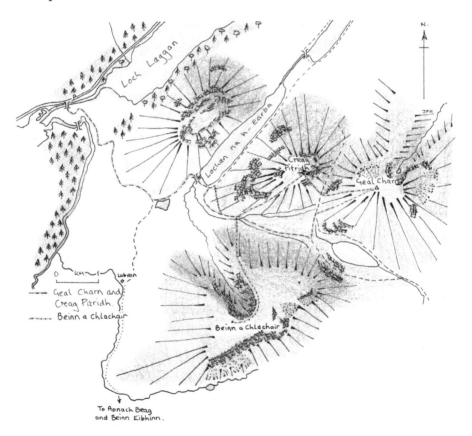

We left the cars by the road about one kilometre south-west of Loch Laggan and followed a good track which wound south-east into the hills. There was the inevitable debate between Fionn and Struan, with Fionn leaving us to climb Beinn a' Chlachair to the south. The rest of the Jolly Boys continued down the track, raising clouds of pale grey dust, an unusual occurrence for the Highlands.

A well-marked path took us north and then east onto Geal Charn. At the top, we stopped for lunch, soaking in the fantastic views, especially to the north and west. Maps were opened up and I was surprised to discover that this was one of four Munros with the same name, the others visible from our lunch spot and within walking distance. Geal Charn means white hill. This is easy to visualise in the long months of winter snow cover. Even in summer, however, these mountains are covered in pale grass rather than dark heather, which perhaps helps to explain the "geal".

It was one of those lunch stops where we wanted to linger but we had to get back to the Borders and be ready for Monday so we were soon off again.

We came through scree and huge boulders contorted by ancient earth movements to a high col then we scrambled up the steep rocky slope to the top of Creag Pitridh, a much more shapely peak than that upon which we had lunched.

Still warmed by the sun we enjoyed the last of our tea on the pale grey summit slabs which form an eyrie above the deep blue waters of Lochan na h-Earba. The mountains of the Highlands were spread out around me, range behind range, an unknown land. I wondered if I would see the same unknown land when I sat on top of my last Munro?

As we strode back to the cars along the dusty track we thanked the weather gods for the weekend.

Pine marten.
Tulloch Station 1/7/00.

Braeriach and Ben Macdui

My introduction to The Cairngorms

July

My son, Tom, had been working in a hotel in Aviemore and we had arranged two days of walking. I had booked us into Jean's hostel in Glen Feshie and ordered one of her legendary dinners. He had been exploring the Cairngorms on his days off and was bursting with the need to show me this wonderful corner of Scotland.

We parked at Loch Morlich and the day began with a delightful walk through Rothiemurchus, one of the largest remnants of the old Caledonian Forest. The sun was shining, the path was dry and we made good progress. The ancient, gnarled Scots pines each had a distinctive character. Twice we stopped to watch red squirrels.

The path began to climb, the trees to thin out and the Lairig Ghru appeared in the distance before us like a great gateway. I have since learned that all expeditions in the Cairngorms are long but on that day I did not properly appreciate the scale of things. It seemed a long walk before we stood in the entrance to this famous mountain pass, once used by hardy drovers to take their black cattle to markets in Deeside.

The Lairig Ghru is U-shaped in cross-section, bleak and stony, with cliff-like walls towering up to the mountains on either side. We walked uphill along this great landscape

Braeriach and
Ben Macdui.

feature for a few miles until we reached some pools feeding a little stream which rushed off to join the Dee far away to the south. Here we stopped to enjoy some lunch. We had not seen another human being all day.

Tom then decided that we should climb out of the Lairig Ghru so that he could show me Braeriach, the massive bulk to the west, rising straight from the pass. I asked what route he had planned and, true to character, he replied by pointing straight up the

The Lairig Ghru.
Cairn Toul (right) and The Devil's
Point (left) beyond.

imposing slope in front of us. By the time we stood on the crest of the northern ridge of the mountain we were tired, hot and sweaty.

The airy walk to the summit soon restored our spirits, however. Fine weather had set in for the day and the Cairngorms looked their summer best, set off against a perfect blue sky. An intermittent hint of a path took us around the rims of scalloped corries, looking down on the Lairig Ghru which was just as impressive from above. We passed patches of snow and a blue jewel of a lochan, both sparkling in the bright sunlight. Near the top we rested among granite rocks, a place with marvellous views to the north, east and south, and ate the rest of our lunch.

The clear air shortened distances and we were tempted to continue south from our summit ledge to climb Sgor an Lochain Uaine and Cairn Toul which towered above the Lairig Ghru to the south. Tom told me that these were, respectively, the fifth and fourth highest mountains in the British Isles, with Braeriach the third and Ben Macdui, directly east, the second highest. It certainly felt that we were sitting on the roof of the country. I was concerned, however, that we would not be back in time for our meal in Glen Feshie and so we packed up and turned north for the return trek.

Looking south down the
Lairig Ghru. Carn a'
Mhaim on left, Lochan
Uaine and Cairn Toul
on right.

A fine walk back it was, along a well-trodden path which followed the crest of the Sron na Lairige which marks the western wall of the Lairig Ghru. It was, though, a long, long walk and it was a weary pair who returned to the hostel with barely time for a quick shower before our meal.

It was Tom's first experience of Jean's cooking and he was impressed. He takes a lot of filling but for the first time in his life he had to leave some of the delicious pudding after his second helping.

The next day we were up early and the sun streamed into the homely common room as we stoked up on porridge and home-made bread to prepare for another day in the Cairngorms.

We stopped in Aviemore to pick up Nikki, Tom's Kiwi girlfriend who had a day off from the hotel. She was great company and it was a cheery party that tramped through the pines of Rothiemurchus on what turned out to be another fine day. Tom's plan was to go up the ridge leading to the eastern rim of the Lairig Ghru and go to the top of Ben Macdui.

We made great time as Nikki told us about the wild beaches and mountains of New Zealand's South Island where she lived. She was working her way around the world as do so many of her compatriots. She explained that her country is so remote and it is so expensive to travel from it that it has become a tradition for young people to do as she was doing, before returning to settle down. Before coming to the UK she had explored the Middle East. She had walked alone, hitching lifts, from Lebanon, through Syria and Jordan to Israel. To pass unscathed through these troubled lands of suicide bombers and shoot-first soldiers was an achievement.

We enjoyed scrambling up and down the rocky tops along the ridge and then started up the long slopes to Ben Macdui. The atmosphere of the walk changed at this point. Wisps of cloud blew over an expansive landscape of grey rocks. Little grows in this bleak arctic environment, yet small families of ptarmigan ran to left and right, the red flashes above their eyes making them strangely easier to spot, despite their summer camouflage. "What do they find to eat up here?" asked Nikki.

On we went, with no other human being in sight, half expecting the 'Grey Man of Ben Macdui' to loom suddenly out of the mist. Our happy chattering had been stilled by this bleak and eerie place. It took longer than we expected to get to the top, which was as devoid of people as the rest of our walk had been. A shelter had been constructed from the litter of stones on the summit and we sat in it to drink tea and have lunch.

"What a pity there's cloud on the top when we saw for miles yesterday," I said, just as a breeze tore a ragged hole in the cloud to reveal blue sky and a view across to Braeriach. Nikki declared that it would all blow away so that the New Zealand visitor could marvel at the beauty of the Cairngorms and it did. The cloud thinned to wisps and the wisps were sucked down into the Lairig Ghru to melt away.

We packed up and walked to the edge of that deep pass, Nikki being rewarded with excellent views to the south-west, of Cairn Toul and The Devil's Point, with Beinn Bhrotain beyond. We could see the path leading to Carn a' Mhaim and were tempted to go on but it was getting late and we had a long return journey to the car.

We had walked many miles over the two days and my legs ached as we ate fish and chips in Aviemore. I would have been sad to leave but we had a walking holiday planned in the first week of August, so I waved goodbye with a smile as I drove away to begin the long road home.

Ben Mor Coigach

 The first summer walking holiday

August

Jane and Faye had outgrown the little white cottage overlooking the Summer Isles at Polbain. They decided that one week of our fortnight would be enough for them and that I should invite friends to stay for the second week to have a walking holiday.

Kenny and Allan rescued Tom from the Freedom Inn (an oxymoron as far as he was concerned) at Aviemore where he endured his holiday job. I fed them a huge dinner when they arrived and then walked them up the Castle Hill which thrusts out of the ground behind Polbain in the way of these mountains of Coigach. Once on the top, the mysterious and unique Fairy Hill (Meall an Fheadain) stood before us. Hidden from the village, it is revealed as a perfect steep-sided cone, described as "a child mountain" by my daughter, Faye.

We scrambled up on this crystal clear summer evening, Tom and I full of excitement with the knowledge of what would be unveiled at the top. It did not disappoint. Kenny and Allan were spellbound by the view east across Inverpolly Forest. This must be the strangest and most individual of all the mountain landscapes of Britain. The mountains of Torridonian sandstone rise like citadels from a floor of knobbly outcrops of gneiss and a myriad lochans. Water sparkled everywhere. The mountains, widely separated, were easy to point out. Suilven, Stac Pollaidh, Cul Mor, Cul Beag.

The light on this summer evening was still good so we walked to the top of the Red Hill, Meall Dearg, which towers above the beautiful natural harbour at Old Dornie. Sitting on top of the sandstone cliffs above the harbour, we watched the sun set behind the islands of the Outer Hebrides. The sky blazed red, soaking the sandstone boulders around us in the same colour. Allan had asked why it was called the Red Hill, the explanation was all around him.

The next morning was bright and clear. We were off soon after breakfast to climb Stac Pollaidh. This was the first time I had used the new path which winds around the east and then north side of the mountain (see map, page xiv). Our visitors were suitably impressed by the towering ridge, capped with dozens of vertical pinnacles of rock. Tom scrambled up each pinnacle, showing off, while Allan struggled with vertigo in places and decided to miss the tricky boulder with the overhang which we negotiated to get to the west top, the highest point.

Once the ridge was explored, we sat together to eat our sandwiches gazing north and east towards Cul Mor and beyond. Kenny suggested the order in which we would climb each mountain over the next few days and I was easily carried along by his dream on this most beautiful of days.

That night we ate in a hotel in Achiltibuie but were not impressed. We had been in the fresh air all day, had used a lot of energy and the portions did not match our healthy appetites. Back at the cottage, however, we enjoyed a nightcap while making grand plans for the next day.

When I looked out of the window in the morning it was grey with sheets of light rain blowing across the Summer Isles. Kenny would not want to climb a mountain if there were no views and Allan would not want to leave the cottage but I feared cabin fever and knew that we must walk.

I jollied them through breakfast and we drove in the rain to Achnahaird Bay. We then walked up through the village and across to Altandhu. The day always seems better out of the car and once the brisk walk had warmed our bodies our spirits had lifted.

We turned west then north, heading for Reiff. The plan was to follow the coast to Rubha Coigach and, having walked around the peninsula, end up back at Achnahaird Bay.

Reiff has a peculiar atmosphere, a straggle of very individual cottages set among and growing out of the ancient rock. The cliffs just north of the village are spectacular. Made of Torridonian sandstone, they rise vertically from the waves far below. There are geos, caves and blowholes to explore and drops to make one's head spin.

Beyond is a lovely sheltered bay with its own little island. The sands are as white as sugar and I can think of few nicer places on a sunny day.

The rain never became heavy and we walked on in good spirits. There was interest at every turn. We explored seabird colonies, lofty cliffs, secret coves and hidden lochs.

It was early evening before we were back at Achnahaird, the rain had stopped and we walked along the sands, enjoying the first blue sky of the day.

That evening we tried the Am Fuarnan Bar at Altandhu. We had driven past it that day and when asked what it was like I replied that I had never been inside. It turned out to be a darkly lit place of interlinked rooms with odd décor but great character. There was an old-fashioned juke box with classics from the 60s and 70s, a long tank with tropical fish, old dark wooden beams and a lovely smell of cooking from the kitchen at the back. We quickly found a table, ordered our meals and a couple of bottles of red wine and decided that this was our kind of place. The food and wine were excellent and we were soon in good form.

The pool table drew Kenny like a magnet. He teamed up with Tom and declared that Allan and I had little chance of victory. Three of us were complete novices, so his prediction was the likely outcome. We played with much enthusiasm but little skill. Competition between the two teams grew more intense with each trip to the juke box and bar. The game became more frenzied as the alcohol kicked in. At a point where there was surprisingly little between the two teams it was my shot. A yellow lay like a sitting duck by a pocket but we were pocketing the reds. I had lined up a good shot at a red when Allan shouted, "What are you doing!" He directed me to the yellow. I replied that we were actually pocketing reds. The argument became heated. Tom tried to join in but Kenny shut him up and then went strangely quiet. We failed to notice the warning signs. Allan pulled rank, "I'm the boss and I'm telling you that we are pocketing yellows!" I gave in and pocketed the yellow.

"Thank you," said Tom and Kenny before roaring with laughter and going on to win the game. Afterwards Kenny described Tom's "touch" as "like an elephant".

When I looked out of the window the next morning it was grey and threatening rain. The prospect of cabin fever came into my mind again so the walkers were reminded why they were described as such and we were soon in the car heading for Lochinver.

I felt they were sluggish, perhaps due to an excess of alcohol the previous night, so I directed the driver to turn left at Loch Bad a' Ghaill. The following narrow, single track road with its steep climbs, dramatic drops and sudden corners was enough to wake anyone up. A momentary lapse in concentration could easily have led to our vehicle hurtling down into the sea, or a loch, or a sea loch. It was a good tactic, everyone being mightily relieved to get out of the car and begin the walk.

We took the track from Glencanisp Lodge and gazed over the postcard picturesque loch towards Suilven, our objective for the day. The wind had picked up and was blowing cloud onto the top of the mountain and then off again, revealing this iconic landmark in all its dramatic glory.

Suilven is actually a ridge but this view of the west end of the mountain makes it look like a massive, vertically-sided tusk rising high above the ancient landscape of bare hills of Lewisian gneiss and a thousand lochs of all shapes and sizes.

The walk in is long but easy along a well-made track. It becomes more difficult when the track is left and the walker heads south to the mountain. It was more difficult on that day because the ground was saturated and it began to rain heavily again.

We slipped and slid around black boggy sections and climbed over a succession of heather covered hills and ridges. Then we traced a way between some little lochans until Suilven loomed up before us. It stopped us in our tracks. A seemingly vertical wall of horizontally-bedded sandstone rose high up into the cloud which covered the upper section of the mountain. "You are not expecting us to go up that?" said Allan, more as a statement than a question. I felt bitter disappointment coming on. My dream of sitting on top of Suilven, gazing at this most dramatic of vistas was draining away as surely as the raindrops were dripping from my jacket. I considered suggesting that it might clear but wisely thought better of it.

It did clear, of course, but by that time we were washed and changed and heading for the Altandhu Bar for another good meal and a glass or two. On the way we had a stroll around the bay at Old Dornie, watching the scattered clouds turn pink against a darkening blue sky, hoping that it would stay clear for the morrow.

When I looked out of the window the next morning it was grey with curtains of light rain moving across the mountains of Coigach. It was to be our last day together so there was no sitting about the cottage. It might clear after all.

We drove through Achiltibuie and down to the road end at Culnacraig, the mountains of Ben Mor Coigach our objective. As we trudged northwards we had to remove layers of clothing. The rain had stopped, but we were in low cloud and the warm air was saturated with moisture. The cruel blow of another day with no views was taking its toll on Kenny and Allan, both of whom were a little grumpy at this point.

The walk soon began to get interesting, however and spirits began to lift. We left the summit of Cairn Conmheall and turned east, walking through a weird and wonderful group of stone trolls, the gift of thousands of years of weathering of the Torridonian sandstone.

Next was Sgurr an Fhidhleir, the famous peak of the fiddler. Tom ran on ahead and came back excited. The cloud was swirling away and he urged us on to see. "Keep going down the path, Dad." I did as instructed and ended up on the very prow of this mountain. It is shaped like a massive ocean liner run aground above the waters of Lochan Tuath far below. My viewpoint was distinctly airy. Vertical cliffs fell 200 metres to my left, my right and straight ahead. I am normally fine when standing on top of a cliff, but felt light-headed in this exposed spot. It is not a place for a windy day.

Once I had back-tracked, Tom urged Kenny to sample the experience of standing with substantial drops to each side and in front. He was so uncomfortable that he immediately picked his way back up the path. Allan had only to look at his face to decide that this particular experience was not for him.

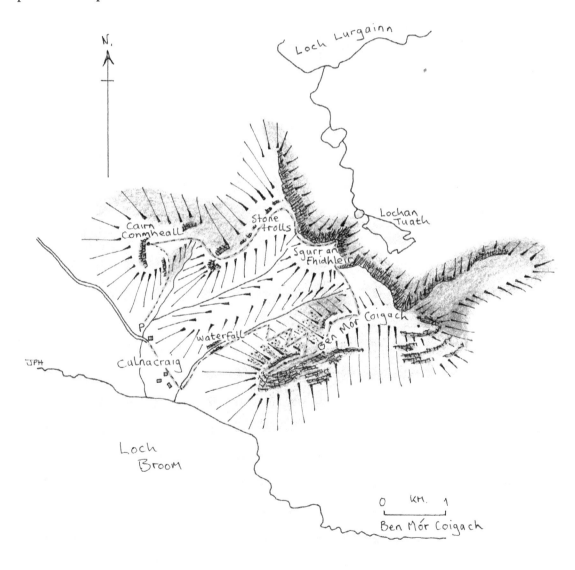

There had been a lull in the wind and rain but they now picked up again. We walked down steep slopes to the head of the Allt nan Coisiche and looked south-east where the massive bulk of the Ben Mor Coigach ridge reared up very steeply into thick cloud. It was my most difficult moment. Kenny and Allan had been disappointed by the weather since their first evening and I was asking them to find the energy to slog up the steepest and hardest slope yet with no prospect of any break in the weather. It was also their last day and they had a long drive ahead. "We've had three days of bad weather," I said, "it's bound to break up soon." I won round Kenny, Tom was game for anything, so Allan grudgingly agreed to give it a go.

The climb was long and hard, with Allan complaining all the way. On the top, the thick cloud made route finding tricky and we had not found the path which follows the crest of the ridge. I stopped to take out my compass and the miracle happened, the cloud blew away as if a weather god had just snapped his fingers. All around was a brilliant panorama of mountain and sparkling blue water. Kenny shouted, "Wow!" I had felt personally responsible for the poor weather and was now both relieved and disorientated. I thought the long stretch of water was Loch Lurgainn until Tom and Kenny pointed out Ullapool on its shore! They enjoyed the irony of the man with the map and compass being re-orientated by those with neither.

Ben Mor Coigach   August '98   J P Harland

My shame was short lived, however, because the sky was blue, the sun was so hot we had to remove our jackets and the ridge before us was wonderful.

We were at the north-east end and before turning to walk south-west we sat to finish our flasks while looking north across a landscape which must be the most photogenic in the British Isles. The mountains and lochs of Coigach and Inverpolly Forest combine to create a fantasy world that is worth all the effort and all the waiting to see.

The walk along the ridge was certainly not an anti-climax. It narrowed and became rockier. We began to scramble over sections with steep drops, especially to the south and east. Always there were the dramatic views. We kept stopping to absorb it all and our progress was slow. Towards the end, the ridge narrowed even more. Spectacular cliffs fell away on either side. The path began to drop down and suddenly all was blue sky and sparkling sea. Ben Mor Coigach had ended abruptly 700 metres above Loch Broom. We stood together admiring the Summer Isles with their mountain backdrop on the far shore of the loch. We could pick out the Cuillin of Skye and the Outer Hebrides beyond. Our reverie ended with Allan's prosaic question, "How do we get down?"

The path appeared to continue straight down the south-west gable of the ridge but the others were not much taken with the prospect of such a precipitous descent. I remembered having passed a zig zag path going down north-west towards the Allt nan Coisiche, so we retraced our steps and worked our way back to the car, passing on the way a foaming waterfall in its rocky grotto.

Soon I was waving goodbye to Kenny, Allan and Tom as they drove up the track from the cottage, heading for Aviemore. I was pleased that they were all in good spirits but relieved that they were going. I needed some peace and quiet.

The next day was almost unique in my life, a day all to myself. It dawned mild but Ben Mor Coigach was veiled again in thick cloud. I drove to Old Dornie and spent the day painting in this special place. I thought back over the week and made up my mind that this summer hillwalking holiday would be the first of many.

Suilven
Ben Mor Assynt and Conival

The second summer
walking holiday

August

Kenny and I drove back up to Rose Cottage in the summer of 2001, full of hope for a good few days of walking, Kenny optimistic that he would get some great panoramic views on his new video camera.

When I looked out of the window on the first morning I was surprised to see blue skies and the sun lighting up the Summer Isles. By the time we had eaten breakfast and were ready to go it was still fine, so I suggested making a dash for Suilven before the weather changed its mind. The previous year's attempt at climbing this iconic mountain had ended at its foot in pouring rain and frustration, so we were anxious to achieve our goal this time.

The drive along the coast road the previous year had frayed both driver's and passengers' nerves, so we went via Loch Assynt instead. We drove slowly so that we could enjoy the exceptionally beautiful road that winds past Stac Pollaidh and Cul Beag, the Ben Mor Coigach range reflected in the still blue waters of Loch Lurgainn.

We were treated to splendid views of Cul Mor and distant Suilven as we drove past the Knockan Cliff. I possibly bored Kenny a little as I explained the geological significance of this special place. Then it was the weird and wonderful Quinag and the blue-black Loch Assynt before we pulled into our parking space just outside Lochinver. The day remained bright, with a warm breeze blowing clouds which touched the top of Suilven and then raced off eastwards. The prospects were good.

We hurried along the track but stopped just before Glencanisp Lodge to watch a slow worm cross the track at our feet. It was fascinating. Rather thicker and shorter than a snake but otherwise similar in the way it moved. I bent down to see if I could see any sign of its residual legs, for a slow worm is a lizard rather than a snake, but I could not.

Slow worm
JPH

I was surprised by its beauty, a bright silver with delicate articulating scales and dark, intelligent eyes. The silver showed that it was a male, females being yellow-brown with a dark stripe down the back.

On we marched, in the highest of spirits. We were impatient to get back to this mountain while the fickle Highlands weather held, so the distance seemed much longer than we remembered.

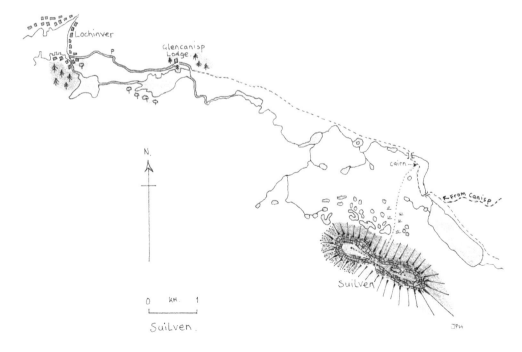

Suilven.

When we did arrive at the base of this massive rock monument we wasted no time. I had used my previous visit wisely and knew exactly where we would climb up to the bealach on the ridge. The climb appears daunting but it is not as bad as it looks, especially in conditions as good as they were that day of high summer. It was hot work, however, and we were soaked in sweat as we sat on the crest of the ridge to take a breather. Looking down, we were surprised to see that an attractive young woman coming up behind us had protected herself from overheating by stripping to her underwear.

It would have been rude to stare, of course, so we were soon on our way to enjoy quite a different spectacle, the views of this wilderness of the most ancient of rocks. All was there before us, the mountains of Inverpolly Forest and Coigach to the south, Quinag to the north and Canisp to the east.

Suilven

A beautifully made gateway in a lovely but incongruous dry-stone wall pointed the way to the main summit of Caisteal Liath. We ate lunch on the top and I drank tea while Kenny recorded the views on his video camera.

We explored the ridge, scrambling up steep sections and climbing down into gullies. The eastern tower of rock loomed before us and we began to climb. The rock was still wet and slippery from recent rain, however, so we decided that it would keep for another day. At that point, a party of climbers appeared on the top and made short work of climbing down, using a rope for security. We walked along a section of the ridge with them and they talked of being on Stac Pollaidh the previous day. Interestingly, they had not managed the summit, being put off by the overhang which must be negotiated. Knowing that we had done it made us feel a little better about not climbing that last tower of Torridonian sandstone.

The next day dawned warm and fair and we were soon driving north past the Knockan Cliff again, this time parking at Inchnadamph, with Ben More Assynt and Conival in our sights.

We had a look at the Inchnadamph Field Centre and the hotel, agreeing that this would be a good base for a walking holiday. We both liked being part of a group where people spark off one another so I decided to organise a summer walking holiday for the following year well in advance to attract a good crowd. Inchnadamph would do just fine.

We walked into the Traligill, the gorge of the trolls, but they were not out on this warm and sunny day. It was strange to be walking over limestone and to see the river disappear down a sink hole. I vowed that one day I would return to potter about this interesting place, taking my climbing helmet and head torch, and explore the caves.

Limestone is unusual in the Highlands and soon enough we had walked off it onto a rock which could hardly be a greater contrast, the ancient Lewisian gneiss. This oldest of rocks mostly forms the lochan-pitted basement of the far North-west but here it rises in massive bulk to form the linked mountains of Conival and Ben More Assynt. It is so hard

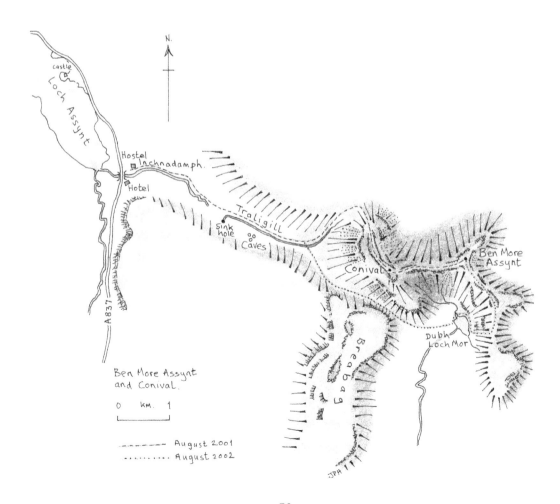

and resistant to erosion that it will outlast rocks like Torridonian sandstone, ensuring that these mountains will be here for a long, long time yet.

We walked up Gleann Dubh, following the river as its course became ever steeper, falling as a series of waterfalls. Our first challenge was to scramble up a craggy ridge to a level grassy place, studded with huge boulders. Leaning against one of these we looked down at the fantastic landscape of Assynt. When we turned to look towards the mountain it was hidden in pale grey cloud. Four stags picked their way among the giant rocks, unconcerned by our intrusion into their world.

Kenny's mood changed as we walked across this little alp and entered the cool and dripping cloud world of the upper mountain. It did not look like he was going to see far on this day.

The ridge was narrow at the bealach and an obvious path followed the crest south to Conival's summit. This was a different landscape again, everything more intimate in the swirling cloud droplets. All was grey in many shades, a high world drained of colour.

The cap rock is pale quartzite, mostly broken into a blanket of large, angular blocks which covers the underlying gneiss. It made walking difficult, especially as the moisture had made the flat surfaces of this finest-grained rock treacherously slippery.

The wind was strong and it was surprisingly cold. On we went to the top of Conival and, without stopping, followed the path along the crest of the ridge to the east, towards our final objective. It did not look too far on the map but it was slow going on the slippery and unstable screes.

There were no views at the summit, so we did not linger. We dropped down in the lee of the wind, into a hole between giant blocks. There we ate lunch and sipped tea, listening to the silence of this high place. Kenny broke the silence by saying, almost in a whisper, "It is kind of eerie up here, isn't it?" At that moment we heard a faint tap, tap among the rocks. It was difficult to judge how far away it might be. Tap, tap it went again, tap, tap. Was it getting louder? Tap, tap and again, tap, tap. We strained towards the sound and a large and sinister figure loomed out of the wreaths of mist. It must have been a trick of the light, however, because the figure shrank to more modest proportions and a walker came over to greet us, tapping the rocks with his shepherd's crook. I told him that I was relieved that he was not Blind Pew from Treasure Island, come to serve us a black spot.

We retraced our steps back to Conival and down to the high bealach, Kenny grumpy about carrying his camcorder when there was nothing to film. A few minutes of scrambling down from the bealach and we were out from under the cloud, looking out at a warm and sunlit landscape again.

The fair weather held for the next day and we headed for the parking space near the Knockan Cliff Visitor Centre, Cul Mor our objective. Kenny had left his camcorder behind, convinced that it would be a waste of time to carry it. Needless to say, the weather held fair and he was annoyed that he could not film the unfolding views.

Our first stop was at the little lochan with its miniature sandy beach. Then we scrambled down the massive sandstone pillows, stopping on the lowest to eat some lunch.

It was with a light step that we walked over the high rolling plateau to the vertical cliffs where we could look south and south-west to Stac Pollaidh, Cul Beag and the Coigach range. We decided to sit on this high perch and drink tea as we admired the panorama. I took off my rucksack, opened the top and rummaged for my flask. When I looked up, I could hardly believe my eyes. Cloud had rushed silently up the face of the cliff and smothered everything. The mountain was dramatically transformed.

Kenny declared that tea could wait, he'd had enough of life in the clouds. I advised caution, we were on a narrow ridge and there were no clear paths on this surface of weathered sandstone. The drops were sudden with a long fall to the bottom.

I led the way back along the ridge by instinct, judging the lie of the land and by recognising distinctive rocks and patches of vegetation that we had passed. We got back to the pillows and then to the lochan. Next was the wide stony plateau surface of Meallan Diomhain before we left the upper reaches of the mountain and properly began our descent.

On we marched, me leading the way, Kenny telling stories about his rugby days. I realised that we were descending into a steep-sided valley instead of the broad ridge I was expecting with its well-used path. I had swung round to the south instead of following the correct ESE line. I consulted the map, worked out where we were and took out my compass. Kenny was none too pleased to have to climb back up to the high dome we had just left.

Once on the top again I kept the compass in my hand and we walked along a bearing. We were soon on the path and descending the ridge. As on the previous day we walked out from the bottom of the cloud to find a pleasant day beneath. Jackets were stowed and we strolled back to the car in high spirits. That was our last hill before driving south and the weather had been kind, holding back the cloud until the point at which we were to finish our flasks and return.

As we drove home, Kenny returned to the dramatic moment when we had been plunged into thick mist, commenting that mountains, even in high summer, should be properly respected. I agreed, adding that a hillwalker should trust the map and compass, not instinct.

Binnein Beag, Geal Charn

 Girls who are boys

September

We travelled up to Tulloch Station after work on a mild September evening, cars arriving at intervals until, by 10 o' clock, 30 of us were gathered there. We packed into the tiny sitting room, many sitting on the floor around the open fire. Some had beer, some sloe gin, some a bottle of wine and soon we were a merry crowd.

The weekend had been organised by Struan in response to comments made by female members of staff about the anachronistic Jolly Boys from which they were excluded. It was certainly a novelty having women present. The diehards had predicted disaster, most turning their backs on such an avant garde venture. I thoroughly enjoyed it, however, the first evening in that snug little room being more fun than most Jolly Boys evenings. An added pleasure was an encounter with Maggie in the small hours while I was on my way to the gents, she returning from a shower and attempting to cover her impressive curves with a small hand towel.

Breakfast was more like the old Jolly Boys in that it was both hearty and riven with arguments about which Munro we should climb. Ray presented the case for Binnein Beag, Struan for Stob Ban. I nailed my colours to Ray's mast, being attracted to the idea of walking the length of Glen Nevis, his proposed route.

We drove to the car park under the massive bulk of Ben Nevis and walked the first mile

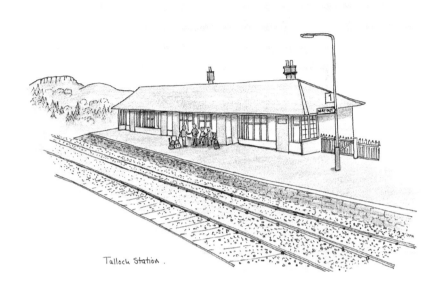

Tulloch Station.

through stunning scenery. Once past the gorge made by the Water of Nevis, its roaring rapids and waterfalls gave way to the calm of the green meadow at Steall. We left the path to explore this jewel of a place, gazing up at the thundering waterfall and trying out the chain bridge. Spirits were high and rocks were thrown into the river to splash those edging their way across the wobbly chains.

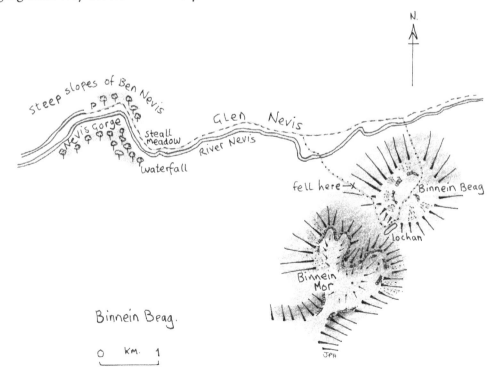

43

Aware that we had a long way to go, Ray soon had us marching along the path which follows the river. It was a day of sunshine and showers. The showers were heavy enough to force us to stop to put on waterproofs but it was so warm that they were back in the rucksacks as soon as the shower passed.

Binnein Beag is a steep, cone-shaped hill. Some of our party were climbing their first Munro and it took quite some time to get everyone safely to the top. We rested in the shelter cairn, a sun trap that day. I looked across Glen Nevis to Stob Ban and could see little dark specs moving near the top, I was sure that these were our colleagues under Struan's leadership.

We decided to go down to the bealach between Binnein Beag and Binnein Mor. Nestled there is a lochan, sparkling on that summer day and taking the colour of the blue sky. I was still full of energy and Binnein Mor looked so near. More than half the climbing was done and it seemed a pity to go back without climbing it as well as its smaller neighbour. I sat by the shore of the lochan, drinking the last of my tea and admired the graceful arêtes which curved around the scalloped corrie to meet at the summit. Ray was not keen. Our group was a mixture of experience and level of fitness and some were tired and had had enough. So we began to descend to Glen Nevis.

As so often in the mountains, our descent proved to be the most challenging part of the day. A stream tumbled down the steep slopes in a series of waterfalls to join the Water of Nevis far below and we followed its course. The rain had made the grasses and other vegetation slippery. I slipped and went quite literally head over heels to land spread-eagled in a sphagnum moss bog. Those watching from above described it as "spectacular" and one asked if I could do it again as she had missed it.

"Could you do it again please?"
Coming down from Binnein Beag 8/9/1.

We got back to the bunkhouse without further mishap, quickly got cleaned up and were soon tucking into a wholesome dinner. The meal was punctuated by many a toast, there was much laughter and impolite behaviour and it was, in all, a most satisfactory occasion.

Breakfast was a strange affair in that there was no argument about which Munro we should attempt. Perhaps the dominant members of our party had drunk a little too much the previous evening.

We headed to Laggan and parked at the Spey Dam. The walk up Glen Markie was pleasant and sociable, the wide path allowing the walkers to chat while the sun winked out from the broken white cloud above. We left the path to cross the Markie Burn and the serious business of the morning began. Ahead were the steep rock walls of Geal Charn's east-facing corrie, an ice-carved notch in the cliffs dividing the summit from Beinn Sgiath, a subsidiary top. We headed for the mountain's north-east ridge, threading through peat hags and bog.

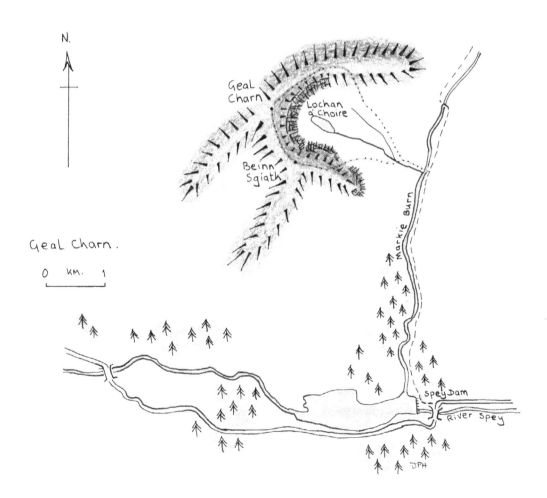

Morag, small, dark-haired, pink-cheeked, caught me up as I jumped across the black pools. She told me that she had been a keen hillwalker when younger, but had not been on a hill for years, tied as she was to her three children. Now that they were older she would love to get back to the mountains, but felt that it was very difficult for a woman. She said that it's a man's world, citing the Jolly Boys as an obvious example. I said that I couldn't change the Jolly Boys if they decided to continue with male only weekends, but she was most welcome to join us on other occasions. She replied that my walking pals might not be comfortable with that and… At that point she had misjudged her jump, absorbed as she was in this conversation and had taken a sudden dive into the semi-liquid black peat. When she emerged, there was a hint of damaged pride but she was back to her theme with barely a pause. I wondered whether this feisty lady would become a hillwalking companion in the future.

The top was wild and windy, with lovely views in every direction. We spent a while picking out landmarks like Ben Nevis and Creag Meagaidh then walked onto the south-east ridge. We dropped down in the lee of the wind and ate lunch perched high above the corrie. The sun came out to warm us and the Lochan a' Choire sparkled blue far below. A buzzard effortlessly avoided the rather lazy mobbing of a pair of ravens, using the updraughts of air which were generated by the corrie cliffs.

All too soon we were stepping from stone to stone across the Markie Burn again and turning back down the glen towards the cars and home.

Ben Lomond

 Kenny's hangover cure

October

Kenny had always wanted to climb Ben Lomond. He had been staying with his nephew in Edinburgh and I was waiting in my car at Harrison Park to meet him. He had asked me to have my phone as he was not sure of the way.

He sounded rough when he made his first call, saying that he was not sure where he was. I opened up a street map and asked him to find a street sign. "Turn right at the end, then take the second left," I advised. I continued to guide him until his car appeared in view. When he got out, he looked worse than he had sounded.

"I'm glad you're driving," he said.

"So am I," I replied.

As we drove the long road to Drymen, I heard the tale of the nephew and his student pals taking Kenny clubbing. How many clubs or what happened at the end he could not remember. "Whatever it was, it involved a lot of garlic," I replied.

We parked at Rowardennan on the shores of Loch Lomond. The morning was fine and I had a strange feeling of having stepped into a Tourist Board poster. We were about to climb one of Scotland's most iconic mountains.

Ben Lomond means Beacon Hill. This seems appropriate for a mountain which is instantly recognisable from so many points south of the Highland Boundary Fault. I had admired this graceful mountain so many times and was thrilled at the prospect of the day ahead.

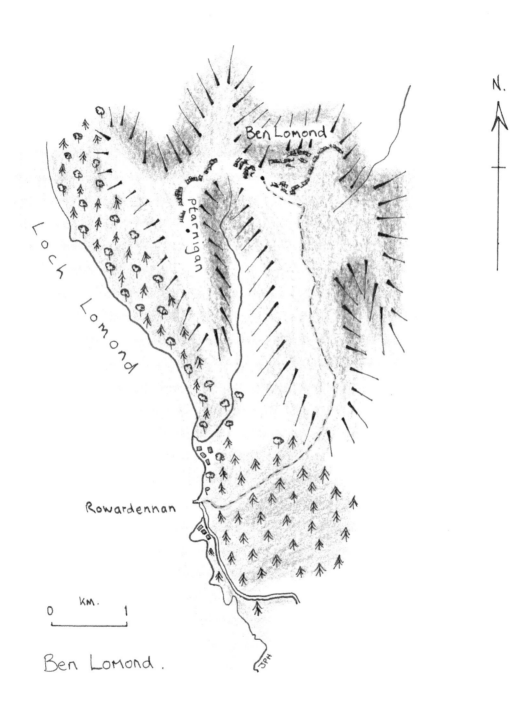

N.

Ben Lomond

Ptarnigan

Loch Lomond

Rowardennan

km.
0   1

Ben Lomond.

Ben Lomond
12/10/1

Kenny had "a bit of a head" and thought he might be sick. I suggested that this might help us solve the mystery of what the garlic had been in.

He decided to go at a good pace and "sweat it out". With that we set out along the path through the forest which skirts the mountain. It was a still and mild autumn day and Kenny was, indeed, soon sweating profusely. I began to find it difficult to walk behind in a vapour trail of what appeared to be pure alcohol, so we swapped places.

We left the trees behind and followed the well-used path up the crest of Ben Lomond's long south ridge. A herd of small black cattle were around the path, some lying on it. We noticed a bull watching over his harem of cows. I told Kenny that I'd often come across this breed in the North-west and never found them aggressive. My optimism proved well-founded as we wove between animals that seemed very much at ease with the world.

By the time we stopped for a cup of tea, Kenny was also at ease with the world, the excesses of the night before sweated out on our brisk ascent.

The walk to the top was delightful, with wide views opening up in all directions. From the summit ridge we could see the Central Valley of Scotland below us, from the Firth of

Forth in the east to the Firth of Clyde in the west. Looking west and north we gazed at the mountains of the southern Highlands, ridge behind ridge behind ridge. The peaks in the far distance were blue against the sky.

We considered a descent down the Ptarmigan Ridge but Kenny thought it best to quit while ahead and we ambled slowly down the path, enjoying the views as we went.

Sitting on a rocky viewpoint above the path while eating lunch, we tried to work out what each of the stretches of water and islands to the south-west were. Then a bunch of pretty girls came up the path and distracted us from our geographical speculations.

We packed up and walked back to the car in good fettle. The fine weather had held and Ben Lomond had lived up to our expectations. As we pulled off our boots, Kenny declared that this was the best ever hangover cure.

Beinn Ghlas, Ben Lawers and An Stuc

 Honey pieces and bananas

October

Dawn broke as we crossed the Highland Boundary Fault. The sun's rays touched the west side of the Tay valley, illuminating the wonderful golds, yellows and browns of the autumn forest. The road followed the river to Loch Tay, looking its very best on that crisp October morning.

Kenny, Allan and I were headed for the Lawers range. Driving along the north shore of the loch, the mountains rose to our right. Their tops were capped with cloud but, always the optimist, I suggested that this may lift as the morning wore on.

We parked at the Ben Lawers Visitor Centre and set off along a good path. The wind was bitter and we walked briskly to warm up.

The path climbed steadily until we were on the long south ridge of Beinn Ghlas. No longer in the shelter of the corrie, we felt the wind's full strength. While putting on our jackets and hats, a father and his two sons passed, the boys bent into the wind and struggling. They wore trainers and light clothes and were already looking blue. I hoped that their father would have the sense to turn back.

Most walkers seemed to be satisfied with Beinn Ghlas on that cold day. We stopped for a photograph on the summit, Kenny commenting that it would look like any other

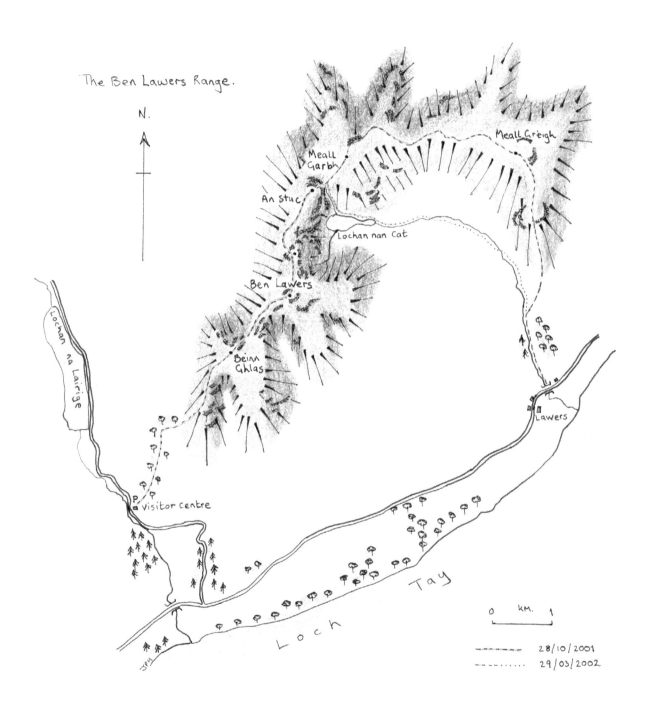

The Ben Lawers Range.

N.

Meall Garbh

An Stuc

Meall Greigh

Lochan nan Cat

Ben Lawers

Beinn Ghlas

Lochan na Lairige

Visitor centre

P.

Lawers

Loch Tay

0   KM.   1

28/10/2001

29/03/2002

Ben Lawers
and An Stuc
from Meall Garbh

cairn in cloudy conditions like this. We were soon on our way again, it being too cold to linger.

The climb up to Ben Lawers was harder than we anticipated. The distance on the map is not great, but this is a big mountain and the wind was in our faces. I thought about this well-loved mountain as I plodded up the path. The tenth highest in the British Isles, it is nearly 4,000 feet above sea level. There is uncertainty about its name. It could be named after a loud stream on its slopes or, more likely, means the claw or hoof mountain. Having seen it now from surrounding mountains on all sides I can appreciate that its shape, with deep, scallop-shaped corries, does indeed resemble a curved hoof from some viewpoints or, with its long, narrow ridges, a claw.

Ignoring Kenny's predictable sarcasm, we took more photographs on the top. Looking back, they can only be distinguished from Beinn Ghlas because I wrote on them when I collected the prints, proving that Kenny was right, of course.

My hands were numb with cold and, again, we did not linger in that cruel wind. We decided to try for the next Munro, An Stuc.

My companions fortified themselves with sweets and we picked our way down the bare rock of the steep ridge. We emerged from under the cloud and could see the path ahead. It curved down to a bealach and then rose steeply again to a peak with thin cloud blowing over its top. Dark crags fell away, especially to the east, down into the huge Coire nan Cat.

The wind was fierce in the bealach and there was no shelter so we postponed our long overdue lunch.

We pushed ourselves hard to climb to the next summit and, in the shelter of a large rock, I looked at the map. This was a Top, but An Stuc was still some distance NNE along the ridge.

Wearily, we made our way along that last stretch and were relieved to reach the last Munro of the day. No one had the energy or inclination to continue along the ridge in such difficult conditions.

Later, when reflecting on the walk, I understood that I had been seriously low on reserves of energy at that point. We had climbed three Munros on a day of strong, bitter cold wind without stopping to rest and, more importantly, to eat. My blood sugar was low and I was not thinking clearly. We should have considered walking back the way we had come only to the first bealach and then dropping down to Lochan nan Cat. We would have been able to walk back to the car south and then south-west, traversing the lower slopes of these hills. We would then have been out of the cloud and sheltered from the worst of the wind. Instead, we simply turned and walked back along the ridge.

It was as we climbed back up to Ben Lawers that I felt my energy drain away. For the first time, it crossed my mind that I might not make it down from a hill. I was still thinking sensibly enough, however, to work out that the problem was almost certainly down to not eating so I shouted ahead and we stopped in the lee of the nearest rock outcrop. The strange thing was that I did not particularly want to eat that sandwich but, washed down with a cup of tea, it did the trick.

We marched back up to the summit of Ben Lawers, then down, then back up to the summit of Beinn Ghlas. As we walked, the cloud thinned and suddenly blew away, leaving us with wonderful views across the Tarmachan ridge and down to the bright water of Loch Tay.

We stopped at a pub in Aberfeldy's square and I ordered roast lamb and red wine. As I ate, I felt a warm glow slowly spread down my cold arms and tired legs, reminding me again of the importance of balancing energy output with input. I pointed out that we had, by walking back along the ridge, climbed five Munros on that demanding day. It was later that I realised that I had been a poor leader not to have come down from the ridge and taken a low-level route back to the car.

The outing made a lasting impression on me in that I always carry plenty of food. I try to stop at intervals, whatever the conditions, for a cup of tea and eat something each time. Two favourites are honey pieces and bananas.

15/2/02

Meall nan Tarmachan

 Winter skills 1

February

The early morning air was cold and clear and we could see for miles under a dark blue sky. The low sun shone on the snow-capped tops, giving them a golden glow. Our car was parked a short distance from the head of Lochan na Lairige and we were looking forward to a day exploring the Tarmachans.

We looked south into the huge Coire Riadhailt and chose a route up onto Creag nam Bothan. Only two of us had brought an ice axe and crampons, so I decided to save weight and leave mine in the car. This, as experienced hillwalkers will be thinking, was a mistake.

After crossing the stream, we made our way across the corrie floor, walking over hard frozen peat bogs.

The going was easy on the ridge. We stopped for a cup of tea and enjoyed the views east over the Lawers range. Shortly after our break, we were walking on snow.

At the narrow bealach at the head of the corrie we turned south-west, having decided to explore the rocky tops on the ridge. This is narrow and quite exposed in places, the path winding between and over steep rocky outcrops. On that day, however, there was no path and we made our way through drifts of pristine snow.

I followed Struan's footsteps across a particularly steep slope and felt uneasy for the first time. I moved faster, aware that I had nothing to stop me should a slab of snow break away under my feet. The rest of the ridge provided a more secure route and I enjoyed the

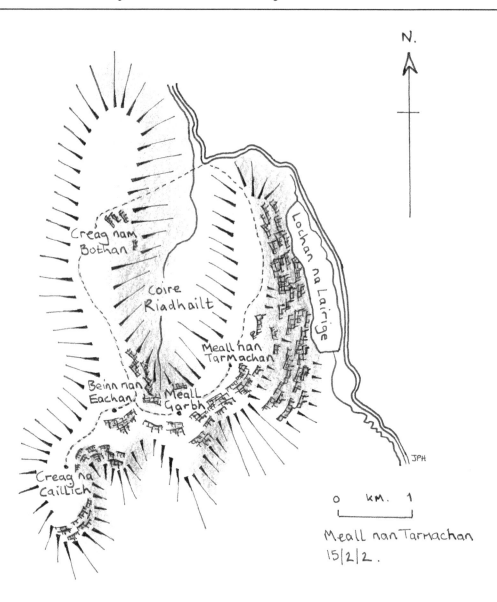

N.

Creag nam
Bothan

Lochan na Lairige

Coire
Riadhailt

Meall nan
Tarmachan

Beinn nan
Eachan

Meall
Garbh

JPH

Creag na
Caillich

0   km.   1

Meall nan Tarmachan
15|2|2.

winter landscape from our viewpoint on Creag na Caillich. Loch Tay reflected the deep blue of the sky and the hills in every direction were transformed into mountains by their blanket cover of new snow.

On the way back, we took a detour around the steep section that had scared me. At the bealach again we looked east along the ridge and the first obstacle, Meall Garbh, looked formidable in these conditions. Here and there were outcrops of black rock, exposed by the strong wind of the previous day but almost all of the daunting ascent was on deep snow.

Morag expressed reservations, wishing, like me, that she had brought her ice axe. I would have liked crampons too. Struan decided to kick steps in the snow to get us to the top. Kenny followed and, as Morag said she would bring up the rear, I went next. About 30 metres up the slope, Kenny missed his foothold. He recovered, but I had my second nasty moment of the day. If he had slipped, he would have carried me with him and Morag would also have been swept down the slope. I stopped for a while to put some distance between Kenny and myself and shouted down to Morag to do the same. All got to the top safely and we enjoyed the airy walk along the ridge to Meall nan Tarmachan, the highest point.

We had decided to return by the long north ridge which runs between Coire Riadhailt and Lochan na Lairige. The initial descent from the Munro summit was very steep.

Kenny began his descent, slipped, did a cartwheel, landed with his head pointing downhill and shot down the slope. We watched, frozen, as he hurtled past rocks before sliding to a stop in the hollow far below. A black object, his video camera, slithered to a stop beside him. In response to our calls he got stiffly to his feet, a little battered but in one piece. It was when we were all at the foot of that snow-covered slope that I decided that I would never again leave my ice axe and crampons behind on a winter outing.

We walked along the ridge until we found a sheltered spot and stopped to have our last cups of tea. The day's walking had been more demanding than we had anticipated and I could happily have nodded off in that sunny place. Struan and Morag felt the same. Even Kenny, normally anxious to get going, was subdued. He knew that he had had a lucky escape.

We stopped at a pub in Aberfeldy for a hot meal and discussed the day. It was agreed that hills that may be straightforward on a fine summer day can be turned into something potentially dangerous in winter conditions. We were uninjured but were not going to push our luck in the future. Kenny drained his glass of wine and declared that winter walking was not for him.

On the way home, I said that it was not just a matter of taking the right equipment on a winter expedition, a hillwalker should know how to use it as well. Struan offered to help.

First he gave me a booklet on using an ice axe, then he took me into the Cheviot Hills to practice. I wore an old nylon jacket and waterproof trousers to increase the velocity of my slide; the session was to be on the principle of do or die.

We walked up past the mountain rescue hut above the Bowmont Valley and stopped at a deep, steep-sided cleugh. The long slope to the stream below was suitably snow-covered.

Struan, being a good teacher, demonstrated. Then it was my turn to deliberately slip and use the ice axe as a brake. I slipped feet-first face down and feet-first on my back, twisting around as I slid down. Next it was head-first face down and, most daunting of all, head-first on my back. I tried the moves again and again, gaining more velocity each time before stopping.

Winter skills in the
Bowmont Valley.
February 2002.

JPH

Later, we sat drinking tea in the rescue hut. Struan commented that I had been a keen student. I replied that knowing my life may depend on this skill probably explained my enthusiasm.

29/3/02

Meall Greigh and Meall Garbh

 Winter skills 2

March

I t was Good Friday and a special day in another way, I had a day out in the hills with my son, Tom, as my companion. The spring morning made my heart sing. The perfect blue sky and sunshine were to last all day.

We could see that the tops still had caps of snow and took ice axes and crampons. I wanted to pass on my newly learned skill of ice axe arrest.

We parked outside a leather and horn craft shop at Lawers on the shore of Loch Tay. A pleasant woman from the shop told us that walkers were allowed to leave cars there but a contribution to the Lifeboats was expected. I dropped my coins into the model lifeboat and wondered why that particular charity was chosen, this place seemed so remote from the sea.

We walked up the southern spur of Meall Greigh, taking rests as Tom's dissolute student life had eroded his fitness. I did not mind in the least, this was a day to stop and stare.

A longer break among some boulders just at the snow line allowed us to enjoy the views. Those to the west towards the snow-capped An Stuc and Ben Lawers were particularly impressive.

We walked on across a blanket of old snow which reflected the sun, increasing its warmth. A long snow slope ran down to the bealach between Meall Greigh and Meall

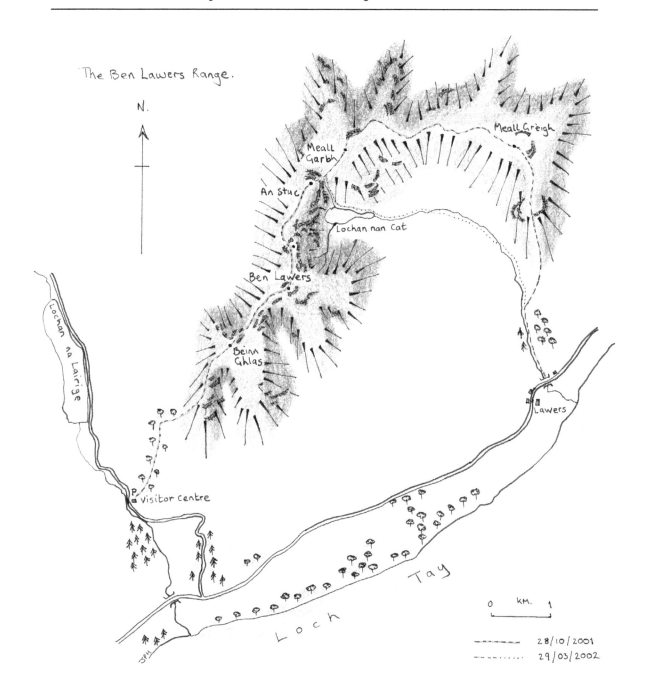

Garbh. Tom could not resist the temptation to slide down. He fashioned a makeshift sledge from his survival bag and pack, keeping his ice axe as a brake and he was off, hurtling down and whooping. The sledge fell apart near the bottom, the various bits arriving separately, but Tom was still in one piece. Dad trudged down more sedately.

Tom descending from
Meall Greigh 29/3/2.
JPH

A deep gully on Meall Garbh was filled with old compacted snow, somewhere between snow and ice. The east-facing wall was about eight metres high, perfect for a bit of crampon practice. We spent a happy hour there, using our crampons and ice axes to scale various sections of it.

The east ridge of Meall Garbh had an icy slope where the sun had not melted the snow and we kept on the crampons to walk up this. After that, the sun had done its job and snow only lay in hollows like our gully.

We scrambled down from the summit to the bealach between Meall Garbh and An Stuc and looked at the north-east face of this middle Munro of the Lawers range. It was steep and icy. Tom declared it too much of a challenge given his relative lack of fitness. We decided to go down to Lochan nan Cat which we could see sparkling in the sun far below on the floor of the giant corrie. This would give us a circular walk back to Lawers.

The descent, following a little stream as it roared down a series of waterfalls, was the hardest part of the day. The stream has cut deeply into the rock and we had to pick our way down and round the massive outcrops with great care. It was, however, wonderfully picturesque and I stopped a number of times to take photographs.

Tom had enjoyed the whole walk but he became most animated when we got down to Lochan nan Cat. The winter floes of ice were beginning to shrink and strips of water, reflecting the blue sky, were beginning to reclaim the surface. Dark spotted trout, still torpid after the winter cold, half-heartedly moved away from the warmer water of the bank as we passed. Tom, a keen angler, declared that he would return with his trout rod and cook his catch on the banks of this lovely lochan.

We came upon a path which followed the Lawers Burn and during the walk back to the car Tom entertained me with fishing stories. The day had been special indeed, one of the best I've had in the hills.

12/4/02

Carn Mairg, Carn Gorm, Meall nan Aighean and Meall Garbh

 A long walk in the Glen Lyon hills

April

We parked the car at Invervar on that fine spring day and set off up the burn, bound for the long round of the Glen Lyon Munros. I explained to Allan, Kenny and Morag that it would be safer to start with Carn Gorm. To start with Meall nan Aighean[2] would be to risk being taken by the fairies. Morag smiled as I got the expected response from my rugby coach friend, Kenny. Scepticism aside, we were soon walking up the long south-east ridge of Carn Gorm.

The name translates as Blue Mountain. Close up, it was more of a dull olive green with browns, the colours of tired vegetation emerging from under the recently melted winter snow. I had seen the mountain a fortnight before from the Lawers Range when it had appeared very dark with a blue tinge, the upper reaches still streaked with snow.

Once past the summit of the blue mountain the ridge walk was delightful, with the sun coming out for long spells to cheer us on our way.

We stopped just below the summit of Meall Garbh, rough hill, for lunch. Looking

---

2   Meall na Aighean on my O.S. map

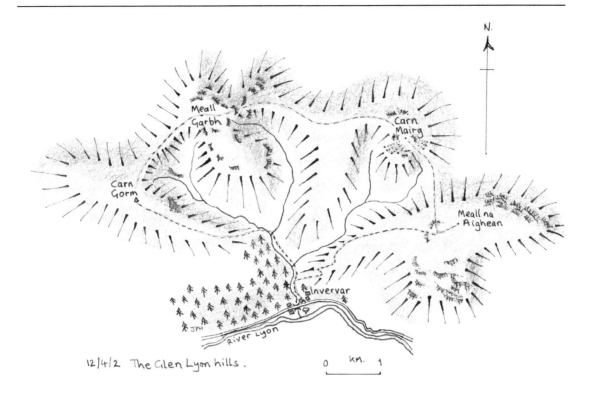

12/4/2 The Glen Lyon hills.

0 km. 1

south across Glen Lyon the Lawers mountains appeared so much more dramatic than the rounded hills we were exploring. There was much exposed rock and steep crags, with An Stuc distinctive as a sharp tooth. Snow patches lay on the summits. This view of the range is certainly more impressive than that from Loch Tay.

On we walked, up to Meall a' Bharr, down to a bealach and up again to Carn Mairg, pronounced marak, the hill of mist. This, our third Munro, is the highest of the range at 1041 metres. It is a massive rounded lump of a mountain with a number of rocky knolls on its flanks. The whole mass is being weathered away and extensive screes of large grey quartz-schist blocks lie on its steep slopes. From a distance it looks as if it is disintegrating, an ancient stump of a once grand mountain.

We made our way carefully down one of the scree slopes and looked up at Meall nan Aighean, the hill of the hinds. This is detached from the others, an east-west ridge running parallel to the main ridge. We had walked a long way and the steep slope ahead was enough for Allan to suggest that we could save it for another day. He was outvoted, however, and we were soon working our way up a north-facing spur. There were no hinds to be seen but we were treated to a lark singing, a small black speck above our heads and a sure sign that spring had truly arrived.

12/4/2
A rest on Carn Mairg, looking across to Meall na Aighean.

There were photographs taken at the top and everyone was pleased to have achieved so much on one walk. It had been a big day.

The light was beginning to fade a little as we clambered down the long ridge which leads back to Invervar. Legs were stiff and knees sore when we got back to the car.

We stopped at Aberfeldy on the way back. A bar on the street leading down to the square had a good menu for hungry hillwalkers. I had hot smoked herring for a first course, followed by a satisfying platter of fajitas, all washed down with a full-bodied red wine.

The meal was a jolly affair but the journey home was mellower, as tired muscles were rested and we looked back on a great walk.

Ben More and Stob Binnein

 A healing day

June

There are a few reasons why I spend time in the mountains, one of them is that it is a time of freedom, mostly freedom from the demands of work, so when hillwalking I avoid talking shop. Yet on that June day I talked shop for the entire journey up from the Borders to Crianlarich. I burned in the heat of an injustice I was sure I had suffered. Morag drove, listened and occasionally said something sympathetic.

That frame of mind is not the best for route planning. We parked to the east of Loch Lubhair, crossed the road, jumped the fence and headed straight for the massive bulk of Ben More in front of us. Finding a path was the last thing on my mind as I pushed hard up the mountainside, still unloading my bitter thoughts onto the ever-patient Morag.

Swirling cloud touched the summit and then blew away, but I barely registered this. I was going at a tremendous pace and was soaked with sweat. My companion kept up without complaint. Then we were on the broad summit and the cloud blew away again, revealing blue sky and the conical peak of Stob Binnein to the south. The sun gently warmed my face. I felt drained emotionally and physically, yet surprisingly better than I had felt since my upset at work.

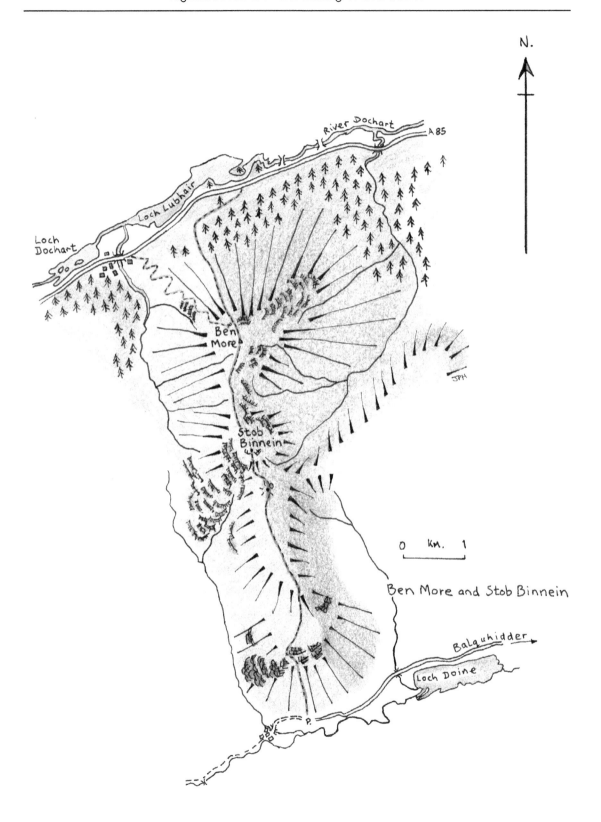

N.

River Dochart

A 85

Loch Lubhair

Loch
Dochart

Ben
More

JPH

Stob
Binnein

0   KM.   1

Ben More and Stob Binnein

Balquhidder

Loch Doine

P.

We sat down below the summit, the ridge to our next mountain before us. I drank tea and ate some lunch, quiet now and calm. Morag ate but said nothing. I felt my mood change, it was rather like curtains being drawn back from windows in my mind.

I broke the silence by asking if Morag was ready to go to Stob Binnein. I was somewhat ashamed of myself. As we made our way down to the bealach a buzzard came silently up the west side of the mountain. It was near enough to see the pale feathers under the wings and the yellow of its talons. The sun must have created a good thermal because the bird soared upwards without even moving its wings.

Our climb up to Stob Binnein was altogether more pleasant than the climb up to Ben More. The views were uplifting, especially west towards Ben Lui, still with a cap of snow which shone like crystal in the sun.

We climbed back up to Ben More to enjoy the last of our tea while sorting out the geography of the mountains which lie to the north. The light gave each range a peculiar two dimensional quality, as if cut from huge sheets of board and laid one behind the other to infinity. The colour of these mountains graded from lilac in the near distance to progressively deeper blues further away.

Using the path this time, we descended to the road and walked along the verge back to the car.

I had a massive appetite, partly due to the emotional energy I had expended earlier in the day. We stopped at the Suie Hotel and ordered a mixed seafood platter for a first course. Once that was eaten, I felt at ease with myself and the world. I sipped a glass of red wine while they cooked my steak. Morag made light of my apology for spoiling the start of the day but I vowed that I would never do that again. Days in the mountains are too precious to be contaminated by such things.

Canisp, Suilven, Conival, Ben More Assynt

 Summer hillwalking trip

August

Our first day had been perfect. Lesley had signed up for the summer walking holiday and Kenny, Allan, Morag, Struan and I had enjoyed showing her the outlandish and wonderful peaks of Coigach and western Sutherland. We had only climbed 600 metres but that was enough to give us an eagle's eye view of Sgurr an Fhidleir, Ben Mor Coigach, Cul Beag, Cul Mor, Suilven, Canisp and the rest.

We checked in to the hostel at Inchnadamph and got cleaned up for the evening. Muriel Gray, in her book about the Munros, had not been particularly complimentary about the hotel which stands on the other side of the River Traligill, the curiously named river of the trolls. We decided that if it was no good we would drive the long road to Lochinver each evening, which was far from an ideal end to a hard day on the hills.

The bar was comfy and we were met by a pleasant couple from northern England who had recently bought the hotel. Mrs did the kitchen while Mr did the bar. By the end of the evening we were more than happy with the service and the wholesome, home-made food.

Sun streamed through our dormitory windows the next morning. We decided to climb Ben More Assynt and Conival. For some it would be a first, for Struan, Kenny and me a previous ascent had been spoiled somewhat by strong wind and low cloud.

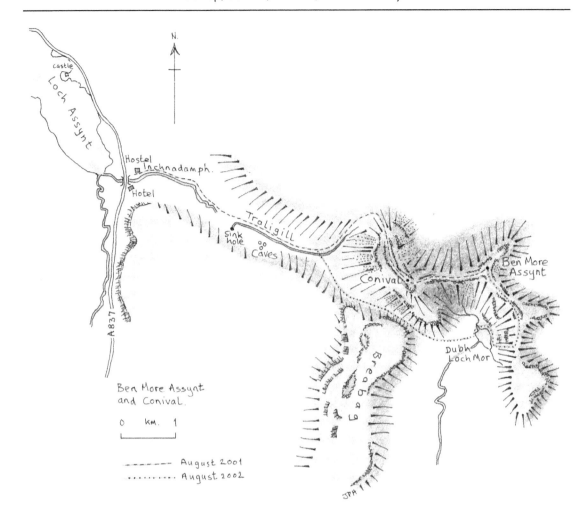

As we walked up the valley of the trolls, Struan told us about his companion being blown flat on his face on the ridge above. Kenny looked up at the blue sky and dared it to spoil his day for the second time.

Over the boulder-strewn pass between Conival and the Breabag ridge we walked and stopped on the shores of Dubh Loch Mor for an early lunch. We looked east at the tall cliff wall of Ben More Assynt's south ridge and tried to pick out a route north of the lochan, as suggested in the Scottish Mountaineering Council guide. Some time was spent over this but the general conclusion was that, for walkers, this would be rather extreme.

We tried south of the lochan instead. I selected a likely gully and went up this with Kenny, Morag and Allan. Struan walked further south where the ridge was lower to ascend with Lesley.

The gully was steeper than it appeared from below and we were using our hands as well as our feet as we neared the top. "This is certainly not hillwalking," remarked Kenny. Morag suggested that a rope might have been a good idea. My gully had not turned out to be an ideal route.

To make matters worse, the clear morning skies disappeared the moment we reached the crest of the ridge. Kenny's colourful language as the cloud blew in is unprintable. This was the second time he had climbed this mountain to have his dream of panoramic views frustrated ("And the last," he assured us).

Then to make matters worse again, we were not sure about Struan and Lesley. Had they come up? How broad was the ridge and could they miss us in this poor visibility? We shouted but there was no reply. It seemed a long time later that two ghostly figures loomed out of the mist. Struan was none too pleased that the party had separated, making it clear that this is simply not done.

The cloud swirled over Ben More Assynt's south ridge, thinning at times to reveal spectacular drops on either side. I was thrilled to be here again in this mountain landscape of such great character and vowed, (although not out loud), to return.

We had tea and a second lunch among the massive quartzite boulders of the mountain, listening in vain for the tap, tap, tap of Blind Pew. Then we gingerly made our way along the boulder ridge to Conival.

Descending into the valley of the trolls I experienced a moment of déjà vu as we emerged from under the cloud, still high up on Conival's western flank, and saw before us a bright sunlit landscape of mountain and loch. A Munro path led down by little waterfalls and I slipped on the smooth wet surface of a quartzite block. My left forearm hit the sharp-angled top of the rock and broke my fall. I was concerned that I'd put a hole in my mountain jacket and it did not occur to me that I might have fractured a bone, which was, as I discovered later, just what I had done. It has made me wary of stepping on wet rocks, particularly if they are fine-grained. I never gave my sore arm a thought, however, and we had a cheery walk back to the hostel in the late afternoon sunshine.

Showers were essential but we were anxious about missing our deadline for bar suppers. Kenny's solution was to shower before we'd untied our bootlaces and he drove the 100 metres to the hotel to give our orders.

The rest of us, clean and changed, walked across. Or rather limped across in the case of Lesley. Her new boots had not been a success and her toes were sore. She said that she was not going to let that spoil her walking holiday and did not complain at all the following day. I found out later that she had lost most of her toenails.

The next day I drove to Lochinver with Morag following in her seven-seater. We left it at the car park on the road to Glencanisp Lodge and I drove us back to Inchnadamph. We then drove down the road towards Ledmore Junction, stopping just north of Loch Awe. Our plan was to walk to the top of Canisp and then Suilven, ending at Lochinver where Morag's car would be waiting.

The day was fine again, with white cloud and patches of blue sky. Our first obstacle was the River Loanan. Some managed to cross with dry feet and some did not. Kenny had wet feet but was in upbeat mood, telling Allan that he was "a wuss", when he complained.

Oddly, Kenny remained positive even when we walked into cloud near the top of Canisp, poking fun at Struan for calling the hill Cansip. He did not have to worry, however, because the cloud was only a thin blanket over Assynt and once above it there were crystal-clear views and blue sky. It was one of my strangest moments in the mountains. Cloud lay in a brilliant white sheet and the mountain peaks sat on top like islands. The scene was made more remarkable by the shape of Suilven and its neighbours to the south, each

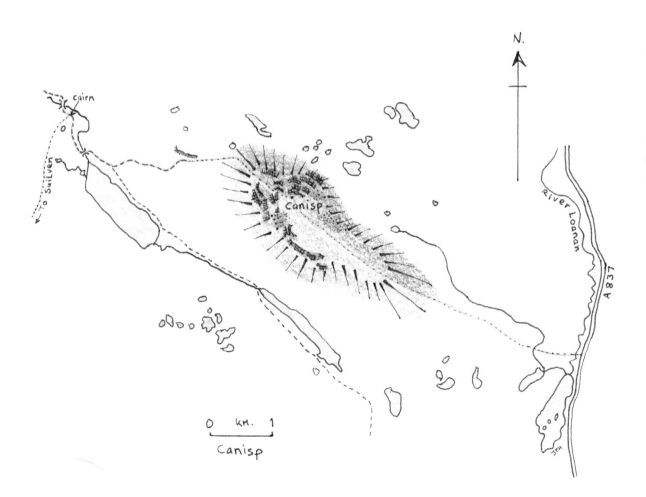

Canisp

rising as a near vertical-sided pillar. Even more bizarre was the second sheet of cloud, 50 metres or so above Suilven's summit, which stretched across the sky from above our heads and in an unbroken layer as far as we could see to the south, west and north. Above this was blue sky and bright sunshine. It was rather like looking out of an aeroplane window.

I explained about temperature inversions while Morag photographed this natural phenomenon. We were just below the quartzite-capped summit, on the top of steep, west-facing crags and it was here that we decided to have our lunch while enjoying this amazing view.

Skies and weather never stay the same for long in the North-west and soon the cloud thickened. All views vanished and we found a way down the steep western side of the mountain, hoping to discover a path marked on the map, a path which crossed the outflow from Loch na Gainimh by a bridge.

I took out my map, Struan produced his compass and we followed his bearing, walking in a straight line to landmarks like large boulders. Not long afterwards, we realised that we were walking on the path, Struan's bearing having been perfect.

The clouds lifted and with them our mood as we approached the seemingly impregnable walls of Suilven. Kenny had been to the top before and he was in his element teasing those who had not.

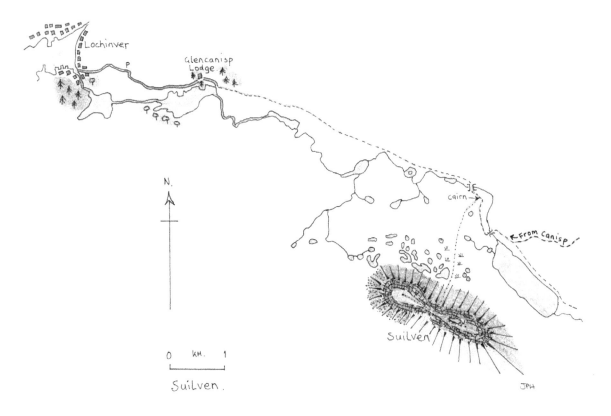

We seemed very small indeed as we stood at the foot of this iconic mountain, looking at the precipitous path up to the Bealach Mor. It was hot work scrambling up and Kenny expressed his disappointment not to have met the attractive young woman wearing only her bra and pants who we had admired last time.

Canisp from Bealach Mór,
Suilven, August 2002.

The fickle weather seemed on our side because the clouds broke into thin tatters once we were on the ridge and there were excellent views south to Stac Pollaidh and its neighbours, towering above a watery wilderness. Knobs and knuckles of ancient gneiss stood among a hundred lochans. In the west, dark islands rose from a sparkling sea.

We drank tea as we drank in this extraordinary landscape and then it was time to continue our walk. The long trek to Glencanisp Lodge was pleasant in late afternoon sunshine but we were weary when we stood on the side of Loch Druim Suardalam. We looked back over the still water of the loch to the fortress-like shape of Suilven, Lesley amazed that we had managed to climb it.

The sky had cleared of all cloud the next morning and it looked like being a scorcher. Lesley's feet were sore and the others had had enough of the hills. I suggested a trip to the beach and no one needed persuading.

We drove south past the Knockan Cliff and turned onto the most beautiful of roads. The fantastically-shaped mountains and the lochs at their feet looked their best in the intense morning light. We parked at Achnahaird. Those who had never seen the bay's pale sands and clear, turquoise water were surprised and we were all impressed.

I had a swim and then lay in the sun to dry off, dreaming of my next trip to this special place.

August

Aonach Beag and Aonach Mor. The Aonach Eagach: Sgor nam Fiannaidh and Meall Dearg

---

I meet an Angel

September

walked along Glen Nevis with Struan and Morag, Struan a little morose. We were staying at Tulloch Station again and the previous evening had been lively, explaining his subdued humour. Subdued perhaps, but he was our leader and just after the ruin at Steall he set off north-east, heading for Sgurr a' Bhuic, taking a straight line to the summit. His pace was relentless, more suited to a machine than a human being. It was hard but it worked wonders in clearing the head.

Glen Nevis seemed to steam as we toiled up its steep slopes, a strong wind tearing the vapours into shreds. We were caught in a heavy shower, the first of a series on that unsettled day.

It was a relief to be up on the high ridge at Sgurr a' Bhuic, most of the hard work over. The shower had blown away and the route to Aonach Beag was clear, curving around a deep corrie cut into the south side of the mountain. Dark cliffs fell away to the north and east. We followed an intermittent path to Aonach Beag, our jackets on to keep out the cold wind. The sun came out and we were treated to a perfect view of Carn Mor Dearg, its knife-edge curved arête an airy stairway to the summit of Ben Nevis.

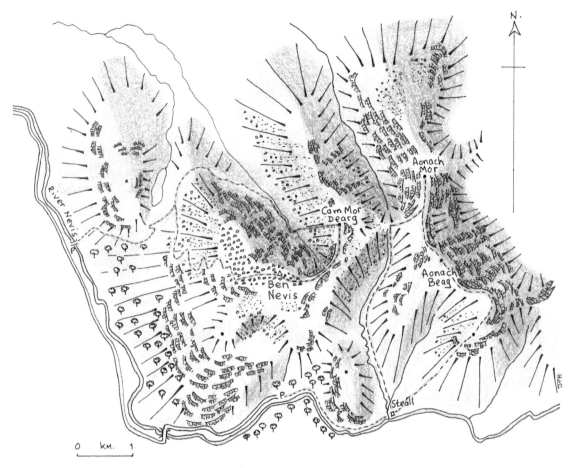

The Ben Nevis area.

After Aonach Beag we descended to a narrow rocky bealach but as this acted like a wind tunnel we kept moving and were soon climbing the south ridge of Aonach Mor. Grey cloud rushed towards us and brought hail with it, the icy pellets rattling off my cap.

As grass gave way to drifts of stones, the path disappeared again and we had to navigate with map and compass in the poor visibility. The map showed that we were walking along an elongated plateau about 200 metres wide with massive drops on either side. Care was vital, but Struan is always reliable in such situations so we were happy to follow him.

The summit was rather uninspiring but we decided to sit on its lee side to have a bite to eat and a cup of tea, hoping for another break in the clouds and the all-important views. Just as we packed up the clouds blew away in ghostly vapours, revealing the Grey Corries, linked by a sinuous ridge stretching away to the east. The range looks impressive from this viewpoint, a wilderness of pale grey frost-shattered rock, covering the long, steep slopes in a mantle of scree.

The sun stayed out as we walked south down the ridge from Aonach Mor, giving us clear views of the Mamores on the opposite side of Glen Nevis. Deep corries have eaten into these rounded mountains, all linked by fine, narrow ridges. The shapely Binnein Mor stood above the other peaks.

Struan led us along a path which ran west down a steep spur to the bealach at the head of the Allt Coire Giubhsachan. As we descended into the corrie the clouds rolled over again, but the weather did not throw anything too extreme at us on our walk out.

The couple who run the hostel prepared an excellent meal for the weary walkers and at the table we swapped stories of our day. Some inexperienced walkers had completed the long walk to the Lairig Leacach, with the majority of that party climbing Stob Ban. One of them was so stiff that she had to be showered by her friends.

After the customary "fast sleep", I was up early on the Sunday, planning to complete the ridge on the north side of Glen Coe with Morag. We were breakfasted and on the road before the others had stirred.

The Aonach Eagach 1/9/2.

As we drove along Glen Coe, we looked up at its grim north wall, the Aonach Eagach (notched ridge). It was difficult to pick out the individual features marked on the map.

We parked a short distance before Allt-na-reigh cottage and found a narrow path which twisted and turned up towards Am Bodach. Walking poles were soon secured to rucksacks and we were using our hands to scramble up to this first summit.

Once on top we could see before us the narrow crest of the ridge, studded with sharp rock teeth. It looked like the most challenging section was over a kilometre away but we were mistaken. A sudden drop of about 15 metres appeared. Morag reminded me to turn and face the rock and I lowered myself over the side, searching for good holds. The ridge walk was already exhilarating and it had only just begun.

At the bottom of this obstacle we made our way with care, still using hand holds, back to the crest of the ridge. There was some first class scrambling on the rest of the route to Meall Dearg. We stopped for a breather on its summit. From our vantage point the Mamores to the north looked majestic in the morning light. The daunting mountains on the south side of Glen Coe were dominated by Bidean nam Bian, pinnacle of the hills, lit on its east side by a broad shaft of sunlight.

The next section of the ridge was hard work. It was a cool day but I was soon down to my base layer as I climbed down gullies, stretched for holds on slabs and climbed up narrow chimneys. There were sections where the exposure produced a rush of adrenaline, these were no places to slip.

Pinnacle followed pinnacle and we began to tire. The previous day had been a hard one and lack of sleep was taking its toll. Finding a place to sit, however, needed some ingenuity. We settled for a perch with barely room for two and had reviving tea and a snack. It was not a place for anyone with a touch of vertigo, there was an awful lot of space in front and below.

Then it was up another narrow chimney to the dizzy height of a tower. From its top we could see that it looked like there was only one (rather scary) pinnacle left. We were soon at its foot and could not see an obvious way up without a rope. A path of sorts clung to the

The Aonach Eagach 1/9/2

north side of this spire of rock, but it was narrow with a long, long drop. We inched our way along, using hand holds for security.

Back up on the ridge we realised that the pinnacle was the last obstacle. We went down to a col and then climbed steeply up to Stob Coire Leith. From that Top we looked back over the notched ridge. I told Morag that my only regret was taking the path along the side of that last pinnacle. I would not recommend that to anyone. If I stand in front of that rock face again I will find the holds and go over the top.

Weary again, we completed the walk to the second Munro, Sgorr nam Fiannaidh, pronounced skor nam feeanee. This is the peak of the Fingalians, those fair-haired warriors of Celtic legend. We stopped here to admire the view before our descent. Sgorr na Ciche, which, given its shape, had to be named after a woman's breast, stood firm and pert above Loch Leven. An eagle glided over from Beinn a' Bheithir, heading towards Kinlochleven.

We noticed a solitary figure coming up from Glen Coe, he was gaining height fast. As he came closer we observed that he wore trainers and had no pack. I guessed from his short, military style haircut and muscular build that he was on leave from the forces. He got to the top barely out of breath and told us that he had left his family down at the Clachaig Inn to break their journey and had taken the opportunity to bag a quick Munro. He then asked about our day. We told him that we were weary and were glad that we were at the point where we could descend from the ridge. I said that it was a pity about the walk along the length of Glen Coe to get the car, but the day had been worth it. We said our farewells and off he sped, soon a small speck far below.

Our brains were not working at this stage and we simply followed the path down to the Clachaig Inn. It was only when we realised how badly eroded and dangerous it was that we recalled reading about other, more sensible, descents. As we skidded down the scree I told Morag that my plan was to walk back to Allt-na-reigh while she sat at the Inn with the packs. She did not, of course, object. My legs, however, were like jelly by this stage and the four kilometre trek on tarmac to the car was a grim prospect.

The Inn grew gradually larger as we made our ungainly approach. A Range Rover stood on the road outside. As we walked up to it I recognised the fit young man from the summit, his family sat with him.

"Come on, hop in," he said, "I'll run you along to your car."

At this point I realised that I had been wrong about his occupation, he was an angel doing good work on Earth and I told him so. I also said that he was especially kind to allow someone so sweaty and dirty into his clean car (but only when safely inside). He just flashed me the sort of smile that I now associate with angels and in a few minutes, there was my car.

Beinn Luibhean, Beinn Ime and The Cobbler

 A surprise outing

September

Struan is not the sort to devote time to long term planning. The telephone rang, "How do you fancy the Arrochar Alps?"

"Great, when were you thinking of going?"

"Now."

Which was how I was surprised to find myself at the Rest and be thankful pass one early autumn day.

Struan also has a direct approach to hills. We crossed the road and went straight up the west side of Beinn Luibhean, the hill of the little plants, scrambling up some easy crags and detouring around others. The SMC Corbett guide book describes this route as "continuously steep" and suggests that, apart from being short, it "has little else to recommend it."

It certainly did not take us long to reach the top, where we sat down to drink tea and survey this interestingly named range of hills. The day was mild, still and grey, the tops all well clear of cloud and visibility excellent. I had thought that the name may be ironic, but was instead very taken with these abrupt, knobbly "Alps", they were certainly mountains rather than hills. Part of the reason for their distinctive character is that there are tough

diorite intrusions among the ubiquitous quartz mica schists. The diorite was much more resistant than the schists to the scouring of the ice sheets. I had no idea that there was such a wonderful landscape so near to Glasgow. It is the sort of area one is drawn to explore and as I looked across Loch Restil to the massive rock walls of Beinn an Lochain I hoped I would return.

Beinn an Lochain triggered an interesting conversation about Scotland's hills and mountains. It is a fine mountain, with a narrow north-east ridge rising by a succession of rock crags to the summit, yet was demoted from the table of Munros following a more accurate measurement of its height by the Ordnance Survey. Does this make it less worthy of the effort of climbing it? So many splendid mountains in the Highlands fall short of the 3,000 feet mark and I told Struan that I would not neglect them. "Mind you," he replied, "we're not getting any younger. It might be safer to climb the highest ones first and then enjoy the rest."

As we dropped down the east side of Beinn Luibhean we lost sight of the road and entered a silent and lonely place, far removed from the busy world only 20 miles away to the south. We had not yet come across a path and I followed Struan as he took another direct line to the top of Beinn Ime, our only Munro of the day.

We sat on the summit to eat lunch, discussing the mountain's name, which translates as the butter mountain. I think that it goes back to a time when more people lived in this area and the high pastures were used in the warmer months. Herders would live in the shielings and, as happens to this day in the high pastures of the Alps, butter and cheese would be made there.

The descent was easy, following a well-worn Munro path which led south to the Bealach a' Mhaim.

At the bealach we had a choice, the left path wound up to Beinn Narnain and the right to The Cobbler. We took the right path.

The mountain is a complex with three sharp rocky peaks, the north-east pinnacle overhanging the rest of the mountain in dramatic fashion. Its proper name is Ben Arthur, probably named after the post-Roman British war leader. The mountain may well have marked the northern limit of the territory he protected from the invaders from across the North Sea. It is known today, however, as The Cobbler, probably a corruption of Beinn Goblach, the forked peak, which is suitably descriptive. I have also read that it may be the peak of the forked loch, Loch Long's name having originally been Loch Goblach.

We sat on top of the great overhanging rock which crowns the northernmost summit and were thrilled by the prospect of the rest of this most interesting of mountains. It seemed like a rocky crown, the points leaning oddly inwards towards the centre.

The middle pinnacle was a treat. We wriggled through a narrow keyhole in the summit rock and gingerly made our way along an exposed ledge to be confronted by a tall tower of rock. The true summit was clearly on the flat top of this tower. It looked like the face in front of us would be for climbers only, so we edged our way around the base to find an obvious route up. From the side, however, it was worse, compounded by a very long drop. I reasoned that generations of agile hillwalkers must have climbed it, so we must have missed something. We back-tracked, looked at the tower again and this time could see a probable route. As often happens, once we got onto the rock it was easier to see which ledges to use. We were so focused on finding safe holds that we shut out the exposure until standing on the rock platform at the very top. I was glad that I have a head for heights. It is a glorious place, with panoramic views over Loch Long, Loch Lomond and Ben Lomond.

On the summit of The Cobbler
28/9/2

Down again, we explored the rest of the mountain. There are other pinnacles, huge slabs, deep cracks and dark caves. I could have spent a whole day up there.

Time was marching on, however, so we dropped down into the valley to the north of The Cobbler, followed the stream down to the old military road and then used the old road to get back to the car at Rest and be thankful.

Struan had got to know the West End of Glasgow when his daughter was a student there. He drove to an Italian restaurant and there I rounded off my unexpected day with an excellent seafood pasta, washed down with a glass of Chianti Classico.

14/10/02

Ben Vorlich and Stuc a' Chroin

 Close encounters

October

Ben Vorlich means the hill of the bay and I started, with Morag as my companion, at Ardvorlich Farm, which means the height above the bay. I looked down to Loch Earn but could see no such feature. The stream running down Glen Vorlich has made a delta in the loch in recent centuries, so the bay may well have been there at one time.

We passed Ardvorlich House and followed the track into the glen, a lovely place of wooded lower slopes with craggy heights above. Before long, we were on the stony path up the NNE ridge of Ben Vorlich. The path runs on the west side of the ridge so we were sheltered from the cold east wind which blew that day. We stopped to put on waterproofs in a heavy squall of rain, but it soon passed and wide views to the north over Loch Earn and the Lawers range were opened up.

While sitting by the path eating a snack and sipping tea, we were joined by a ghillie leading two smart matching grey ponies. He wore a tweed cap, jacket and breeches with traditional woollen hose and leather brogues. We had an interesting chat and I shared my sandwich with his springer. There was a party shooting deer, but over the ridge on the east side of Ben Vorlich. If we stuck to the path and the high ridges we would be well out of the way.

We said farewell and continued up the path, surprised by the number of red grouse we saw, some clattering up from under our feet and setting my heart racing.

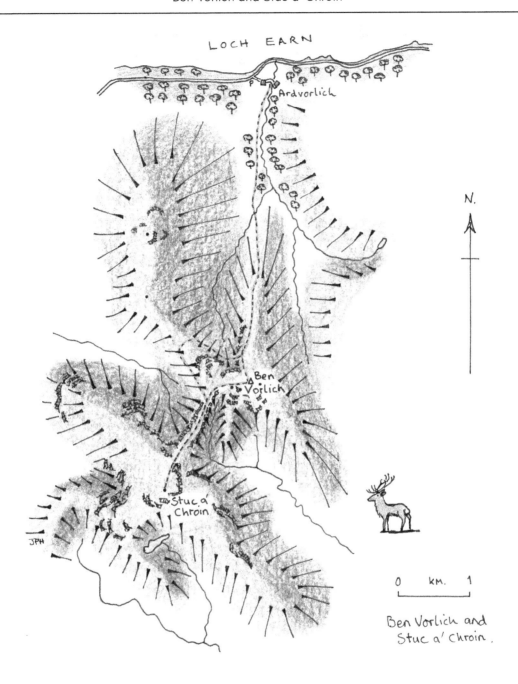

Ben Vorlich and
Stuc a' Chroin.

Just before the summit there was another heavy squall, the rain almost horizontal. It did not last long but left cloud on the mountain top. We reached the triangulation pillar and then took the path to a large cairn about 100 metres to the south-east. I remembered that the SMC guide book made reference to a line of fence posts which should be followed to point the way to Stuc a' Chroin. There was a clear path in the right general direction, however, so we went down it. It was the lack of fence posts that made me stop. I looked at the map and, from the topography, decided that we were probably on the south-east ridge. We had made the classic mistake of walking off onto the wrong ridge simply because there was a path down it. I was not happy with myself as we toiled back up to the cairn.

More wary this time, we took the next ridge to the west. This one, however, barely had a path and this soon petered out. We stopped again and as we did so the cloud blew away in rags for a few minutes. We saw a line of steep crags to the west, with a deep gully between us and them. "Our route," I declared, "lies along the crest of those crags." So we turned again to make our way back to the cairn but stopped in our tracks as a stag bounded up the slope from the east, steam blowing from his nostrils. He stood his ground just in front of us while his hinds crested the ridge and dropped down into the gully. Once they were safely over, the stag turned and joined them. He was moving them well out of the way of the guns on the east side of Ben Vorlich.

We were a little fed up with the cairn as we climbed up to it for the third time. I stopped to think and had a brainwave, what if the true summit was the triangulation pillar? The fence posts would then show us the way from it, not from this cairn. We walked back to the pillar and, of course, all was revealed. The broad path, complete with old fence posts, led us onto a craggy and narrow SSW ridge which was the correct route.

The clouds blew away again and we could see our next mountain rising before us. We still had a fair climb before we were done.

We stopped on rocky ground at the foot of crags. I remembered the guide book informing walkers that one route to the top was by scrambling up these, but warned that it was somewhat challenging. As we considered our options the next squall, of sleet this time, slammed into us from the east. That decided matters, we put our heads down and followed the path around the side of the crags. We could enjoy scrambling on them on another, more benign, day.

Putting our heads down
on Stuc a' Chroin 14/10/2

By the time we had climbed to the summit ridge the sleet had stopped, but the cold wind made it feel like we were in the Arctic. This impression was strengthened by a group of ptarmigan, their feathers turned to white in patches, reminding us that winter was near. They ran off to disappear among the rocks, not over concerned about our intrusion into their high sanctuary.

We reached the summit and agreed that the day had been hard work. At that point the cloud blew away to the west, the sky brightened a little and we were treated to the fine views we were denied on Stuc a' Chroin's more famous neighbour.

The walk out was straightforward. We followed a path which skirted the west flank of Ben Vorlich, having no desire to climb up there for a fourth time. It took us to a col on the mountain's north-west ridge and then we followed a high path which took us round the back wall of Coire Bhuide. This led us to the point where we had met the ghillie.

The walk down into Glen Vorlich was delightful. We were sheltered from the wind, it seemed positively mild and the sky had brightened up. It was a joy to walk among the rowans, alder, birch and hawthorn, all in their autumn yellows, browns and golds.

On the other shore of the loch we ate a bar supper in the Clachan Cottage Hotel, watching the sky turn pink and dark orange as the sun set in the west.

Driesh and Mayar

Dreich on Driesh

November

O n a rather bleak last day of November, more early winter than the end of autumn, I drove up Glen Clova with Morag. It was raining steadily and most sensible souls would have turned back by then. But, as so often happens, it seemed worse from inside the warm car looking out than it actually was. We stopped in the car park in Glen Doll and put on our boots and waterproofs.

It rained steadily as we followed the pathways up through Glendoll Forest and we talked about what makes us do this. The answer, of course, was all around. The cool, rainwashed air; the rushing burns; the sad yellow of the larch needles; the springy, soft carpet of moss on which we walked; these were some of the reasons.

We came out onto the open hillside on the old Kilbo Path, cut into the side of the Shank of Drumfollow. Considering that it rained all day, the visibility was surprisingly good. The crags on the far side of the corrie, blackened by the downpour, had wide ribbons of white water tumbling down them. Driesh was a massive rounded lump looming above.

At the point where a path branches off to the south-east lies a massive boulder. It was the best shelter we could see so I spread out my survival bag and we sat under the boulder's overhang. Despite the weather we were both upbeat, our moods infectiously cheerful. Two hillwalkers arrived as we drank our tea. They stopped for a chat and laughed to see us sitting in a puddle.

The ridge to Driesh is at first steep and rocky and then it broadens out to a wide, stony plateau of arctic tundra. The hill's name is supposed to mean thorn bush or bramble, but there was nothing much there except lichen and dwarf juniper clinging to the ground. The wind howled and the rain turned to sleet.

I was wondering what could possibly survive there when I saw the first ptarmigan. They were in their white winter plumage, which seemed appropriate. As we walked we saw more and I remarked that I had never before seen such a large number together. They generally just run away to hide among rocks but something spooked them and they rose into the air together, their small wings beating furiously. The strong wind caught them and they compensated by flying sideways.

Ptarmigan flying sideways
Driesh   30/11/2

We did not linger at the summit but returned to cross the Kilbo Path and follow the well-worn track to Mayar, our second Munro of the day. Its name is a mystery, perhaps a distortion of the Gaelic magh ard, high plain.

Brighter patches began to appear in the sky and the hills to the north were revealed, looking curiously two dimensional in shades of grey. Morag picked out Lochnagar, almost due north from our viewpoint at Mayar's summit cairn. We looked from west to east across the Mounth, a wild and lonely place it looked on that day.

The wind dropped a little but the rain continued. We had considered returning by the path down the Fee Burn but decided that it might well be slippery and difficult in those poor conditions, so we were soon back on the Kilbo Path.

There was nowhere sheltered to stop so we plodded on until we were back in the forest. We rested under some young larch trees, sitting on a bank of fallen needles and cushions of moss. A little burn gurgled by. In companionable silence, warming my hands on my

cup of tea, I felt perfectly content. It had rained all day and we had not seen the wide views from the tops, but the charming micro-landscape in front of me was compensation for this.

Not long after, we were driving down Glen Clova when Morag said, "We forgot to check whether we left anything behind."

"Best go back then," I replied.

It was just as well that we did for there were Morag's boots, already half filled with water.

14/2/03

Carn nan Gabhar, Braigh Coire Chruinn-bhalgain, Carn Liath.

 ## Return to Beinn a' Ghlo

February

Beinn a' Ghlo had lived up to its name, misty or clouded hill, the last time I had climbed it and I was hoping to see it properly on that February day.

Struan, Morag, Kenny and I had driven up to Pitlochry the previous evening and checked into the hostel there. We had eaten a meal in the pub next door and drunk rather too much.

Despite having a bit of a hangover, I was up and away with the others in the dark of the winter morning. We parked at Loch Moraig and set off along the track in the dawn light.

We passed the hut and took the track straight up the face of Carn Liath, Beinn a' Ghlo's westernmost Munro. Struan set a fast pace and, despite it being well below zero, I was soon sweating. By the time we reached the high snowfields my hangover had gone and I felt great.

There was a light but cold south-west wind so we walked beyond the summit cairn and down the slope a little to find some shelter. The sky was now deep blue and the pale winter sun, though not able to raise the temperature much, lifted our spirits. Kenny was particularly cheerful as his two previous visits had been spoiled for him by low cloud and he had vowed never to return.

We sat in the snow to have a hot drink, our route to the next summit clear before us. Beinn a' Ghlo is a mountain range rather than a single mountain. To climb everything and be back to the car in daylight would mean making fast progress. Struan asked if we had torches.

N.

Loch
Loch.

Carn nan Gabhar

Braigh Coire
Chruinn-bhalgain

Red
deer
rut

Carn
Liath

JPH

0   km.   1

—— Carn Liath and
Braigh Coire Chruinn-bhalgain,
14/10/99.
...... Carn nan Gabhar, 14/2/3.

Beinn a' Ghlo.

P
Loch
Moraig

It was easy walking down the ridge to the bealach and then we were climbing again up onto Braigh Coire Chruinn-bhalgain, the strangely named height of the corrie of round blisters. Snow and ice covered the rocks of the summit dome. Ptarmigan trotted away from us but did not seem too perturbed. We stopped at the cairn to enjoy the views and take photographs. The view in every direction was superb. To the west, a cream coloured mist lay like a blanket over the land, the brilliant white mountain tops sticking up above it. Around us the snowfields were tinged with yellow. The sky at the horizon was a deep golden yellow, fading to pale yellow, pale blue and then the very deepest of blue as the eye travelled upwards.

The descent from Braigh Coire Chruinn-bhalgain was interesting. The view ahead (east) of the final Munro, Carn nan Gabhar, was so impressive that we stopped on a slope of iced-up boulders to have our lunch and enjoy it. It was still well below zero and the wind, although light, was adding a significant wind chill factor. Our boulder field was well placed to give us shelter.

14/2/3
On Beinn a' Ghlo.
Looking west to the peaks
around Ben Alder, which
are rising above a sea of
white mist.

Fortified by our hill food and hot drinks, we walked down to the bealach and then began the last climb up to the ridge leading to our final summit. There was a fair distance between us at this point and my companions seemed tiny in that winter wilderness. We had not seen another soul, it was silent and forsaken.

We passed the cairn and walked on to the triangulation pillar. It was built on a platform of rocks, rocks and pillar thickly coated with ice crystals. Horizontal icicles stuck out from the pillar, pointing the way the wind was blowing. I walked to the north-east edge of the summit plateau until I stood on the very edge of the crags making the headwall of the Coire Cas-eagallach. From this high vantage point I looked down into the deep, steep-sided Glen Loch. The glen was in shadow, still and mysterious, with the curiously named Loch Loch's black surface patterned by ice floes. I wanted to stay but knew that Struan would be leading the others back by now and looking over his shoulder for me to catch up.

We retraced our steps in the snow to the bealach at 964 724 and climbed onto Airgiod Bheinn, the south-west top of Carn nan Gabhar. From there we looked west and south-west, the sun now low and the sky already turning pink along the horizon.

Struan chose a long snow slope and we managed to slide down most of it to reach the broad glen to the south. It was heavy going over the snow covered heather, detouring around deep drifts, until we reached the Allt Coire Lagain. It had been too cold to melt any snow so the water was not high and we crossed without getting soaked.

We made good time on the track to the south-east of the burn, but there was still a long way to go to get back to the car. Our legs were tired but the sky was turning deep red to the west as the sun began to set before us and the prospect of walking in the dark spurred us on.

The sun set with a golden halo around its red core and the pink drained quickly from the sky as the February darkness took over. Our last kilometre or two was walked in growing darkness but the snow helped to magnify what little light remained and we did not have to use our torches.

As we drove home I was tired but relaxed and content. We had made the most of every minute of that beautiful winter day.

Ben Chonzie (Ben-y-Hone)

 ## The hill with two names

April

It was a warm spring day, the sky was blue and Kenny, Morag and I were in good fettle. The car was parked at the Loch Turret dam and we walked along the track on the east side of the reservoir. One of our friends had described the hill we planned to climb as "boring", so we had no great expectations.

At the head of the reservoir the track led us through undulating terrain studded with rocks, the overgrown remains of glacial moraine. As we drank tea on a rocky mound a red grouse posed on a boulder a few metres away, showing off its plumage in the bright sun.

Lochan Uaine, the little green loch, was a surprise in that it was so picturesque. It sits among lush green water meadows, a horseshoe of crags and steep slopes providing a contrasting and dramatic backdrop.

It was not a day for hurrying. We followed a narrow path as it twisted up and around the first of the crags. It was surprisingly steep with sheer drops. Hot and sweaty, we flopped down onto a patch of sun-dried grass and stretched out for a rest. "We" in this instance being Morag and I, as Kenny doesn't rest on mountains. It was perfect lying there, my head on my rucksack, my eyes picking out a route up through the next crags and onto the summit. A bee buzzed by. A butterfly landed on my hand. Morag had almost nodded off to sleep, but we were not to have our nap in the sun.

"What are you like, you two?" enquired Kenny, "We're here to climb hills!"

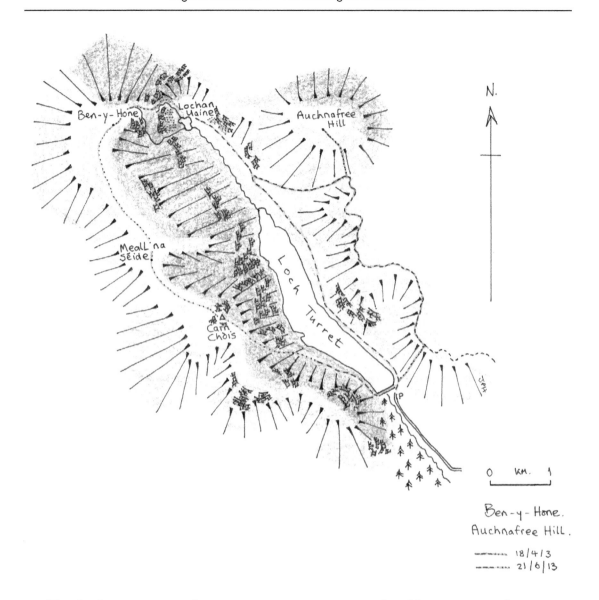

N.

Ben-y-Hone.
Auchnafree Hill.
------- 18/4/3
--- --- 21/6/13

The final section up to the summit cairn was steep, with a false summit to keep us on our toes. Sitting on the cairn, I wondered about the name, Ben Chonzie. It seems that it must be an anglicisation of an earlier Gaelic name, perhaps to be expected in a hill just over the Highland Line. I think that it is unusually ugly, not at all in keeping with the graceful lines of the corrie and its pretty lochan.

The views from the summit on this perfect day were wonderful. We expected a spectacular view of the Ben Lawers range to the north but the best view was to the west. Hill after hill led the eye to the distinctive shapes of Ben More and Stob Binnein, with Ben Lui rising behind.

We decided to go back over the tops that rise above the west side of Loch Turret. It was fine walking on such a day, the path so good that we did not have to watch our feet and could enjoy the changing views. We climbed up onto Meall na Seide and then up onto Carn Chois. A comfy perch was found among the crags which surround the summit trig point and there we finished our tea. This time I did nod off, waking to see Kenny chatting to another hillwalker, the first we'd met all day.

Ben-y-Hone
18/4/13 .

I went down to join them and the walker, a man who had grown up in the area, told us that the Munro we had climbed was actually called Ben-y-Hone. He did not know what this means. I felt much the same about this new name as I felt about the first, that it is rather odd, not representative of Gaelic language and traditions. Perhaps Gaelic never took much of a hold in this area.

We said our farewells and then began the steep descent to the loch. It was easier than it looked and we were soon changed and on the road again. Morag remarked on the perfect weather. "This is what I signed up for," replied Kenny.

Stuchd an Lochain, Sron a' Choire Chnapanich and Meall Buidhe.

Jelly legs

June

Two lochs, Loch Lyon and, to the north, Loch an Daimh, feed the River Lyon. Both were dammed long ago when hydro-electric power generation was a new technology. The dams have now mellowed with age, the narrow roadways leading to them are old and worn and they are now an integral part of the landscape.

Morag and I had driven up Glen Lyon and parked at the Loch an Daimh dam, our plan to walk across all of the summits surrounding the loch. When looking at her map, Morag had spotted the area of flat land at the head of the loch and hoped that there was a beach of sorts where we could have a pleasant lunch at the half way point. The map showed that this is a lonely place, at least five kilometres of rough hillwalking to get to the nearest track in any direction and further again to get to a proper road.

It was warm and sunny and looked like it might be settled for the day. We crossed the outflow and were soon climbing very steeply up towards Creag an Fheadain. The first section was muddy and wet but higher up the path became dry and stony, making the walking a real pleasure.

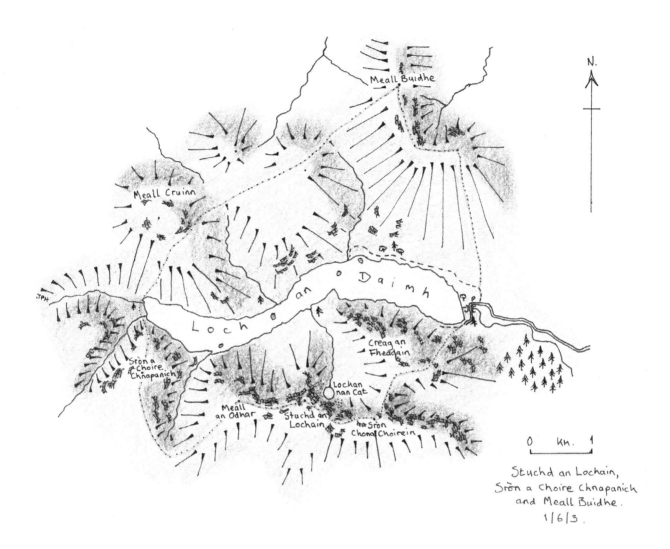

Stuchd an Lochain,
Sròn a Choire Chnapanich
and Meall Buidhe.
1/6/3.

On top of the crags we were almost 900 metres above sea level and the views had opened up. We decided to enjoy them over our first cup of tea. The air was clear enough for us to pick out the fine detail of Glen Coe and its mountains, with Ben Nevis rising up grandly behind. Despite the June date, Ben Nevis was holding on to its cap of snow.

We packed up and began descending to a low col, stopping to watch a large number of hinds with calves, the first of many deer we would see on that day.

After the col, the path climbed up onto Sron Chona Choirein, giving us clear views down into Coire nan Cat, its lochan bright blue on that day of early summer sunshine.

The great cliffs of the corrie headwall led our eyes up to Stuchd an Lochain. This is a fine pyramidal peak, with corries eaten into it on three sides, separated by craggy arêtes

Stuchd an Lochain
1/6/3.

leading to the summit. The very top of the peak has gone, removed by ice when, at the height of the last great Ice Age, an ice sheet covered all of this area's hills. A short and narrow rocky plateau is now the summit, probably giving the mountain the stuchd part of its name. We agreed that this is a fine Munro.

The path grew indistinct after the summit, the reason being that most hillwalkers turn around after bagging the Munro and return to the car park. The high ridge going west to Meall an Odhar was a real pleasure, with rocky crags dropping on each side, particularly to the north. Loch an Daimh sparkled in the sunlight far below.

We then followed Meall an Odhar's south-west ridge to avoid a deep, steep sided valley which cuts into the ridge at this point. As we crossed the bealach at the head of this valley we disturbed another large group of hinds and calves.

Our next hill, a Corbett, lay ahead in a NNW direction. Its south ridge did not look too steep but I was already tired. It crossed my mind that we were not yet at the half way point. We postponed our next tea stop until we reached the top to give us extra incentive to make the climb.

Sron a' Choire Chnapanich is another fine hill, a steep-sided pyramid with, on a day like that, grand views on all sides. As we drank our tea we could see Morag's little meadow at the head of the loch, directly below us. There was a coppice of Scots pine, bright green grass, an old ruin and what could have been a beach. It looked very tempting, the only hurdle being the way down, which was going to be steep and long.

The sron bit of the hill's name refers to a steep spur or nose and it was down that we went. My knees were sore when we got to the bottom.

We plodded slowly to the trees and sat on an old trunk to have our lunch. The food soon hit the spot and gave us the energy to look around and enjoy our surroundings. Looking back at the sron we had descended, we could not see a trace of a path. Looking north across the head of the loch to Meall Cruinn, we searched for a path but were disappointed. It was going to be harder work than we anticipated.

Morag had nurtured the idea of a paddle but the unpredictable Highland weather spoiled her plan. Thin cloud rolled across and a light rain began to fall. It was as if it was hurrying us on because we had barely begun to climb the south-east ridge of Meall Cruinn when it stopped. That climb was hard work for my tired legs and it was with some relief that I reached the crest of the ridge.

The next part of the walk was hard for both of us. We followed a north-east line, keeping to the high ground. The going was rough, over peat, heather, hardy grasses and screes. The four kilometres seemed far longer. Eventually, however, we slowly climbed up onto the Meall Buidhe ridge, too tired to decide whether the hill really was yellow, as its name implied. We knew that we had set ourselves a major challenge and it was with real satisfaction that we stood by the cairn of this, our second Munro of the day. Very weary by this stage, we had the sense to sit, finish our tea and eat a little more to fuel the walk back to the car.

The Munro path was a bonus because it provided a clear way down the ridge and was so much easier than the rough terrain we had crossed. I remember little of that last stage. I was perfectly happy, but the long and strenuous day had numbed my body and mind. Seven hours after starting, we were back at the car. My legs were like jelly.

We drove down Glen Lyon to the pub at Weem, looking forward to a hot meal. I had used up a lot of my reserve of energy but a panful of mussels with crusty bread and a tender Aberdeen Angus steak was a satisfactory way to top it up again.

Cairn Toul and
Sgor an Lochain Uaine

 "...a jam sandwich and a bag of crisps."

June

The Jolly Boys began arriving at the Newtonmore Hostel, bunks were bagged and no time was lost in crossing the road to the pub.

It was Friday night, a guitarist was singing pop classics and country songs and the early arrivals were already merry. Kenny kept the singer going long after his session was officially over by buying him drinks and the Jolly Boys were a bit worse for wear as they made their way back to the hostel in the wee small hours.

In the morning, Fionn must have caught the smell of frying bacon on the air because he stirred and came in from the lawn where he had slept. He sat at the table in his underwear and ate the substantial leftovers of black pudding, sausages, eggs, bacon and tomatoes. Substantial because there were some delicate stomachs that morning.

It was later than Ray and Struan, our leaders, would have liked before we were parked at Auchlean in Glen Feshie and ready for our walk.

The Foxhunter Path up onto Carn Ban Mor was a challenge for those in the party who had been a bit reckless the previous evening. We all reached the top, however, and

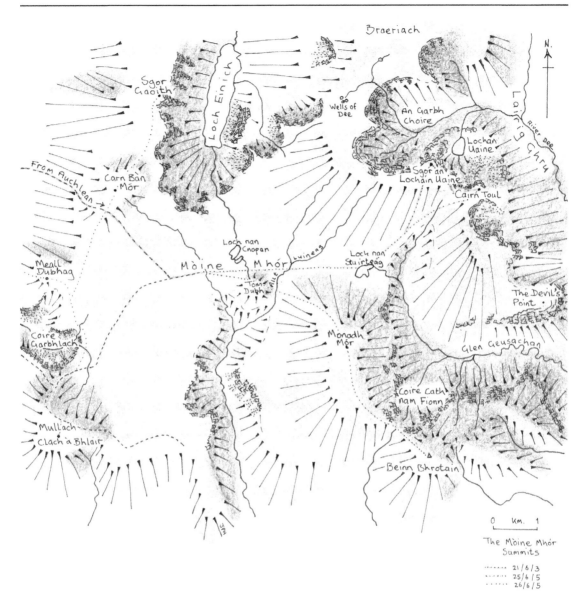

The Mòine Mhór
Summits
········ 21/6/3
······· 25/6/5
······· 26/6/5

it was there that the traditional arguments began about which objective was best. One group followed Fionn on a northerly path to Sgor Gaoith, this appealing to those less experienced/fit/desperate to bag Munros. The rest of us followed the path to the south-east. It joined a wider track at a point which was to have great significance later in the day.

The track took us east for little more than half a kilometre and then ended abruptly. The high wilderness of the Moine Mhor spread out before us. This is a place of big skies and big distances. There are no paths and careful navigation is essential. In bad weather it can be dangerous and deadly.

The day was cool and cloudy, the cloud base just touching the tops of the 4,000 foot peaks to the north-east. It was dry underfoot and I began to enjoy the wide space of this high plateau.

We stopped for a break and I noticed a dotterel on a pile of rocks nearby. It was a handsome bird, with a chestnut brown chest marked with a white crescent and a white flash over the eye. When we moved off I began to spot others, birds well adapted to rearing their chicks in this subarctic environment.

We had our second break on the banks of Loch nan Stuirteag and it was there that the debate about who would do what began again. Struan was for climbing Monadh Mor, which rises to the south of the lochan, while Ray had his eye on Cairn Toul and Sgor an Lochain Uaine to the north-east. I had been looking towards Cairn Toul as I walked across the plateau, admiring the snowfields which, even in late June, patterned its slopes. Its neighbours to the north had similar patches of old snow. We had been walking since climbing the Foxhunter Path at altitudes around the 3,000 foot mark, Cairn Toul and its adjacent peaks were all over 4,000 feet. It was these I wanted to climb and so joined Ray's group. Kenny had to pick up a friend that evening at Edinburgh Airport and knew that if he did not turn back he would not make it.

It was Kenny's decision to return that was to be memorable. Allan and a couple of other weary souls decided to go with him, none were experienced hillwalkers. I tried to get Kenny to take my spare map and compass but he said, "You'd be as well giving me a jam sandwich and a bag of crisps for all the good they would do me." Struan gave instructions to head due west until they hit the track and then follow it down into Glen Feshie. "Do that and you can't go wrong," were his parting words.

Struan led his group south to climb Monadh Mor, setting a fast pace as he was uncomfortable about Kenny's party.

I walked with Ray's group up steep slopes to the north-east, heading for Cairn Toul's summit. The ground became more rugged, with more rock than vegetation. Dwarf juniper and willow grew horizontally, strong roots clinging to what looked like gravel rather than soil. We kicked steps up a snow patch and then entered the cloud which sat on the summit.

The cloud was thin and moving all the time. I hoped that it would lift so that I could enjoy the spectacle of the view down into the Lairig Ghru. It continued to swirl about the summit, however, so we had a quick snack and began the steep descent to the col between Cairn Toul and our next objective, Sgor an Lochain Uaine.

We could see the sun through the thin mist as we clambered down the massive blocks of a truly impressive scree. A young man appeared, quickly catching us up as he lightly skipped from rock to rock. He had two large collies. He stopped to talk and I made friends with the two dogs. They were search and rescue trained and especially skilled at sniffing out bodies under avalanche snow. The young man asked why I was looking at their paws and I told him that my dog's paws had worn red raw on Beinn Eighe. He said that the granite of the Cairngorms is particularly abrasive and that's one reason why the dogs have to be in the mountains as much as possible. Their paws had hardened to a stiff leather. He had camped the previous night at Loch nan Stuirteag and often did this with his precious canine companions. We said farewell and I was sad to see him go, sure that he had many interesting tales to tell.

As we scrambled down more blocks the cloud blew away to reveal an ice-sculpted landscape on a grand scale. Below us was Lochan Uaine, occupying the bottom of a deep, crag-lined corrie. This gives its name to Sgor an Lochaine Uaine, the peak of the little green loch. That day, however, the lochan was brilliant blue, reflecting the summer sky. Beyond was the deep trough of the Lairig Ghru, with steep, scree-covered slopes falling from the massive bulk of Ben Macdui.

The cloud returned in thin patches as we climbed up to our second summit, given the strange name of The Angel's Peak in Victorian times. This was done at the time Bod an Deamhain, the demon's penis, which lies three kilometres to the south, was renamed The Devil's Point. Given that we no longer have to consider offence to Victorian sensibilities, is it not time to restore the original colourful name?

We sat on the angel's vantage point sipping tea and enjoying panoramic views, the cloud having obligingly melted away. More than satisfied, we turned for home and set off on a south-west bearing across the trackless Moine Mhor.

While crossing the Allt Luineag we looked up to see Struan and his group against the skyline to the west. They waited and we soon caught up. Struan had been looking out for Kenny's party but had not seen them.

We found the track again and followed it uphill to the point where the path to Carn Ban Mor branched off to the right. I was chatting to Struan and we walked straight past the junction. Ray had kept his eye on the map and he called us back. "I hope Kenny, Allan and the others didn't make the same mistake," I said.

Struan began to worry as we reached the path down into Glen Feshie. It was a clear afternoon and we could see large stretches of the path below. No walkers could be seen. Some of our group were footsore and very weary by this stage, they were content to plod slowly down with Ray while Struan and I stepped up the pace to get down to the floor of the glen.

Our hearts sank when we saw the cars, the others had not returned. I suggested that

To Carn Bàn Mór.

We walked straight past
the junction.
Jolly Boys 21/6/3.

JPH.

they could have done what we did so easily and missed the path which branched off from the main track. We looked at the map and guessed that they were somewhere to the south on the flanks of Mullach Clach a Bhlair.

I called Kenny on my mobile phone and, surprisingly, I got a signal and we were connected. He was not in good cut. I suggested that they consult a compass and tell us what way they were walking. They did this and Kenny replied that they had been walking east but would now appreciate some help in getting off this f****** mountain.

Struan asked for the phone and gave them instructions to turn around and follow the track west down into Glen Feshie. He asked how the others were bearing up and the answer he got was that they had very little left in them. He said that he would walk up the glen to meet them in case they needed help.

I was feeling surprisingly good and so offered to go with Struan. We set off up the glen, meeting the advance party of our walking companions and passing on the news.

Much later, my phone rang. Kenny had got to the end of the track where it met a path by the River Feshie. He wanted to know whether they should turn left or right. "Right," I replied, thinking with horror of the consequences of them turning left. Cold, hungry and very tired, they could have wandered into the wilderness at the head of Glen Feshie.

Struan and I had made good time and shortly after Kenny's call we caught sight of the forlorn walkers. They were pleased indeed to see us, although Kenny's grumpiness probably had the edge over his pleasure.

Back at the hostel we had plenty of tales to swap. Dave had gone on a low level walk and laughed loudly as the "lost boys" described their confused wanderings.[3] It was his 60th birthday and he produced a bottle of Speyside malt. I told him that I was not a whisky drinker but was given one on the grounds that I must join in the toast. Later, Fionn noticed that I was making little progress and he suggested that I dilute the malt with a splash of water, "to bring out the aroma and unlock the flavour." Later again, noticing that I was still making little progress, he relieved me of my whisky and replaced it with one from his own bottle. He downed my first in a quick gulp and told me about my new drink. It was Ardbeg, an Islay malt. He asked me to compare. I replied that it was completely different. This was warm and smoky. I told him that it reminded me of the reek from a peat fire. The aroma seemed every bit as important as the taste. I warmed the glass in my hands and as I sipped, this magical potion seemed to spread a glow of well-being through my tired body, down my weary limbs and right to my fingertips and toes.

---

3   Postscript.
    "But we thought we were walking in a straight line," said the lost boys. They had walked in a big anti-clockwise loop and were heading in the opposite direction to their intended line when we contacted them. This, it seems, is to be expected as most people unconsciously walk towards the left. It is because most are right-handed and have a stronger right leg. The right leg has a longer stride than the left. Also, when pushing off from the right foot, the bias to the left is greater than the bias to the right when pushing off on the left foot. Without use of a compass or clear landmarks, most people would move in an anti-clockwise direction during a long walk.

Am Bathach, Ciste Dhubh. The Saddle (An Diollaid), Sgurr na Sgine. Sgurr na Ciste Duibhe, Sgurr na Carnach, Sgurr Fhuaran (The Five Sisters).

 ## Heatwave in Glen Shiel

August

t had rained all summer and it rained as we drove north on the first morning of our hillwalking holiday. Our destination was the white hotel at the head of Loch Duich. Those who had signed up last were in the little bunkhouse with the corrugated iron roof which sits in front of the hotel. The early birds had the more spacious accommodation with separate bedrooms which sits to the side of the main building.

After checking in with the hotel staff I shared some lunch while we waited for the others to arrive. The elusive sun came out and the setting was perfect.

I was anxious not to waste the afternoon, knowing that it might be the only one of the holiday with blue sky. We left messages for the latecomers and Tom, Kenny, Allan, Morag, Alex and I set off to drive along Glen Shiel, on the same road we had travelled a couple of hours before.

We parked a little east of the Cluanie Inn and walked up the south-east ridge of Am Bathach, a fine, steep-sided Corbett. There were moans about my choice of route and

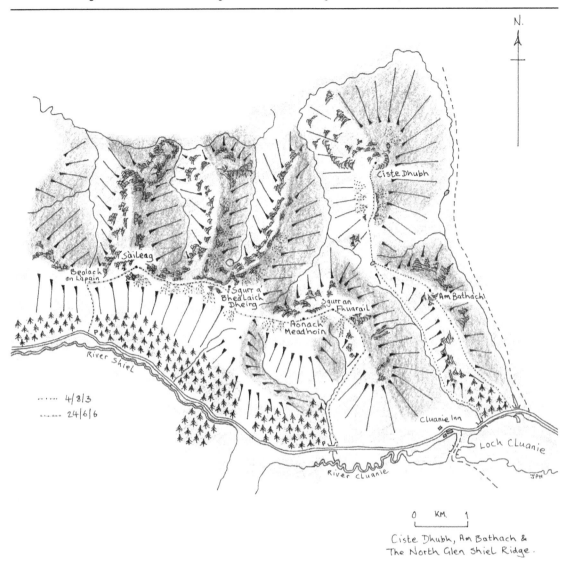

Ciste Dhubh, Am Bathach &
The North Glen Shiel Ridge.

I was asked why we had not followed one of the tracks along the floors of the adjacent glens. I explained that I expected the glen paths to be boggy after all the recent rain and, in any case, I fancied a nice ridge walk.

Once we had done the worst of the climbing they began to shut up, all except my son, Tom. A member of Edinburgh University Mountaineering Club, he was wearing his expensive, little worn, winter boots. They did not fit and were causing him terrible discomfort. In the end he took them off and completed the ridge walk in his walking socks. I was grateful that there was a good path and that it was warm and dry.

The air was now hot. We dropped down to the Bealach a' Choinich, walked past a tiny lochan and then climbed up onto the south ridge of Ciste Dhubh, the black chest (or coffin). Tom mocked my pronunciation, stating that no self-respecting mountain could be called keesta goo. He also left his boots at the bealach, to pick up on the way back. We were shocked by his reckless abandon. What if there was an injury and a mountain rescue? What would they say when they found that one of the party had only socks on his feet?

It grew steadily hotter. A lizard was making the most of this rare opportunity to bask on a warm rock and was not disposed to be disturbed by the likes of us.

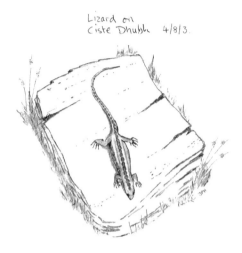

Lizard on
Ciste Dhubh 4/8/3.

The ridge grew narrow and bare, with crags falling down on the east side. The rocky summit was a superb viewpoint. Cameras were taken from packs and I surveyed the surrounding peaks. We had, I announced, come to the right place for a hillwalking holiday, it was splendid. I could have stayed there into the evening, soaking up the beauty, but Alex took on the role of our conscience and said that we should return to meet up with the others.

We collected Tom's boots and, bowing to pressure, I led the way down into An Caorann Beag. It was very boggy, a fact that I was careful to point out to the others more than once.

We were a hot and sweaty bunch when we got back to the hotel. The blue water of Loch Duich looked very tempting. A few minutes later we were in swimwear at the jetty. There was some chat about how icy it was likely to be. I decided that the slipway might be the best way to get over the pebbles and into deeper water, I would cautiously ease my way down it. As soon as I put my feet on it, however, I was propelled down its slippery surface like a rocket into the water. The top 60 centimetres was as warm as a bath but below that it was very cold. The trick was to keep as much of the body as possible in that 60 centimetres.

Soon, most of the party were in, diving off the pretty fishing boat and having great fun. We stayed for some time but the lure of a hot meal began to draw the swimmers back to the shore.

JFH

Swimming in Loch Duich
Summer 2003.

We ate in the hotel bar and finished the evening in the hostel kitchen, enjoying a nightcap.

I woke early and walked down to the jetty, surprised to see that there was not a cloud in the sky and the wind was no more than a warm breath.

Tom's feet were sore and he mumbled from his bed that he would go fishing in the River Shiel instead of climbing another mountain that day. He and Fionn had stayed on in the bar long after the rest of us and I guessed that this might well be a second reason for his decision.

Everyone else was up for a walk and we were soon parked in Glen Shiel, at the foot of the path which leads up to the Forcan Ridge. At either side of the way grew bog myrtle. Fionn and I picked bunches and rubbed it in our hair and on exposed skin, it being a natural midge repellent. The sun was shining brightly so there were no midges but, as Fionn said, it would never last.

The stalkers' path is beautifully engineered and it was not long before we were on the bealach between Meallan Odhar and Biod an Fhithich. We stopped to have a drink, our clothes already wet with sweat. Our exertions were rewarded by the wonderful views, north-east to the Five Sisters and south-west to our first objective, An Diollaid (The Saddle). It was the Forcan Ridge, a serrated knife-edge leading steeply to the summit which attracted most comment. Were we really going up it? Is there another way?

While we talked a large herd of red deer appeared on the shoulder of Biod an Fhithich and we watched while they made their way down into the Choire Chaoil.

As we packed up I commented that we could have done without the bog myrtle as there was not a cloud in the sky. Fionn's practical response, however, was that it was just as well because it masked the smell of the sweat.

At the start of the ridge we split into two groups, those prepared for the scrambling and those who would follow the path to the south. We would meet by the lochan on the Bealach Coire Mhalagain.

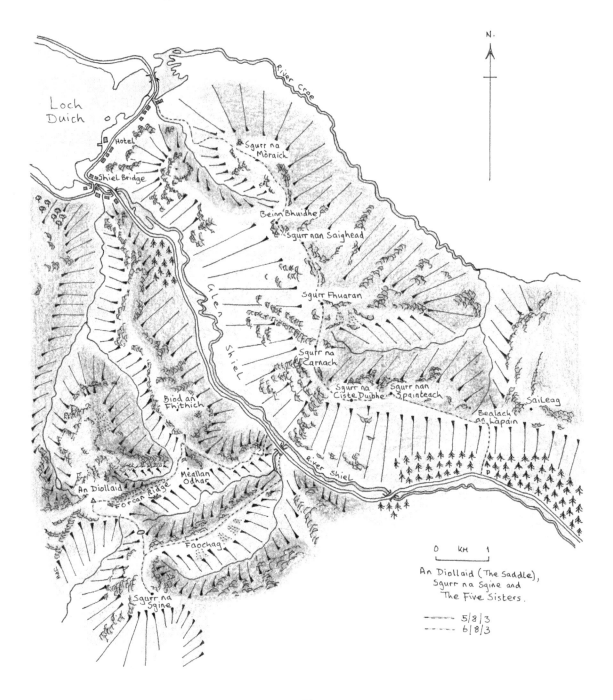

An Diollaid (The Saddle),
Sgurr na Sgine and
The Five Sisters.

----- 5/8/3
- - - - - 6/8/3

The rock was warm and dry and the Forcan Ridge was exhilarating. We climbed up huge slabs and turned to face the rock as we picked our way down narrow chimneys. Those who were ahead would stop to shout advice about good routes up the rock. The ridge grew narrower and steeper as it got higher. Some of the sections were tough, with long vertical drops on either side. There were always good holds, however, and it was clearly safer to climb up the crest than to attempt to work round the obstacles.

One by one we came out on the top, each thrilled by such an exciting ridge scramble. We made our way to the summit of An Diollaid and stood together to enjoy the panorama from one of the finest viewpoints in the Highlands. I could easily find Ben Nevis to the south, the Cuillin to the west and the Torridon hills to the north-west, but the group's expert was Fionn. His outstretched arm slowly swept round as he pointed out the islands, mountains and landmarks of this most beautiful corner of Scotland.

On such a day it was easy to spot those who had decided that the ridge was not for them, they sat far below on the banks of the lochan in the bealach. We traversed across An Diollaid's southern slopes and soon were eating lunch with our friends while telling them about the scariest bits of the ridge. I could easily have dozed in the hot sun but some of the party had not yet climbed a Munro and Sgurr na Sgine, the peak of the knife, rose impressively above our picnic spot.

It was hard work to get to the top, the shimmering heat making it seem more than the 250 metres of ascent. We enjoyed the views, particularly of the South Glen Shiel Ridge to the east. Then we turned to walk along the crest of the mountain's north-east ridge, a route which would lead us back to the glen and the starting point.

The ridge was long and sharp like the blade of the knife in the peak's name. There was a good path and we did not have to watch at every step where we put our boots. The walk allowed us to soak in the views. Heads often turned to the north-west to admire the jagged teeth of the ridge which had been our main challenge of the day.

We climbed up to Faochag, our last summit of the day and then followed the ridge down to the floor of the glen. The slope was relentlessly steep and there were some sore knees by the time we got to the bottom. Those suffering most from heat and knees lay on a grassy bank while the others walked along the roadside to the cars.

Soon we were in our swimming gear and cooling off in the salty water of Loch Duich. A perfect way to end a perfect day.

Tom joined us for a swim and we swapped stories. He had fished in the River Shiel and had caught some lovely sea trout, removing the hooks and returning them to the water. Fionn commented that anglers were prone to such tales and he would have to see the evidence.

Later, in the bar, Fionn returned to Tom's story and again expressed scepticism. "I could pop out now and bring a sea trout back to show you," was Tom's reply. Fionn snorted with derision and said that he'd bet Tom a fiver that he wouldn't bring back such a fish. "Throw in a pint of Guinness and you're on," said Tom, and he was off.

We asked for the menus and had just ordered when Tom returned with a beautiful silver sea trout which he slapped down on the table in front of Fionn. "I'll have that Guinness now, thank you," he said with some satisfaction.

Later, we met in the hostel kitchen for our nightcap and Tom made a good job of cooking the fish for our supper.

I woke early the next morning and walked down to the jetty, even more surprised to see that, again, there was not a cloud in the sky.

Tom covered his heels with pads of Elastoplast and I gave him a pair of my loop pile socks which he wore over his own. Morag, Kenny, Allan, Alex and Fionn joined us and we drove back along Glen Shiel.

We parked by the forestry due south of the Bealach an Lapain and were soon toiling up to this notch in the ridge which forms the spectacular north wall of the glen. It was very hot and as we sat drinking on the bealach we realised that replenishing our water was going to be important. Fionn was carrying neither water nor food. He was wearing old fell running shoes and told us that his preference was always to travel light. I worried that carrying no liquid would be a real problem if, as was likely, the tops and the ridge had no running water. He replied, "In that case, I'll have to complete the walk quickly," and he was off! He headed west to Sgurr nan Spainteach, the first rocky peak of the Five Sisters range, our objective for the day.

We followed at a more steady pace. From the first summit we could see Fionn near the top of the second, a pattern that was to be repeated throughout the day.

There was little ascent to the first Munro, Sgurr na Ciste Duibhe, the peak of the black chest (another one, interestingly). The view of the Five Sisters ridge was wonderful. Narrow, rocky and sinuous, it stretched out before us. Our attention was diverted by a deep crronk, crronk call. It was a pair of ravens, circling overhead in the powerful thermals with outstretched primary feathers.

The next section involved a considerable drop to a narrow bealach and then a rocky climb to Sgurr na Carnach. Viewed from the west, this Munro is particularly elegant, with three sharp arêtes soaring up to a steep conical summit.

On top was a tiny lochan. Allan rushed over, removed his boots and sat with his feet in the cooling water. We all stopped for a drink from our bottles. It was difficult to eat on such a baking hot day, particularly as our water supplies were already beginning to run out. This was all the more concerning because there was no likelihood of replenishing bottles on this parched, rocky ridge.

As we rested we noticed ptarmigan looking, I thought, somewhat out of place in the shimmering heat. One in particular seemed fascinated by Allan soaking his feet in the lochan. I suppose I would be surprised if someone put his feet in my drinking water and I imagine that the ptarmigan's thoughts would be unprintable.

When we got down to the next bealach, the water situation had become critical for some in the party. We could see a narrow gully below on the west side. Tom and Kenny volunteered to climb down with the water bottles and try to fill them. It was a steep scramble down and very hot work to get back up but the mission was a success.

Rehydrated and in good spirits, we climbed our third Munro, Sgurr Fhuaran, the wolf's peak. This was the best of the three, the meeting point of scalloped ridges with dramatically plunging cliffs. Everything was on the grandest of scales. We were sure that the tiny figure near the top of our next objective was Fionn, still going fast. It was the last we would see of him on the ridge.

The next section, over Sgurr nan Saighead and Beinn Bhuidhe, was a hillwalker's dream. The dry, narrow path wound along the crest of the ridge, often following the very edge of the massive cliffs and screes of the eastern flank.

By the time we stood on Beinn Bhuidhe we were all very tired. Sgurr na Moraich rose ahead, with the path an arc around the head of Coire na Criche. We knew that it was our last challenge so we took deep breaths and got going again.

The views had been opening up of Loch Duich with the island-studded sea beyond and we were treated to this panorama as we climbed the gentle slopes to our final summit.

There was little conversation as we descended its steep slopes to pick up the path which follows the Allt a' Chruinn. We were spread out in a long line, legs feeling as if they were made of lead. At this moment we had a little bit of luck. Those at the front reported that attractive girls with shorts and bikini tops were heading down the path just ahead. We never did catch up but the pace certainly quickened.

The thought of our dip in the cool, salty water of the loch had kept us going and we wasted no time in peeling off sweaty clothes and plunging in. Fionn had already cooled off in this way and was enjoying a cold beer. He pointed up to the blue sky above Sgurr an t-Searraich where a pair of golden eagles were slowly circling.

I floated on my back, letting my tired legs sink down into the colder water below. I watched the eagles and wondered what they made of me and my companions. If there is a heaven, I thought, it could well be like this. I floated in a dream-like state but my spiritual reflections were interrupted by Kenny shouting, "Come on, we're STARVING!"

Golden Eagles above
The Five Sisters.

Meall Corranaich and Meall a' Choire Leith

 Woken by a bee

August

When Morag and I said that we would like to climb Meall Corranaich and Meall a' Choire Leith, some of the more experienced hillwalkers had expressed derision. They dismissed these hills as "boring lumps" and invited us to join them on their planned routes which would, we were assured, be much more interesting.

The conversation moved to the weather. Those who had been on our recent summer walking holiday were full of doom and gloom. Every day of that trip had been one of perfect blue sky and it was just too much to expect the same on this one.

As we drove westwards, heading for the boring lumps, Morag remarked on the perfect blue sky, but would it last? To our right was the Ben Lawers range, its southern slopes rising steeply from the roadside. The mountains looked close in the clear light of early morning, the beautiful succession of peaks lifting our mood.

We turned onto the narrow, unfenced road that winds its way through the range, hugging the shore of Lochan na Lairige before crossing the high pass and descending into Glen Lyon. We left the car just past the top of the pass and looked at our mountains. They appeared to be BIG lumps.

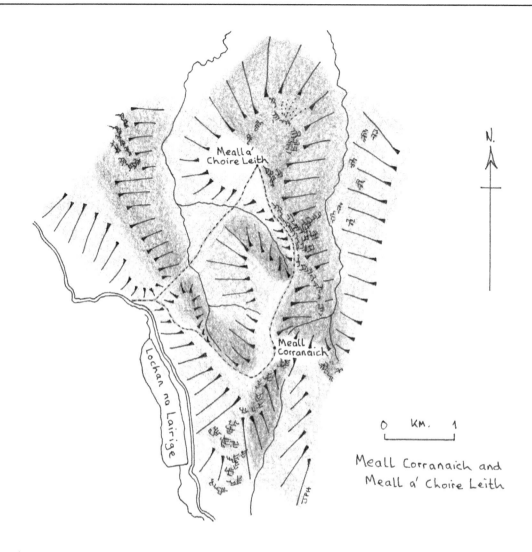

N.

Meall a' Choire Leith

Meall Corranaich

Lochan na Lairige

0   KM.   1

Meall Corranaich and
Meall a' Choire Leith

Our line was south-east. We scanned the hillside for a path but there was none to be seen. The going was fine for the first kilometre but then the slope became steep as we climbed up to Meall Corranaich's south-west ridge. It was hard work but easier once clear of the heather.

The ridge itself is stony, with sparse, short, yellow grasses and pale lichen. It was bone dry. We stopped for a cup of tea and from our 1,000 metre high vantage point surveyed the landscape. To the east, the Ben Lawers range rose in rugged crags, matched by the gem of the Tarmachan ridge to the south-west. To the south, far beyond the sparkling water of Loch Tay, Ben Vorlich stood above a sea of surrounding hills.

We finished our tea and walked up the dusty ridge to the summit of Meall Corranaich, the strangely named crooked hill, our first Munro. From the top, a narrow, elegantly curving ridge led to Meall a' Choire Leith (hill of the grey corrie), our next objective.

The easy path down the crest of the ridge was a joy to walk. We were both tired after a busy week's work, a late night with our pals and the climb up, but it is possible to be tired in a good way. The warmth from the sun and in our muscles conspired to produce a feeling of well-being. As so often when on the hills with a friend, we walked in silence, enjoying the peace of this lovely day. I woke from my reflective mood feeling that something was wrong, surely we did not have to walk down to the floor of that valley ahead of us and then climb all the way up that long slope? I consulted the map and found that we had begun to walk down the main ridge which drops to the north-west instead of the narrower ridge which runs to the north and would take us to our second Munro.

We backtracked, worked around the head of the narrow valley and found the path on the crest of the north ridge. There was agreement that it is not a good idea to switch off one's brain in the mountains, even on such a benign day.

The narrow ridge has steep cliffs along its east side and great views across to An Stuc's sharp peak. The climb up to Meall a' Choire Leith was not demanding and we were soon on the little bare summit plateau.

We found a spot on the north-west edge and unpacked our lunch. The views to the north and west in particular were stunning. Glen Coe looked almost near enough to walk to. We could see its steep walls and name the famous mountains on each side. Beyond stood the Mamores and the unmistakeable profile of Ben Nevis. Near at hand, Glen Lyon seemed a linear green oasis, with its lush meadows and woodland.

After eating a good lunch, I lay back and pulled my old sun hat over my eyes. Morag was already asleep. I listened to the tiny sounds of insects and was surprised to hear bees buzzing by, at over 3,000 feet above sea level.

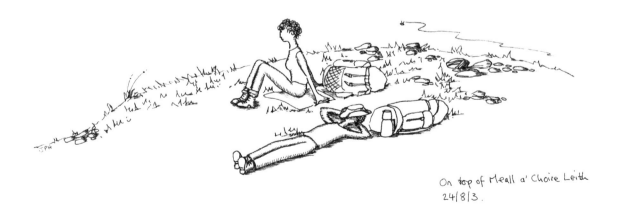

On top of Meall a' Choire Leith
24/8/3.

I think that it was a particularly loud bee droning by a few inches above my hat that woke me. My companion was already awake, sitting quietly and dreamily admiring the landscape.

We packed up and set off on a south-west line back to the car, ending one of my best days on the hills. I would recommend this pair of "boring" hills to anyone.

Beinn nan Imirean, Meall Glas and Sgiath Chuil

The day we accidentally climbed a Corbett

November

At Boreland Farm I parked in the yard, scattering the hens. A black pot-bellied boar came trotting up to check out the new arrivals. Brightly coloured prayer flags fluttered in the wind. The hostel was warm, as was the welcome from the Dutch family who run it. Morag declared that it was homely, with its guitars and other musical instruments hanging on the walls, and perfect for a jam session.

In Kenmore, Struan found us a pleasant bar in which we discussed our options for the next day. We spread out a map on the table and looked at the mountains on the north side of Glen Dochart.

The next morning I woke well before dawn. It was pitch dark and I could hear from the cracking and snapping of the prayer flags that it was windy. Struan stirred, muttering, "What unearthly hour is this?"

We ate breakfast, fed the scraps to the pig and were bumping out of the yard before there was light in the sky.

I drove along Glen Dochart and parked on the grass verge near the road to Auchessan. As we crossed the bridge over the River Dochart, the prospect of the day ahead and the cold, clean air combined to give me a much needed boost of energy.

Our first objective was the Munro of Meall Glas. We left the little group of houses and walked onto wide, steadily rising slopes. There was no obvious track and we ended up following deer paths or making our own way across peat bog and heather.

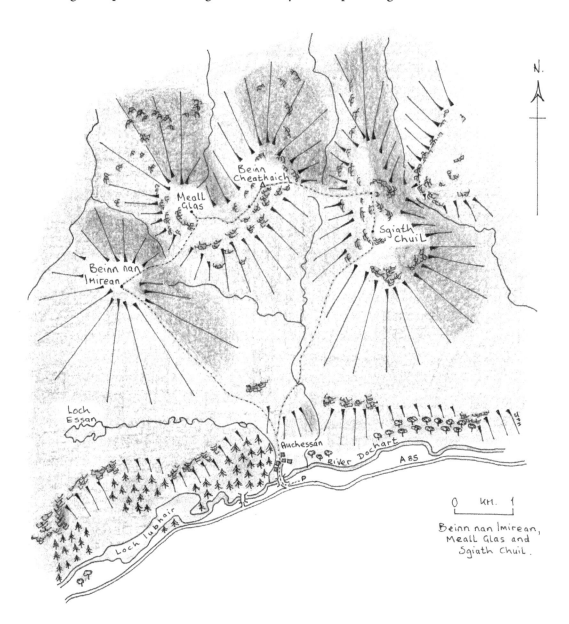

Beinn nan Imirean, Meall Glas and Sgiath Chuil.

There were a few breaks in the cloud and, ever optimistic, I suggested that it might turn out to be a fine day. This comment was promptly followed by the clouds sealing up the small blue patches and releasing a steady downpour. The wind was strong but was not a major problem at that stage as, being a south-easterly, it was blowing on our backs, blowing us up to our first top.

There was no lingering on the summit as the wind was blowing sheets of rain almost horizontally across it. We moved a short way down the north-west side until we were sheltered from the worst of the weather and sat down for a cup of tea. I said that I remembered crags on the map but we had seen none on the way up. Struan and I got out our maps to check. There was enough visibility at that point of the day for Struan to use his compass and map to check our position relative to the landmarks in Glen Lochay to the north. I had worked out what we had done before he announced that we were on the wrong mountain. This was Beinn nan Imirean (pronounced yeemaran), a Corbett to the south-west of Meall Glas and a feature I have since admired many times when driving along Glen Dochart.

I drank my mug of tea and ate a sandwich but was not disposed to sit long in those conditions. I suggested that someone should design a lightweight shelter which could quickly be erected in bad weather. Struan replied that such things can, indeed, be purchased. In the absence of such comfort we were quickly packed again and working our way down steep slopes to the bealach between the Corbett and the Munro. The south-east wind howled through the gap between the mountains and the going was hard.

As we climbed the steep slopes to Meall Glas, I wondered how long my clothing would keep me dry. The rain was whole water, driven into us by the gale. We scrambled up some crags, the rock black and slippery, to reach the top of our first Munro. It was too exposed to sit and rest, so we set off east along the ridge to Beinn Cheathaich, the gusts threatening to knock us off our feet, looking for some shelter. The wind was still in the south-east, so we went down from the old triangulation pillar to shelter among rocks on the north-west side. My body temperature dropped quickly and I barely managed a cup of tea before I needed to be moving again.

We clambered back up to the top and then made our way down to the bealach before our last climb. The day had been characterised by walking without the help of a clear path and this stretch was no exception. Water seeped into one of my walking poles and a section collapsed. I could not get it to lock again, perhaps due to water inside the pole or because my hands were numb and not functioning properly.

As the ground levelled out, we had our heads down, battling into the teeth of the wind. Great curtains of rain were thrown across the bealach (and us), one after another.

We stumbled up a peat hag and almost stepped on a young stag and two hinds. The wind had been blowing from the deer to us and they had no warning of our approach. The bewildered stag rose up and, strangely, stood his ground while the two hinds ran off. We waited until he turned then followed them.

Sgiath Chuil is the highest point of a knobbly north-south ridge. We began to climb the steep, grassy slope to Meall a' Churain, the northernmost top. The 300 metre ascent was the hardest thing I had done since a mountain rescue in the Alps when I was a teenager. I felt as if all my energy had drained down into the saturated ground. I was reduced to fixing on a rock a short way above then willing myself to make the steps to struggle up to it. I began to count my steps, twelve before the next rest, ten before the next rest. I was too exhausted to have willpower and can only suggest that I must have a hidden strength that can drive me when my normal systems have just about burnt out. Whatever it is, it did its work and I stiffly made the last steps onto the crest of the ridge. The wind hit me so hard that I was nearly knocked flat on my back. The rain had turned to sleet. I could see the others bent low and making slow progress ahead so I leaned into the wind and followed.

8/11/3
The stag and hinds
under Sgiath Chuil.

This bleak and exposed ridge was a weird place indeed on that wild day. None of us could stand upright. Morag and I stepped onto a recumbent slab of polished rock, black and glistening with a veneer of water. The tread on our boots was neutralised and, with almost no friction, the wind was able to blow us back across the slab like a pair of synchronised skaters. Further on, we came across some little white footballs. They were ptarmigan in their winter coats, heads tucked under their wings, huddled in tight against the storm. I lifted one gently above the ground and then replaced it, the bird showed no reaction at all. I smiled when we reached the cairn of Sgiath Chuil, its English translation is sheltering hill. I could not share this observation with my companions as speech was impossible in those conditions.

Struan led the way down the steep south-west spur of the Munro, gravity helping my tired legs. As we could not find the path and the terrain soon became one of heather and peat hags, it was hard going. We were all weary by this stage and the four kilometres back to the car seemed much longer. At one point we had to climb a deer fence and even the stoic Morag began to think that some higher force had decided to throw everything at us.

As the light began to fade, the car was truly a welcome sight. Past caring about propriety, I peeled off my wet clothes, encouraging passing motorists to give a blast of their horns. I had expected my dry clothes to give me more comfort but my body temperature had fallen too low for that. I needed warmed up.

I switched on the headlamps and drove the short distance to the Suie Hotel. The owners were surprised to see visitors on such a wild and wet day. They were even more surprised to find that we had been hillwalking. More logs were thrown on the fire and I soon began to thaw out. Conversation was limited as we got down to the serious business of tucking into bowls of home-made soup and piping hot dinners. It was not until we were sipping mugs of tea round the roaring flames of the fire that we began to reflect on the day.

I had been worried by my energy drain on the last climb but understood what had happened. I had not been disposed to eat my normal hill food in such miserable conditions and hit a point where my body had no energy left. It needed fuel. I decided there and then that I would never again put myself and others at risk by repeating this mistake. I vowed that I would always carry more than I can eat in a day and that most of this would be high energy food. Just as important, of course, is that I must eat enough of this, no matter what the weather is like.

That decided, we looked back over the rest of the walk, remembering the slashes of blue in the sky in the morning, the courageous stag, the ptarmigan and our fierce struggles against the elements. We all agreed that it had been a grand day.

3/1/04

Meall Ghaordaidh

 Winter light

was still reeling from a busy festive season, the last of my family's guests had departed only hours before and I needed the walk up Meall Ghaordaidh as an antidote.

Morag and I started in Glen Lochay on that lovely mild winter day. Occasionally a low-angled shaft of sunlight would cut through the clouds, intensifying the golden light. All was snow covered, the mountains wonderfully luminous against the grey clouds. Colour had been leached from the landscape, leaving a beautiful monochrome world.

We stopped not far from the summit in the lee of a huge rock for tea and a sandwich. Visibility was excellent to the Ben Lawers range in the east and to Ben Vorlich and Ben More in the south. All was peaceful and I was in no mood to hurry. A young woman stopped and told us that she had left her partner watching an Old Firm match. A man with a terrier stopped and said that his wife was shopping with her mother.

Terrier on Meall Ghaordaidh
3/1/4.
JPH

Next came a man of 70 wearing only a shirt, unbuttoned to the waist, on his upper body, protesting that it was too warm. He had fallen in love with the Highlands and was heart-warmingly enraptured by his climb.

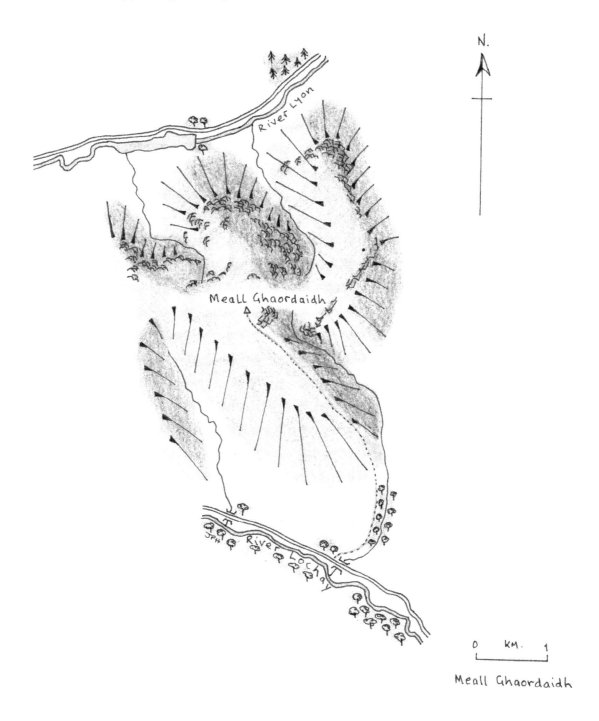

Meall Ghaordaidh

Crampons were put on for the final push to the top as a crust of ice had formed over the snow. The summit was blasted by a strong, intensely cold north-west wind. Horizontal icicles on an old iron post pointed south-east. It was hard standing upright to take a photograph.

We stopped under the same rock on the way down to finish our tea. The light began to fade and the mountains became even more luminous.

The golden light changed to pink as we quietly trudged down to the car. The moon rose as we drove off.

In the Clachan Cottage Hotel on the banks of Loch Earn we ate steaks in front of the roaring wood fire, a fitting end to a perfect New Year walk.

Beinn Dorain and Beinn an Dothaidh

When a good day became a great day

Kenny, Struan, Morag and I woke up in our little wooden cabin to a grey morning of steady rain. Kenny was in a Victor Meldrew mood and argued that we should spend such a day in the pub but, after some debate, we decided to stick to our plan, despite the weather.

As we drove north from Tyndrum, Beinn Dorain (doa-ran) looked very impressive, a steep cone like a child's drawing of a mountain. Its name might be mountain of crying or pain because the wind makes a high-pitched crying sound as it blows over the deep gullies cut by the streams that hurtle down its sides.

We parked at the old station at Bridge of Orchy, went through the tunnel under the railway line and headed east for the obvious notch between Beinn Dorain and Beinn an Dothaidh. The first stage was heavy going in the mild, humid air. There is a grand amphitheatre of precipitous crags cut into the mountainside under the bealach. The rain turned to sleet at 600 metres and snow at 800 metres.

On the bealach, we stopped for tea. My father had given me some Kendal Mint Cake

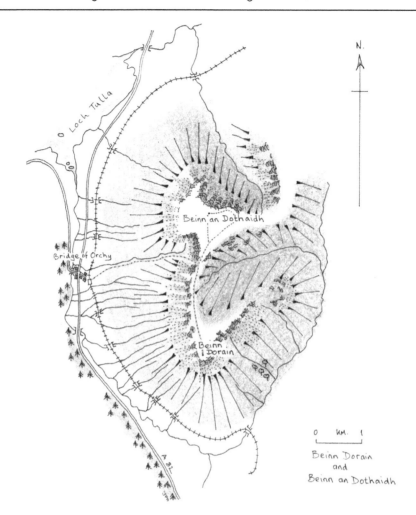

Beinn Dorain
and
Beinn an Dothaidh

bought in the Lake District when on holiday there in 1994. I opened the packet and tried to break this fossil into squares for everyone but it was too hard. I used my ice axe in the end but it proved impossible to eat, even by Kenny. It would have broken teeth if bitten and stubbornly refused to melt in the mouth.

We turned south to walk up Beinn Dorain. There were no grand views due to low cloud and snow but we had a few hundred metres of visibility. The cloud swirled and broke to reveal the shadowy snow-covered peaks of neighbouring mountains. Bright white light reflected up to the grey cloud. Black crags and boulders jutted out of the snow and there was a complete absence of colour. We had read that the big cairn was not the true summit so we went further to the smaller cairn before turning to follow our tracks back to the bealach. The descent was hard on the legs because about 6 centimetres of fresh powder snow lay on top of older snow which had compacted to ice. It was slippery and needed much care.

Beinn Dorain 16/2/4

A ptarmigan in its white coat flew away from where we had tried to eat the squares of Kendal Mint Cake, looking distressed. "Poor bird, I hope no one dropped a piece," commented Kenny. We stopped for lunch. Snow fell into my tea. I was warm and happy. Kenny was still grumpy and refused to sit down. "Look at you," he said, "sitting there in a puddle of slush looking so cheerful, you're stark raving bonkers." Looking at the forbidding slope of Beinn an Dothaidh rising steeply into the cloud he added, "You lot are not seriously thinking about going up there?"

Up there we went and it turned out to be treacherous underfoot. Struan and Morag slipped, Morag landing on a sharp rock and bruising her hip.

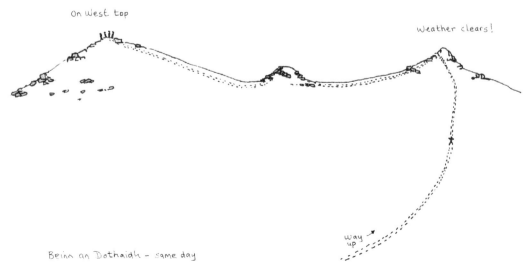

On West top

weather clears!

Beinn an Dothaidh – same day

way up

Tough going but on the east top the sky suddenly cleared. The hidden landscape of snow-capped mountains and brown, desolate moor was revealed and what had been a good day became a great day. We walked along a beautiful, sinuous ridge, just south of its massive sculpted cornice. At times we could see the cornice's compacted layers of old snow and bands of ice. In places, bright blue ice shone like gems, dramatic colour in that monochrome landscape.

It was with a light step that we walked to the middle top and then on to the west top, perched on top of the great wall that is this side of the mountain. We felt like eagles in a high eyrie, looking down thousands of feet to the beginning of Rannoch Moor and the Etive mountains beyond. All was grandeur. All was splendid. A horizontal slash of turquoise sky to the west showed us fine weather heading our way. Kenny had stopped being grumpy the moment the sky had cleared and was almost poetic as he drank in the views. He commented that the temperature would fall when the clear sky spread east and over our heads and he was right. The difference was so noticeable that the cold air burned our lungs.

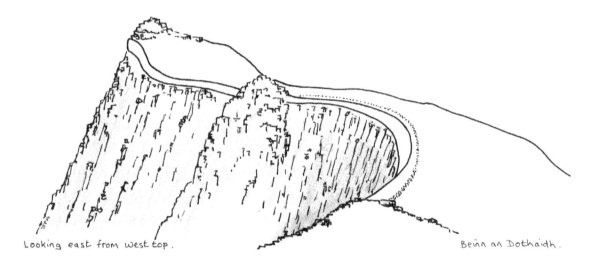

Looking east from west top.   Beinn an Dothaidh.

On the way down we met a man toiling up to the bealach dressed in a cotton shirt and jeans, holding his jacket. He stopped beside us as we finished our flasks of tea, taking a long time to get his breath, which rasped out from his chest. When he was ready to speak, he pressed a button on his neck and spoke with a metallic, robotic voice. He was a victim of throat cancer. He said that he was determined to get up onto the bealach and then he would feel that he had earned his beers in the pub that night. We were touched and watched in silent admiration as he struggled slowly upwards.

Ben Cruachan and Stob Diamh

Ice axe arrest

April

When Kenny, Morag and I woke up in the little wooden hut the morning was grey and dreary. As we drove west to Loch Awe the blanket of cloud began to tear, allowing the sun to illuminate patches of loch and hill. There was some snow on the highest peaks so we decided to take crampons and ice axes. There were complaints about adding the weight of these to our packs when we probably would not need them.

The car was parked near the power station and we followed the abruptly steep path on the west side of the Cruachan Burn's waterfalls. After the dam, we walked up the south ridge of Meall Cuanail. The sun warmed our backs but cloud swirled across, bringing hard showers of sleet and there was fresh snow on the top. It was shaping up to be a day of typical April Highland weather.

The new snow made the boulders slippery on the slope down to the high bealach before Ben Cruachan and we had to place our steps with care. The south spur looked dauntingly steep and its ascent was made worse by the snow, poor visibility in the low cloud, the sleet that rattled onto our hoods and the intense cold. So it was with a sense of achievement that we stood on top of this mountain. The cloud began to break up, revealing Ben Cruachan's fine narrow summit from which sharp, rocky ridges fell away. Walking poles were strapped to rucksacks when we saw that we would need to use our hands climbing down the ice and snow covered rock.

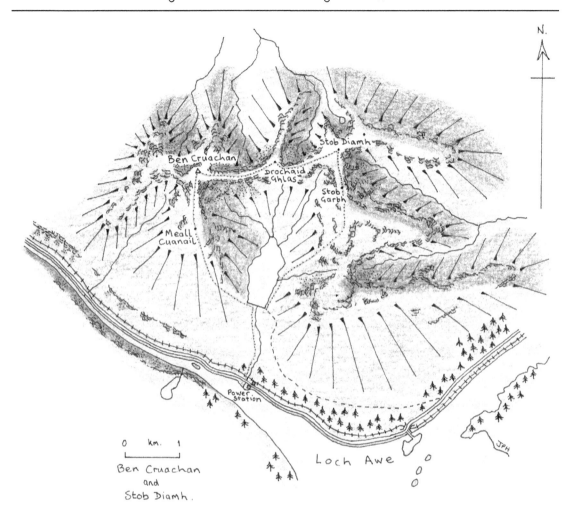

N.

0   km.   1

Ben Cruachan
and
Stob Diamh.

Loch Awe

JPH

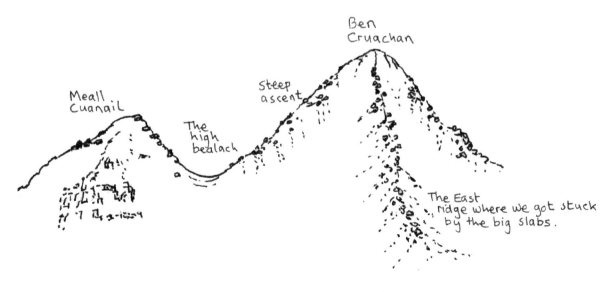

Ben
Cruachan

Meall
Cuanail

Steep
ascent

The
high
bealach

The East
ridge where we got stuck
by the big slabs.

After some tricky scrambling down the east ridge we hit an obstacle on the way to Drochaid Glas. The way was over the top of raised slabs dipping to the south. These were covered with thick ice on top of which lay the fresh snow. To go across them would be to risk slipping (even wearing crampons) and the drop to the south was considerable.

We decided to detour below the slabs, traverse the steep slope, then climb back onto the crest of the ridge. This entailed crossing a patch of snow with no rocks for footholds. Morag was leading but I stopped her to suggest that ice axes might be needed. We unstrapped them, Morag made one step, slipped and used her axe to brake a certain dangerous fall. I followed her across the slope, slipped and used my axe to stop the fall, feeling a rush of relief that the technique I had been taught worked so well. Kenny followed nervously but did not slip.

When we were back onto the crest of the ridge we were quite blown but were distracted from dark thoughts of what could have happened by the clouds lifting off the peaks, giving us absolutely stunning views. At first we could only see Lochs Etive and Awe but the cloud continued to roll away to reveal the mountains of Glen Coe, snow-capped Ben Nevis and a blue and sparkling sea studded with mountainous islands from Arran in the south to Rum in the north. Looking back along the ridge, Ben Cruachan appeared as a fine, pointed pyramid of a mountain with sharp arêtes leading to its gleaming, snowy summit. Kenny described it as "a beast."

The ridge became less difficult to walk as the gradient eased and the snow cover thinned. We huddled in the nook of a giant boulder for a much needed lunch and hot drinks then enjoyed as fine a ridge walk as you could imagine, soaking in the spectacular views.

On Stob Diamh we met two climbers without ice axes and warned them about the ridge going up to Ben Cruachan but they went on regardless. We finished our tea there then turned south for Stob Garbh and the walk back to the reservoir.

We got back to the car almost nine hours after leaving it. Our sunburned faces glowed as we drove to the pub for a well-earned meal but we also had a deeper glow of pleasure after that hard day.

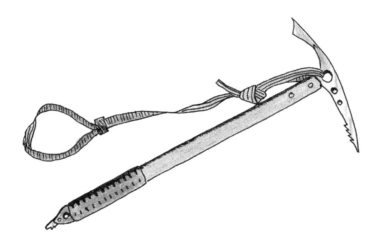

4 – 6 June 2004

Ben Nevis, Scafell Pike and Snowdon

 The Three Peaks

June

Our team set off on a Friday morning on a journey of over 1,000 miles, which would have taken us from our workplace in the Borders to Toulouse. George was our leader and minibus driver. Kenny, Morag, Struan, Alex and I were the climbers. We stopped at Loch Lubnaig on the way north for a picnic lunch on what was a glorious June day.

In Fort William, we registered at the hotel. It was late in the afternoon and we were the last team to do so. The charity organisers and marshals were curious to see what our team members were like. All the other teams had fancy names like The Mahon Marauders but George's seemingly innocuous choice of team name was clearly open to misinterpretation as they expected young women dressed as schoolgirls. Disappointment in our attire aside, they seemed to find us odd and we worked out why later in the evening when we saw the other 27 teams. They were all youngsters and they smiled politely at the old timers as we plodded past.

We checked in with the officials at the foot of the Observatory Path[4] and set off at a brisk walk. The weather was still good but, sadly, there was little time to take in the

---

4   The map on page 75 shows the Observatory Path.

splendid views as Kenny and Struan got that competitive thing and kept up a gruelling pace. There were mutterings from the rest of us and the word mutiny was used. Each time we caught up with them as they sat to have a drink of water they quickly replaced the caps on their bottles and said, "Right, on we go!"

At 1,000 metres we walked into cloud and my ears popped. We had entered a different world, a world of mountain rather than hill. Bare rock, frost-shattered scree and slushy tracks made by walkers across the snowfields.

Some of the walkers wore boots, many wore trainers and one young man wore white socks and sandals in which he slipped and stumbled across the snow. The Lochaber Mountain Rescue Team were acting as marshals and if looks could kill…

The summit had a peculiar quality. There was a strange construction of dry stones like a beehive with a door near the top; it seemed to grow out of the mountain. I decided that it could be part of the old observatory and thought of the man who used to rise at 5.00 am every day to walk up and take readings. Through most of its history, however, the observatory was permanently manned by an intrepid crew. They recorded mean annual precipitation of 4.08 metres per year, similar to that received by the Amazon rainforest. The average temperature on the summit is 0.3 degrees Celsius. The extreme mountain climate confirmed by these and other readings made this an ideal place to harden up Antarctic explorers who signed up for a term of duty.

Not far away was a pinnacle of rock with dry stone walling around its base. It was a shrine, with offerings to the gods. There were rosaries, photographs in silver frames, necklaces, crosses, St Christopher medallions, plaques, bunches of dried flowers, and various strange totems made of wood, leather, beads and suchlike. On my return some years later, all of this had gone without a trace.

The cloud blew away in ragged wisps, revealing a fantastic landscape beyond the summit's snow cornice. I hoped that the man with the sandals realised that there was an enormous drop beyond the cornice as he wandered onto it.

I did not, however, have much time to take in all this as I had barely finished pouring a cup of tea before Kenny had strapped on his rucksack and was pointedly staring at the lesser mortals of the team. I drank the tea too hot then hurried to catch up my companions who had already started the descent across the first snowfield.

It was good to be out of the cold cloud on the way down and the three normal team members at the rear stopped at intervals to marvel at the views up Glen Nevis and across Loch Linnhe. The officials at the bottom told us that we had taken exactly five hours which seemed fine to me.

Kenny was sitting in the River Nevis to allow the cold water to take the ache from his leg muscles. We had learned this trick the previous summer when walking in Glen Shiel. It seemed a good idea but it wasn't. I stripped to my underpants and waded out. I had barely sat down when the first swarm of midges found me. They seem to cover large distances remarkably quickly. Most of the population of Western Scotland came to take their little blood supper before I could get back to the minibus and put on some clothes.

That evening, Fort William was a curious mix of the worst of Scottish hospitality and the Wild West. Drunken young people roamed the main street. We had to intervene to prevent a girl's trousers being pulled down by a youth. The pubs were packed and noisy. Nowhere sold food (it was after 10.00 pm). At the far end, the dire situation was redeemed by a Chinese restaurant which appeared to be the sole provider of nourishment.

The journey south was surreal. I seem to be able to sleep sitting up in any vehicle and missed George dodging the red deer on the road in Glen Coe. I have a shadowy memory of the services at Gretna Green and of George driving endlessly around diversion signs in Carlisle but only really surfaced as we rocked and jolted along the narrow road that twists up the deep dale to mountain number two, Scafell Pike.

It was very early morning when we stumbled from the bus to eat a rudimentary breakfast by the side of the road. George rigged up a stove and boiled hot water for our flasks. We checked in with the marshals and set off, still half asleep, the wrong way. We had walked a fair way down the dale before Struan noticed other teams climbing a path far away on the mountainside in the opposite direction. Grumbling a little, we retraced our steps. This little detour was to cost us a place in the rank order at the end of the challenge.

It was a typical Lake District summer day, warm and damp with low cloud and rain that regularly switched on and off. The humidity made walking difficult. Kenny and Struan had lost some of their electric energy and so I set the pace as we climbed the wet slabs of the steep path to the summit. Crossing a river by gingerly picking our way over the stepping stones, we met The Bolton Beer Bellies coming down at a cracking rate. Unwilling to wait while we crossed, their leader took a less secure route some metres below, slipped and banged his knee on a rock. The loud sound of bone on rock made us all stop and there were many hands to lift the horizontal, wet and bleeding Beer Belly out of the swift current. He was made of strong stuff, however and he stood up, shook off the excess water and strode away rapidly down the path, followed by his team in Indian file. We watched this determined group with admiration until the flagpole and pennant attached to the leader's rucksack disappeared from view. We wondered whether the injury would put the leader out of the challenge but it did not.

The Bolton Beer Bellies.

Onwards and upwards. We stopped for a quick cup of tea and a cereal bar on a slab of wet rock underneath dark crags. At the top, the marshals told us that some of the teams had taken a long time to complete the Ben Nevis walk and it was nearly midnight before the last team was back in the car park.

We passed a few of these teams as we walked down, struggling and weary but brave and determined. No one was for giving up.

Down again and satisfied with our time of four hours we quickly changed clothes, posed for the official charity team photograph and then we were off to Wales. As I was nodding off to sleep I had the sense to suggest to George that he stop in one of the charming Lakeland towns for lunch before hitting the M6 and being subjected to motorway services food.

I woke up at 11.30 as he drove into Broughton-in-Furness. We parked in the square, strolled about and decided to try the Black Cock. As we had seen hundreds of Herdwick sheep with their straight, greeny-grey fleeces and contrasting white heads I was of a mind to sample a local dish of lamb. I was brought Lamb Henry, a joint on the bone with fresh mint and delicious gravy. This, with a large bowl of new potatoes, crisp vegetables and a glass of red wine, made a memorable meal.

While George had a post lunch nap in the minibus, we explored this agreeable little town. The church was the highlight, with its beautiful Norman doorway and mellow, romantic stained glass.

On the road again I fell asleep with a sense of well-being that can only come from fresh air and physical exertion followed by a good hot meal.

I woke up at motorway services. The day had begun to heat up and George stretched out beside the minibus to sleep. I was impressed by his ability to fall asleep in busy car parks.

George takes a nap

The day was bright as we drove into the Pass of Llanberis, the first time most of the team had seen the mountains of Snowdonia. It was so different to the Highlands, a landscape with more people. There were little villages and houses perched on the mountainsides like in the Alps. The rhododendrons were in bloom, carpeting the lower slopes with purple. I mentioned that they were being cleared in some parts of the national park as they are native to the Himalaya and were swamping our native flora, damaging the ecosystem and associated food chains. Our views were mixed, with me in favour of clearing them and Kenny leading the faction in favour of leaving them on the grounds that they are pretty. Either way, the pass was spectacular with giant boulders dwarfing miniature fields enclosed with dry slate walls. Pinnacles of rock rise from the valley floor and massive screes lie in great fans down the mountain walls.

Our bunkhouse consisted of damp little green sheds and rudimentary facilities. It was good, though, to have a shower and change before we drove to nearby Beddgelert for some supper. The old pub by the bridge was busy but we were lucky to find seats and to catch last orders for meals with minutes to spare.

I remembered the old tale of Gelert. The chieftain had gone out with his men to hunt a wolf that had taken livestock and a child from the village. He left his best and most faithful hound, Gelert, in his hall to guard his baby son, still in his cradle. When he returned, the cradle was knocked over, the baby screaming and blood was everywhere. Gelert was panting, with staring eyes and blood on his muzzle. The chieftain took in the scene at a glance and, wild with rage, killed Gelert. Then he noticed the dead wolf against the wall, killed by his hound to protect the child. Full of remorse for his action, he renamed the village Beddgelert to immortalise his brave dog.

The last morning was bright and full of promise as we set off early to walk up the tourist path which follows the railway to the top of Snowdon. It is a broad mountain with a curiously Alpine feel. Perhaps the Halfway House Café, the narrow gauge railway and the café on the summit made me recall trips to Chamonix.

L. to R. Struan, Kenny, Me, Morag.

June 2004
Half Way House
Mount Snowdon.

We made good time, checked in at the top and were heading down out of the cloud and back into the bright morning before most teams had reached the Halfway Café. The exceptions were the Mahon Marauders in their military uniform, who were running down and the Bolton Beer Bellies, following their flag in close formation with their determined look. Their leader sported a large bandage on his knee.

Stopping for our first real break, we had time to take in a sunlit mountain scene on a grand scale. Tea drunk, we went down at a steady pace to finish in 3 hours 45 minutes.

The event finished at a grand old hotel where we had a shower. I emerged wearing a small white towel and my teammates gasped when they saw the number of midge bites I had. I think it made an impression because I was presented with various anti-midge sprays when I returned. We were treated to a pasta feast and the young officials showed us the timings. Alex (a mathematician) corrected their arithmetic and we discovered that we old timers were third out of the 28 teams, beaten by the Marauders and the B.B.Bs. The B.B.Bs had beaten us by minutes only and we reflected that we would have been second had we not taken the wrong turning at Scafell Pike. The Marauders told us that they had two days R. and R. but it was the long journey home for us and work the next day.

Bidean nam Bian and Stob Coire Sgreamhach. Ben Challum

 A lost world

June

The Jolly Boys were in Inchree, near Onich on the shores of Loch Linnhe. The hostel had a TV and when we came back from the pub, Struan switched it on. By chance, it was the weather forecast and it was grim in the extreme. Cold northerly wind, very strong on the summits; heavy and prolonged showers, merging around lunchtime to set in for the day; snow on the highest ground; a maximum of three degrees Celsius on the mountains. One by one the Jolly Boys found reasons to do a low level walk along the West Highland Way. I briefly toyed with the idea that I was unwell but the lure of the mountains was too strong. As the weather was to worsen, we decided to get up early and only four of us set off for Glen Coe next morning.

Within minutes of leaving the car, we had put on waterproofs, warm hats and mitts. The NNW wind was very cold and the rain was tending to the horizontal. We took the well-made path up the steep valley which leads to Stob Coire nan Lochan, the first peak of the Bidean nam Bian massif. The rain eased and the towering black walls sheltered us from the wind. The clear air allowed great views of this landscape of soaring rock buttresses and wild waterfalls. We stopped to watch a bachelor group of 12 stags on the other side of the stream. They were aware of but unconcerned by our presence. The senior

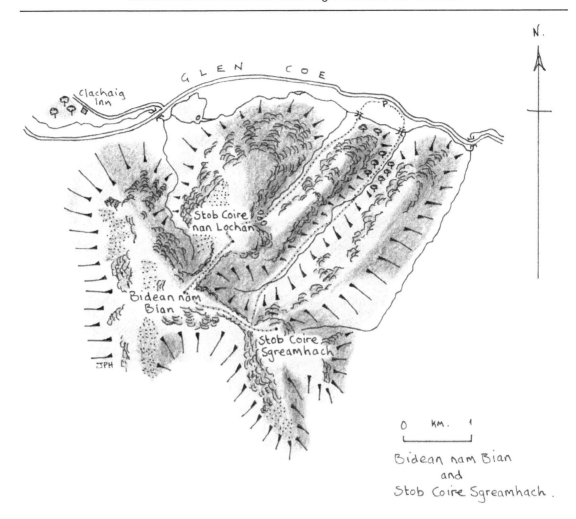

Bidean nam Bian
and
Stob Coire Sgreamhach.

stag had a coat more bright chestnut than the rusty brown of the rest. We stopped at three little lochans for tea and a snack, but it was not the weather to linger.

After a steep climb we were on the bare, boulder-strewn, pinched ridge leading to Stob Coire nan Lochan, a mountain worthy of Munro status if ever there was one. We walked into cloud but it was thin and visibility was good for a few hundred metres. The storm-swept ridge has big drops, Alex was careful not to look down.

The route up the arête leading to the summit of Bidean nam Bian leads south and in places is very narrow with spectacular cliffs plunging down to the corries below. The sketch of this mountain on the next page is from the road, the arête to the left of the summit.

At its narrowest point, Ray had stopped to explain his theory that women's breasts were more attractive covered up than exposed when he slipped on the wet rock. Had he

Bidean nam Bian

fallen east, the Glen Coe mountain rescue team would have been searching for bits of him but he fell heavily the other way. He stopped himself with his face, which was deeply cut. I thought he'd smashed his teeth but he had only bitten his tongue. The padded strap of his rucksack probably prevented a snapped collar bone and his leg was gashed and bruised. He lay in shock for a minute or so and we fussed over him, checking that his limbs worked and his eyes could still focus. When we were sure that he had no serious injury we reverted to normal, asking him the time (his watch was in fragments) and pointing out the vertical chute on the east side with some relish. It was a proud Ray who limped into work the following Monday, a deep scar on the side of his face.

As it began to snow, I reflected that there was always the risk of a fall and it is better to have companions if it happens.

Ray explains his theory

It was cold as we made our way to the top of Bidean nam Bian, there were icicles on the grass stalks, all pointing away from that bitter wind. My hands were frozen as I picked my way through the patches of snow and slippery boulders. We had started on a raw November day and now it was January.

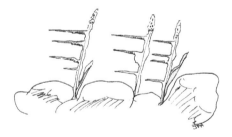

At the summit, I made the pledge made many times before when cloud had obscured the views, I'll be back! Almost as I said this, the cloud began to thin and blow away. As we descended to the col at the head of the Hidden Valley, the views opened up and the world was suddenly sparkling, with spectacle in every direction. We stopped to look north to the Aonach Eagach; down into the great pass of Glen Coe; east to the wonders of Buachaille Etive Beag and Buachaille Etive Mor and south to Glen Etive, with Ben Starav's distinctive profile dominating the skyline there.

We ate our lunch on the summit of Stob Coire Sgreamhach, looking south down Glen Etive, with sharp and clear air and the sun sparkling on the loch. We had been through autumn and winter on this walk and now it was glorious spring.

The fine day continued as we made our way into the remarkable Hidden Valley of Glen Coe. At its head there are ravines and spectacular waterfalls. Then it opens into a wide area, the flat floor of which is carpeted with lush bright meadow grass. All around are massive walls of black rock, sheltering this special place. The valley narrows to a gorge as the track winds down towards Glen Coe. The mouth of the gorge is filled with a jumble of boulders, some as big as houses. Growing around and out of the boulders are deciduous trees, making a little wood which fills the gorge right down to the River Coe. I could smell the wood long before my other senses were aware of it. The sweet scents of rowan and elder carry right to the head of the valley at this time of year.

We walked through the curious wood, the path twisting and turning around the monstrous boulders, sometimes hugging the steep side of the gorge with sudden drops for the careless down into the rushing water far below. Black, ice-polished rock loomed high on either side, streams spreading thinly over it to give the rock a gem-like quality. Elder, rowan, birch, alder and even oak grow there. I wondered how this relic of the Highland's natural woodland had survived but the deer fence lower down provided the answer. The stream we followed plunged over waterfalls then abruptly changed mood as it ran into crystal clear pools, leading us down towards the River Coe. The trees seemed to compete with each other to grow in ever stranger ways in this lost world. I would not have been surprised had an elf appeared from one of the dry-floored caves under the boulders.

A lost world,
Glen Coe, 19/6/4

We crossed the River Coe by a bridge and as we walked back to the car the weather changed again to November mode. The sky grew dark grey and a steady cold rain began to fall. It was set in for the day.

Once changed into dry clothes, we ate good food and shared a well-earned bottle or two. The company was on form, there was much laughter and the evening seemed to pass in minutes.

We rose early and the morning was bright and full of promise. I suggested that we walk up Ben Challum on the way home, despite it being described as "rather boring" in one of the guide books. This time, most of the Jolly Boys came, partly because the sky was blue but also because of the shame of returning without a Munro bagged, a shame compounded by the achievements of the four adventurers the previous day.

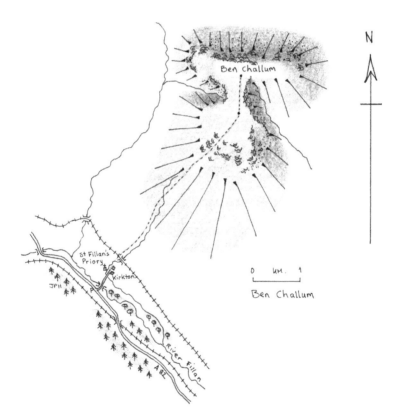

On the way up the long grassy slopes the air rang with the exuberant song of larks. As we climbed, we left the more benign country of this joyous bird and entered the high land of rock and space. There we saw ptarmigan with their summer coats, still with patches of white on their undersides, but mottled with beige, grey and brown on top, a perfect camouflage and impossible to see unless they moved.

The walk was excellent and Ben Challum was anything but boring. It has twin summits, the higher being the furthest away from St Fillan's priory, our starting point. Along the side of the lower top there is a boulder-filled gully. As the wind was still in the north and cold, we went into the gully for a cup of tea and some lunch. We had to share it with some hardy mountain frogs but it was a perfect spot, a sun trap and soon too hot for both the amphibians and the humans.

A short, narrow, rocky ridge then led the way to Ben Challum itself. The north and north-east sides of this mountain are sudden cliffs on a scale that we could not have imagined as we approached from the south-west. The best thing of all, however, was the cool, clear air and the long views. We lingered to discuss Ben More and Stob Binnein to the south, Ben Lui and Ben Cruachan to the west and the Glen Dochart mountains to the east. All had special memories of these places and it was good to share them.

On the way down, Allan asked what I was going to do when I retired. When I replied that a priority was to walk in the hills, he smiled as a father would smile at a naïve child and said, "Has it not occurred to you that you'll be too old to climb mountains when you retire?" I replied that I hoped not and that I would climb hills until my body will no longer allow it. "And what then?" he asked.

"Then I'll walk in the glens and look up to the hills I climbed when I was a younger man."

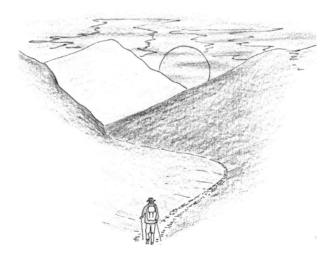

Beinn Alligin: Sgurr Mhor, Tom na Gruagaich. Liathach: Spidean a' Choire Leith, Mullach an Rathain. Beinn Eighe: Ruadh-stac Mor, Spidean Coire nan Clach.

 Torridonian sushi

June

T he sun shone, the Highlands looked their absolute best and Tom and I were full of expectation as we drove to Kinlochewe.

The bunkhouse stands next door to the Kinlochewe Hotel on the main road. It was very basic, a little kitchen with a large wooden table and wooden benches, a dormitory with four triple bunks and a washroom. The hotel is old and was rather down at heel. We talked to the owner, who had a blunt manner which verged on rude, particularly when he was coping with too many customers. As the days went by we saw that he is a man with a dry sense of humour, he just needs more staff. Morag and Cath arrived and were quick to grab the lower bunks, agreeing that those on top looked precarious. Kenny and Allan arrived and we ordered bar suppers. The food was a surprise in that it was skilfully cooked from good ingredients. This was a relief as the nearest alternative was many miles distant, the last thing to contemplate after a long day on the hills. We relaxed in the pub and later drifted off to sleep in our bunks with high hopes of the next day.

I was abruptly woken by an alien person who shone a torch into my face. "Are you comfortable in that bunk?" he enquired.

"Yes," I replied sleepily.

"Well, I wonder if you might consider getting out of my sleeping bag inner so that I can go to bed too?"

I had assumed that this was provided by the hotel and climbed in. I apologised, climbed out (looking down quickly to see if I was wearing my boxer shorts), returned the bunk to its rightful owner and after a quick rummage for a sheet was asleep in a vacant bed in 30 seconds.

At breakfast, there was the night time spectre again, this time with his walking companion. I apologised again but he seemed to bear no ill feeling. The two men were from Lancashire and had a peculiar relationship. They had walked together in the mountains for many years but the owner of the sheet, christened Wallace, nagged incessantly at his pal who endured it all in silent good humour, so he was named Gromit. Very occasionally, Gromit would make a retort which flew across the kitchen like a bullet. Wallace gave a gasp, looked hurt for a moment or two and then started again.

By late morning the others, with the exception of Fionn, had arrived so we decided to climb Beinn Alligin. Morag, Tom and I had earlier been down to Loch Torridon for a

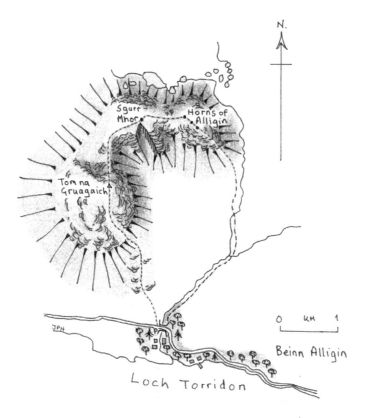

recce and the strange mountains looked so wonderful in the morning sunshine that we were desperate to start, especially while the weather was so uncharacteristically fine.

We got the last two spaces in the little car park and headed north into the Coir' nan Laogh.

The climb up to Tom na Gruagaich was hot work, with each of us sweating out as much liquid as we could consume. The ridge, however, repaid all the effort, with views in every direction that took our breath away. To the west the sea twinkled in the summer sun, to the north was a panoramic wilderness of mountain and loch leading to Loch Maree. To the south, the curious basin of Upper Loch Torridon with its ring of fantastically-shaped mountains. It was to the east, however, that our eyes mostly turned, to admire the unique shapes of Liathach and Beinn Eighe, our objectives for the next two days. While Cath and Tom took off their boots to nurse their blisters, I looked across to these two dramatic ranges. They are made of horizontally-bedded Torridonian sandstone, that extraordinary ancient rock that makes some of the North-west's most photographed and painted mountains. On the highest peaks, especially on Beinn Eighe, were what looked like ice caps of Cambrian quartzite, giving them an atmosphere more akin to lands above the Arctic Circle.

We walked along the ridge with light hearts, stopping for tea and a snack on Sgurr Mhor. When scrambling down a rock outcrop below our rest place, Allan took heavy fall, bruising a leg. Once we had him back on his feet, he decided to go down at the col rather than tackle the Horns of Alligin. Three others opted to go down with him. Struan, Ray, Morag, Tom and I went on to clamber up each of these famous rock towers. The walking poles were stowed and it was time for hands as well as feet as we sought out the high routes on this best section of the mountain.

Beinn Alligin and Liathach across Loch Torridon, 1/8/4.

Back at the hotel, we were in good spirits. We had ordered our meals in the morning and the food was much appreciated. Tom and I had roasted local lamb with a delicious mint gravy. The evening took an unexpected turn when the owner asked if we would consider allowing two Italian women the spare bunks. Kenny announced that there was no question about this and went into raptures of speculation about these women. We left earlier than we might have to enjoy the company of our exotic guests but Kenny was fated to be sorely disappointed. Morag remarked when walking the next day, "It's encouraging to learn that there are plain women in Italy as well as in Britain." The women were an odd couple indeed, with curious habits like pulling on pyjamas over their outdoor clothes when they went to bed. We ended up friends of course, with the Italians taking our photographs before we parted. The only exception was Cath, who swore that they had used her pink towel and invoked the fierce Scottish motto, nemo me impune laccessit.

The second day was to be our most challenging as we were to attempt to scale the imposing wall of rock that is Liathach. There was cloud and those with gloomier dispositions such as Kenny and Ray predicted heavy rain and dangerous thunderstorms.

We started at the small car park a few hundred metres east of Glen Cottage. My car had been left about three kilometres further west near a small conifer plantation. The route was basically straight up a very steep gully and the plan was to get onto the ridge near the east top. We were soon strung out along the well-made path and as I sat on a rock for a breather I saw what I thought at first was a bird but the flight was peculiar. It turned out to be a giant dragonfly and soon there were others, looking prehistoric but wonderfully in place on this most ancient of mountains.

Tom was suffering from the previous day's blisters and decided that it would be easier to cut across the bends in the steep path and go straight up the mountain on hands and knees. All we could see as he approached from below was a head moving through the rocks and heather, a sight which had a singularly unsettling effect on Kenny.

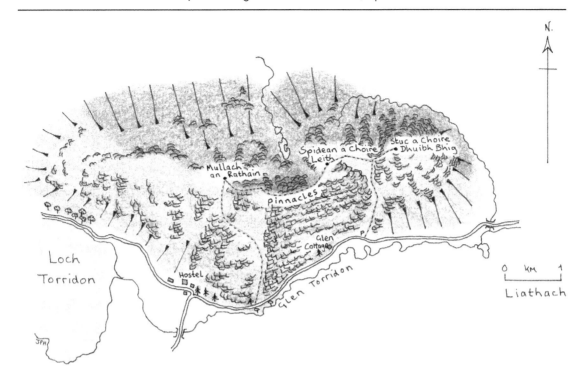

Waiting for us at Stuc a' Choire Dhuibh Bhig, Liathach's east top, was Fionn. He had climbed up the near vertical east face, saying that it was to try out his new fell running shoes bought in a little shop on the Gorgie Road in Edinburgh.

We had lunch together then Allan, Kenny, Alex and Cath went down the way we had come up. The rest of the party began to walk westward along the crest of the ridge, resigned to not having the views we had on Beinn Alligin as the cloud had come down to 900 metres or so. There was enough visibility, however, to tantalise us and on we went.

The most interesting part of the day came as we descended from Spidean a' Choire Leith, Liathach's highest peak. Fionn led us down a tenuous path through the frost-shattered quartzite rocks which cover the summit. He has enormous experience of the mountains, far more than anyone else in the group, having climbed all Munros bar one (a deliberate choice), most Corbetts and lesser peaks and many mountains several times. He has been in the mountains in all weather conditions and has an uncanny knack of finding his way without reference to map or compass. Strange indeed then that we began to realise that we were not following the path to Liathach's Pinnacles. We back-tracked, this time Struan, our next most experienced hillwalker, taking the lead as Fionn fell back with his head down, tutting to himself for having led us astray. Struan had just declared that we were now on the right path when Tom pointed out that we had passed a particular rock outcrop with a distinctive window on the way down and were now heading back up to Spidean a' Choire Leith.

A young man and his father had asked to join us earlier as they were unsure about navigation in such conditions, so, obviously, were we. They looked at us with slightly anxious faces. Ray broke the uneasy silence which had descended by declaring that we should retrace our steps and get off the mountain while the going was good. At that moment, a group of three fit young men appeared out of the mist and announced that they, too, were disorientated and could not find the path to the Pinnacles. They had tried once and retraced their steps to the right, then again and retraced their steps to the left and they were now giving up, returning the way we had all come. We said our farewells and Ray again insisted that we should follow them off the mountain. At that moment an Irish couple loomed out of the mist and joined the discussion. Struan asked what I thought we should do and I suggested that we should carefully check our exact position, set a bearing and pace it in short sections until we either found the path or agreed that we were again disorientated. Ray asked why we should do this when we had already been forced to retrace our steps and I replied that this was an opportunity to learn from experience. So we agreed to give it one last shot. Struan took the lead, everything was done with textbook precision and we found the path in about 50 paces. We had been going parallel to it and had wandered from it when it lost definition in the scree.

On we went with some relief, our party plus our new companions. Relief only lasted, however, until we reached the first of Liathach's Pinnacles which towered up into the mist. Ever positive, I declared, "At least it's not raining and we don't have to deal with wet and slippery rock." The rain started as I said "rock".

Not to be daunted at this stage, we tackled this well-known section with its "serious pitches" and "considerable exposure". Morag got an adrenaline rush and her face lit up with excitement. At one point, I pulled myself briskly up out of a narrow chimney and realised that if I had been a little more vigorous I would have gone straight over the crest and down the other side. I warned Morag who was immediately below and when she in turn pulled herself onto the narrow eyrie of rock her eyes widened as she peered down the other side. "I'm glad that we are doing this in such poor visibility," she declared, "I'm not sure I would have coped if it had been clear." A walker needs a good head for heights on this stretch.

I found it all exhilarating and announced that I had added this to my list of mountains to which I would return on a fine, clear day so that I could properly appreciate its features.

We came down a chute of loose scree from Mullach an Rathain and out of the cloud to an overcast, still and humid day, perfect for midges. And midges there were in their millions. However tired, this was no time to stroll and we were incredibly efficient in getting into my car as I became taxi driver to shuttle everyone back to the starting car park.

When I walked into the hotel, those who had come down early from Liathach were sitting there wearing sly grins. They had eaten scones in the café, had an afternoon nap and were quite smug in the knowledge that they had done the right thing. "What was it like then, atmospheric?"

"Yes," I replied lamely, "very."

At the bar getting the drinks I asked Fionn whether having a positive outlook and an eternally optimistic nature could grate on others. He was in no doubt that it could, suggesting that people tend to be more comfortable with the morose.

Considering our last day, Kenny announced that the forecast was for a band of heavy rain to sweep across from the east. Ray added that he was sure that there was a risk of thunderstorms. It was clear that most did not want to go on to Beinn Eighe as planned. In the end, Morag and I went to climb on that mountain, thunderstorms or no thunderstorms, Struan and Tom went fishing for trout below the Triple Buttress, Fionn went for a ride on his bike and the rest walked along the north shore of Loch Maree.

The start of our walk was the car park at the end of the path which has been made between Liathach and Beinn Eighe, up into the Coire Dubh Mor. Tom parted from us and trudged away to find his angler's dream of a lochan. We crossed the stream and headed north up the steep slopes of Beinn Eighe towards our first objective, Spidean Coire nan Clach, one of the two Munros on this complex of ridges. The day was mild and dry, with good visibility across the great bowl of Upper Loch Torridon and towards its encircling peaks. We rested and talked about attitudes to the weather in the Scottish mountains, agreeing that a properly equipped walker should not necessarily be put off by a poor forecast or a morning that starts wet and grey. Those who are discouraged by inclement weather are not going to see many of Scotland's wonderful peaks and ridges. Other factors to consider are the number of times the forecast is not accurate, like on that very day on Beinn Eighe and the walks on which an unpromising start undergoes a metamorphosis into a great day.

Up on the ridge we turned east and marvelled at the landscape before us. The cloud was thin and wispy, giving us tantalising views down to the bottom of the precipitous cliffs on either side. Grotesque pinnacles of rock loomed to our left and Morag declared that, with the previous day's cynicism in mind, it was undeniably "atmospheric". The Torridonian sandstone is capped with Cambrian quartzite and we walked up angular blocks of this ancient rock to the top of our first Munro of the day.

Doubling back, we followed the fine ridge west and then north-west, taking it easy and stopping for tea and snacks. At the head of the Triple Buttress, the path turns to the north and at this point we stopped to admire the view. Cloud was settling down over the Beinn Eighe ridges, leaving the highest peaks standing like islands in a white sea.

On we walked to Ruadh Stac Mor, Beinn Eighe's second Munro. As we sat on slabs at the cairn, a beautiful snow bunting in his mating white hopped across the rocks towards us. He cocked his head to one side as if inviting conversation, so I talked to him (in a mixture of bird and English) and he hopped closer.

Torridon
1st to 5th August
2004

The snow bunting

I asked Morag for a piece of her peanut butter sandwich and held it out. The dapper little bird ate from my fingers and then took a chunk of sandwich to his nest. Morag had taken a quick photograph but regretted not having time for a good close-up. "I think he'll be back," I said, breaking off another piece and back he came. I felt honoured to be feeding this uncommon bird.

Feeding a male snow bunting:
Beinn Eighe.

We went down a stone chute from the ridge into the massive corrie famed for its spectacular Triple Buttress. The cloud, however, seemed to have come to a rest in this special place and all we could see was the base of the giant columns of rock. This was my second visit and I had been denied sight of this wonder the first time. Never mind, third time pays for all. We made our way across this eerie place of rock and lochan, shouting for Tom. Our voices echoed in turn off the back wall of the corrie, but there was no reply. Morag talked of the wreck of a Second World War aeroplane underneath the Triple Buttress and her description of the place on a clear day stiffened my resolve to return.

Struan had joined Tom to fish for trout. We had shouted and passed so near to them but the mist had muffled our calls. It cleared as we left the corrie and we had perfect views of the surrounding mountains on the long walk back, the fantastic landscape at its best in the late sun and long, dark shadows.

Back in the hotel with the others, we reported on our day. It had been miserable. We had no views, had got lost and the rain had been relentless. Exhausted, we agreed that this had been one of our worst days in the mountains. At the bar, Fionn, who had been listening to our account, said, "Well, that seemed to go down better."

Late that evening, back in the bunkhouse, we sat sipping the Drambuie that Fionn had brought back from his bike run while Tom and Struan told us about their day fishing in a lochan below the waterfall which drains Coire Mhic Fhearchair. Tom had been teaching

Struan the noble art of fly fishing and they had caught 40 trout, bringing some home for supper and putting the rest back. Tom slit open one of the fish. Allan gagged and Kenny laughed, declaring, "You're a true Weegie; you've only ever experienced fish battered and stuck on top of chips." A string of roe emerged from the fish (more gagging) and I asked Tom to save that for me when he cooked the trout. I did not get the chance, however, as Fionn leaned over, pursed his lips and neatly slurped the string of fish eggs from the trout's belly. This had an interesting effect on Allan and Kenny thoughtfully passed him a bowl. We then debated the best method of cooking the trout and decided to bake them. "I'm not tasting them, that's for sure," said Allan. Fionn asked Tom which one was the smallest, took the fish in his hand and ate it raw, stating between mouthfuls that it would be a pity to cook such fresh fish. He ate with relish, leaving only a head, backbone and tail with a piece of skin which, when licked, he assured us, would make a purse. I'll leave the effect on Allan of this impromptu sushi snack to your imagination.

The baked trout made a memorable supper, eaten with brown bread and washed down with the remainder of Fionn's Drambuie.

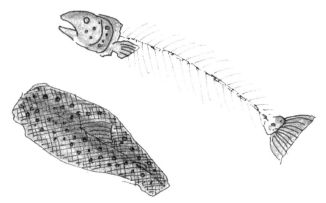

"I'll keep the skin for a purse."

Creag Mhor, Beinn Heasgarnich. Geal-charn, A' Mharconaich

 Gorillas and other wildlife

September

I drove up to Weem on a fine Friday evening to stay at Stuart Wagstaff's new hostel. The Jolly Boys were in the pub and we stayed up late.

Early on Saturday, Morag and I set off for upper Glen Lochay. Ray was to come with us but he groaned when I got out of bed and declared that he had changed his mind. The others were all asleep and planned to climb Schiehallion later that day.

We parked at Kenknock and walked along the River Lochay. At Batavaime Bothy we started a steep climb up a spur leading to Creag Mhor. My head was thick and I was weary at first, but the strenuous exercise began to energise me. My heart was leaping around in my chest and banging off my ribcage. I knew that this would either clear my head or kill me.

The day was fresh, with blue sky and sunshine. White clouds blew across from the west. After a lot of hard work, we thought that we were at the top but then we saw another mountain looming up through wispy white cloud and knew that Creag Mhor was a big one.

After another hard slog the steep slope levelled off and we reached the cairn. At that moment the cloud began to blow up and over the summit.

We knew that we had to walk down north-west from the top and then north for about a kilometre before we turned east, so set off briskly before the cloud thickened further.

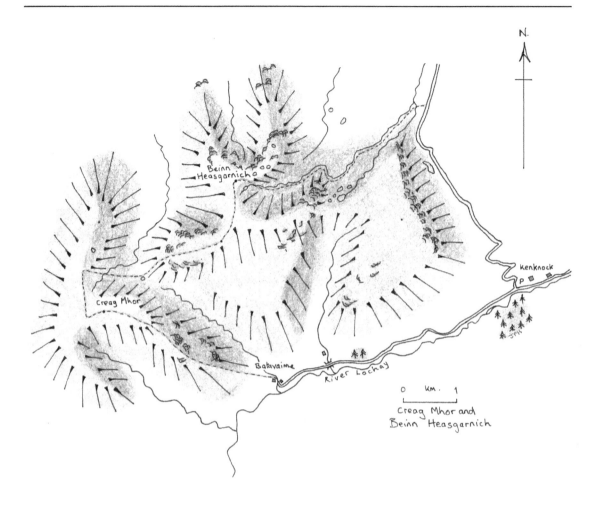

Creag Mhor and
Beinn Heasgarnich

After a while, I noticed that the ground was rising to our right, we had lost the path in the boulder fields and I knew that we were going too far west. I took out my compass and we set off on an easterly bearing, back the way we had come. Our difficulty was knowing how far we had walked from the summit cairn. We both vowed to buy a GPS to help at such times in the future. The easterly bearing took us back the way we had walked and out of the cloud. A huge corrie was revealed and the ridges of Beinn Heasgarnich rose steeply up on the far side. We sat there to eat our lunch, smiling to see that the cloud had blown off the summit behind us. While drinking a mug of tea I felt the silence of this lonely place and wondered where the wildlife had gone.

As we walked across the peat bogs on the floor of the corrie, we talked about the absence of other walkers and the chances of meeting someone we knew on a day like that.

It was wonderful to walk along the ridge up to Beinn Heasgarnich. The path is over 3,000 feet high and the views down to Glen Lyon on the one side and down to Glen Lochay on the other side were crystal clear. The mountains beyond had the odd quality of cardboard cut-outs, each a different depth of shading and positioned one range after another. The bright sun played tricks with the perspective, sometimes making us wonder which range was nearer.

The path wound ahead to the summit and I smiled again as white cloud rolled up to cover it just in time for our arrival. Two figures loomed through this cloud like gorillas in the mist. They metamorphosed into two hillwalkers and then again into my brother-in-law and his friend. They were climbing the same mountains as we were, but their route was counter-clockwise. After the introductions and surprise all round at this chance encounter I commented on the risk they were taking in walking widdershins, especially so near to Schiehallion, the fairy mountain.

gorillas in the mist.
Beinn Heasgarnich, 4/9/4.

We left them puzzled and continued on our clockwise route. The compass was needed again to get us safely off the summit and we sat down on the east side of the mountain, just below the cloud. As earlier in the day, we had just made some tea when the cloud above us dispersed and soon there was not a trace of white in the sky. Morag had a large scale map of the Highlands, cut into A4 sections. We sat identifying distant peaks, using the map to check those we were not sure of. Ben Lui to the south-west was particularly imposing. That high tea on the side of Beinn Heasgarnich was the highlight of the walk and it provided a mystery. Our maps confirmed that we should have been able to see Ben Vorlich and Stuc a' Chroin to the south-east but they were nowhere to be seen. I had an uneasy feeling about this for weeks until I next saw that these mountains were still where they should be.

We had a good walk out, following a stream as it tumbled over waterfalls and rushed through rocky gorges, until we reached the narrow road which runs from Glen Lochay to Glen Lyon. Along the way we disturbed a pair of ravens, the only two creatures, (with the exception of my brother-in-law and his pal), that we saw on that long walk. The road took us back to the car, which we reached exactly nine hours after setting off.

The others were in the pub and there we swapped news of our walks. I ate a big bowl of mussels with garlic bread and a delicious shank of roast lamb. The evening was rounded off with a pleasant malt whisky which I think was called Pretty Vague. Whether this is correct or not, it accurately describes my comfortably numb state after such a splendid day and excellent meal.

I was up at six the next day and was soon driving along deserted roads with Morag, heading for the Drumochter hills. She had chosen these because there was no long walk in from the road and it seemed ideal for a Sunday morning. We discussed these mountains as I drove, agreeing that they do not look very exciting as one passes on the A9. My memories were of plain, rounded lumps, often shrouded in cloud or screened behind grey curtains of rain. That morning, however, was glorious as we parked on the far side of the Drumochter Pass at Balsporran Cottages.

We followed a well-used path up through heather, heading south-west to Geal-charn.

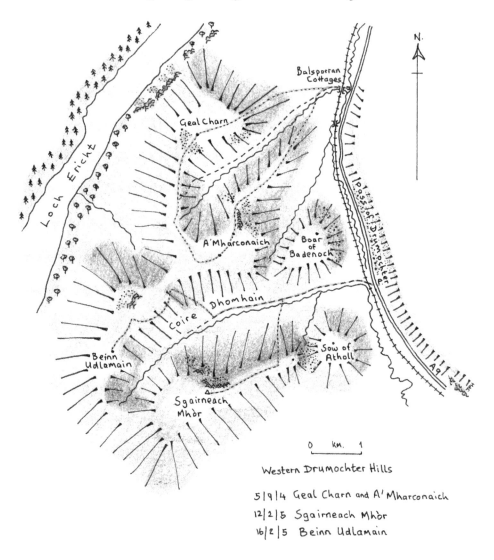

Western Drumochter Hills

5|9|4 Geal Charn and A' Mharconaich
12|2|5 Sgairneach Mhòr
16|2|5 Beinn Udlamain

Small flocks of red grouse flew off to left and right and birdsong filled the air. Higher up, where the heather gave way to boulder fields, ptarmigan trotted away from us in their characteristically unhurried manner. A young red deer stag and three hinds slowly ambled away until they were silhouetted against the blue sky on the very top of the mountain. We also marvelled at the large number of particularly well fed mountain hares, already changing to their winter white. All had white legs, throats and bellies, while one had white ears. What a contrast to the barren and empty wastes of the previous day!

Mountain hares on Geal-charn,
Drumochter, 5/9/4.

Hungry again, we ate an early lunch on the top of Geal-charn where we could see a majestic panorama over Loch Ericht. We knew that the highest part of this group of finely sculpted mountains was Ben Alder, but needed our maps to identify the others. We picked out routes into this complex landscape, up to the scalloped corries and sharp-edged, curving arêtes.

Then it was an airy ridge walk around the crest of the large corrie occupied by the Allt Coire Fhar and on to A' Mharconaich, our second Munro of the morning. We went a hundred metres or so east and sat on a high perch above the pass. The mountain's name translates as the horse place. I looked over my shoulder and imagined mounted Celtic warriors appearing over the skyline. Our view was of mountains to the east and to the distinctive shape of Schiehallion in the south. Meall Chuaich, with its steep slopes rising above a blue loch, looked especially attractive. I thought that the Drumochter hills on a clear day were anything but dull.

Carn Dearg and Sgor Gaibhre

 Fighting the elements

October

Stuart Wagstaff again made Morag and me feel welcome at The Adventurers' Escape at Weem. We spent the evening drinking tea with him in front of the fire in his worn and comfortable sitting room.

Next day, we were off before dawn and drove to Loch Rannoch. As the sky lightened, the views of Schiehallion were so good that we stopped the car a number of times. The autumn colours of the trees on each side of the glen were at their very best, reds competing with browns, yellows and burnt orange. We did not know what to expect of the day as the weather forecast had stated that it was to be a day of sun and showers with a 12 mph south-west wind but already the wind was rocking our vehicle. When we reached the east end of Loch Rannoch the waves were high enough to surf. As we travelled along the loch shore the grey and choppy waters were more like the North Sea than a Highland loch. The first rain splattered across the windscreen.

We parked at Loch Eigheach and looked at the sky. There were tiny patches of blue and the light squalls of rain were the sort that might pass, so we decided against waterproof trousers. Before we set off up the track, the old Road to The Isles, we tried out our new GPS navigators, getting an accurate grid reference for our parking place.

The rain seemed to be getting heavier and the sky was ominous over Rannoch Moor to the west. We decided to take the track north up the glen which leads from

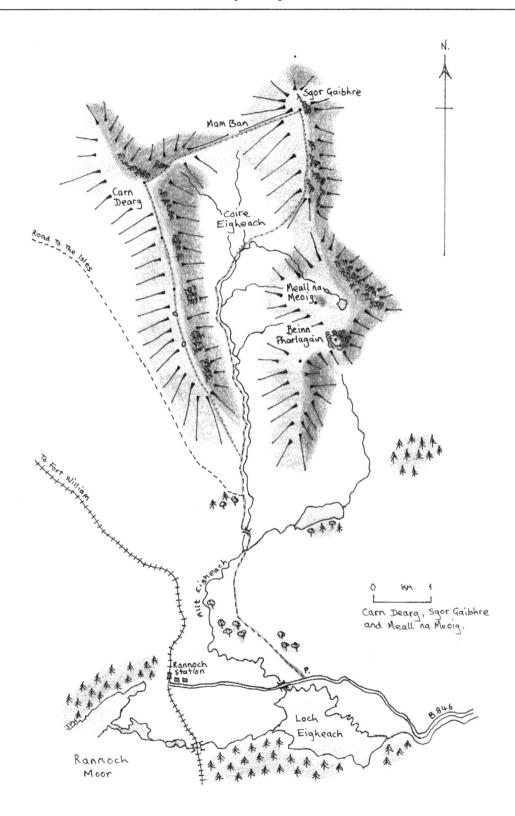

Carn Dearg, Sgor Gaibhre
and Meall na Meoig.

the giant bowl of Coire Eigheach where vast amounts of ice gathered in each of our Ice Ages.

The waters of the Allt Eigheach roared over rapids and waterfalls, swollen by the heavy rain which had spoiled the previous few days. We stopped to look at the last bright spot, far to the east, in a darkening sky and noticed the first red deer of the day. A stag lay on the other side of the river, curiously unconcerned by our presence. Another rose and stared at us while his hinds made good their escape. Further up the hillside another dozen deer headed briskly up the glen in a straight line, lifting their knees high to step over the heather.

We went north-west and began to climb the long south ridge of Carn Dearg. The ground was saturated and I realised that, despite careful waxing, my boots were not going to keep my feet dry that day. Halfway up the hillside, Morag shouted against the wind, "Look, a patch of blue sky!" At that moment the patch disappeared and the wind strengthened, bringing sheets of rain from the desolate and waterlogged Rannoch Moor. We struggled on, heads bent down, wishing we had, after all, put on our waterproof trousers.

Hillwalkers in Scotland have to have an optimistic perspective when it comes to the weather. If there is even a glimmer of hope, one has to go for it. Even weather as grim as we faced that day might blow over by afternoon.

On the ridge we caught the full force of the wind as it drove water into our clothing. We were pummelled and buffeted for the three kilometres to Carn Dearg.

Punch drunk, we sat down in the shelter of the fine cairn. I was uncomfortably wet, my walking trousers having wicked water down under my gaiters and into my boots. I removed my boots, peeled off my wet socks, dropped one into a puddle and then peeled off my soaked trousers. I pulled on my waterproof trousers, wrung out my socks (making a mental note always to pack spare socks) and put on my boots again. I felt surprisingly warm and fairly dry as I wrung a couple of litres of water from my trousers before stowing them in my pack.

Tired and sore from the pounding of the wind, we set off north-east with the wind at our backs to go down to the Mam Ban Bealach and then up again to Sgor Gaibhre, our second Munro of the day. We brought out the GPS navigators again and the grid reference was spot on.

We decided to walk south for two kilometres along the long ridge leading down from this second summit and then drop down into the giant Coire Eigheach so that we could walk back along the valley floor and avoid the worst of the wind.

There was a bit of a path in places but this disappeared whenever it met the extensive stony patches. Visibility was poor and I marched with my compass in hand to make sure that we did not wander the wrong way off the ridge.

When we scrambled down into the massive basin of the corrie, the compass was essential to help us cross that vast space without landmarks to help navigation.

The floor was a wet sponge and the streams feeding the Allt Eigheach were swollen to rivers, each a pale grey rushing torrent. The map showed that the path was on the far bank of the river and we knew that we had to cross it at this upper stage as a lower crossing would be impossible in those conditions. We found a narrow section where the river surged under a steep bank which was collapsing into it as we watched. "How good are you at long jump?" shouted Morag above the noise of the wind and water. We took a good run to the bank and made it across, landing with a splash on the far side.

The walk back was through sheets of rain, boots squelching, the river roaring by our sides and the stags roaring on the wind. We stopped where the river had cut a shallow gorge and sat on rocks to have our last cup of tea, watching the sinuous curves of the huge volume of water hurtling past our feet.

A little further on, a bend in the path revealed a small boat, the sort used by anglers for a spot of sea fishing. On a day like this it was easy to believe that a catastrophic flood was the explanation, with the boat left stranded here, 500 metres above sea level.

Boat by the Allt Eigheach 22/10/4.

We stopped at the pub in Weem on the way home and had venison steaks with a glass of red wine, an appropriate dinner following a day spent among so many red deer. After a walk in the Highlands fighting the elements, (water in particular on that day), it is delightful to sit in dry clothes in a warm pub enjoying a good hot meal.

12/2/05

Sgairneach Mhor

 ## White-out

February

The internet weather forecasts for Saturday 12th February looked fine, so I drove north after work on the Friday evening to stay with Stuart at his place in Weem. Morag had joined me but Struan was recovering from a cold and dropped out.

The Adventurers' Escape was as welcoming as ever, which is why we had chosen it. We chatted to Stuart in his cosy sitting room until well past midnight.

I woke at 7.30 and went to the window. Snow had fallen during the night and had covered everything, including the road, with a thick white blanket.

We lingered over breakfast with our host while passing vehicles reduced the snow to a thin strip along the middle of the road. We were on our way north by 9.00, sun shining, sky blue and scenery a winter wonderland.

I parked at Drumochter and we put on our winter clothing. Two men from Sheffield arrived. They told us that they had not been hillwalking in the Highlands for some time and were a little edgy about the conditions. They asked if they could walk with us and we told them that they would be most welcome.

Coire Dhomhain was stunning in the winter sun, the light sparkling from billions of points on its snow-covered walls. We stopped to look at the red deer, well over a hundred had come down to the floor of the glen. It was one of my closest encounters with them, like being in a wildlife film. There were many small, young deer, obviously not used to deep

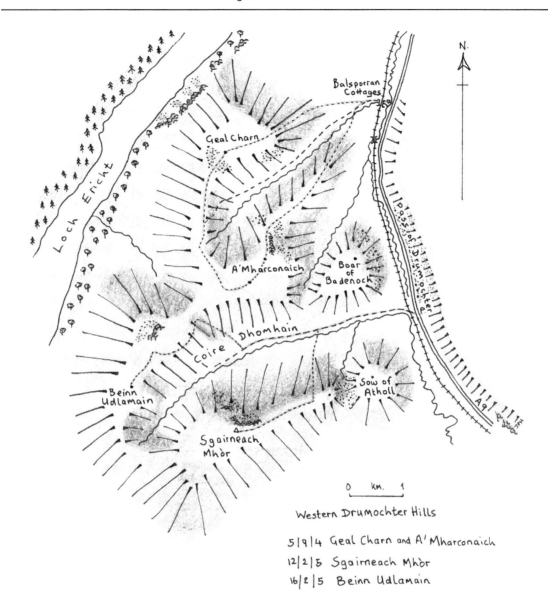

Western Drumochter Hills

5|9|4 Geal Charn and A'Mharconaich
12|2|5 Sgairneach Mhòr
16|2|5 Beinn Udlamain

snow. They lifted their legs high to take exaggerated steps and wobbled as they moved across the slope. It is said that the deer come down to the lower parts of the glens when the weather is severe, we should have taken the warning!

We crossed the river and trudged through deep snow, heading for the bealach between The Sow of Atholl and Sgairneach Mhor. After climbing the latter, the plan was to follow the ridge around the head of the glen, climb Beinn Udlamain, a second Munro, drop down the north side of Coire Dhomhain and walk out.

Stopping in a little grotto decorated with grotesque icicles, we made some tea and had a snack. A ptarmigan flew low over our heads, plump and white against a grey sky, its flash of red a jewel in this colourless landscape.

On our climb up to the col we found the snow soft and squeaky at first, lying in deep drifts and sculpted into fantastic shapes by the wind. Later, the top layer became frozen into a hard crust. At the top, snow skipped and bounced over a surface of solid ice.

The weather was changing fast. Grey clouds had covered the sky and there was an eerie light which foretold snow. The wind was picking up.

Conditions were severe on the bealach. The wind blew incredibly hard from the west, with gusts which picked up our walking poles. Hard pellets of icy snow were being driven into our faces as we turned into it. We stopped to find snow goggles. I was particularly glad that I was wearing a balaclava under my warm mountain cap and that I had pulled on mitts over my wool gloves. Despite having good clothing designed to protect, I was beginning to chill. The wind caught Morag's snow goggles case and it flew off like a bullet.

The struggle along the ridge is something that will always stay in my mind. The wind was so strong that one of our companions was knocked 12 metres back down the slope, this despite being a well-made man.

The snow was mixed with spindrift, making visibility difficult. At one point I noticed that I was near a snow cornice and realised that this was above the steep cliffs of the corrie which eats into the north side of the mountain. I shouted back to the others and we stopped to get a GPS reference and take a bearing from the map. Moving on was difficult, however, because the wind became even more fierce and there were no landmarks at all. With each step I was aware of the cornice to my right. At that point we were faced with complete white-out. There was no sky, no land, no perspective, only white. I stood still as the others slowly caught up. I was on the point of turning to say that we would have to get to safety when there was a brief lull in the howling wind and a dark shape appeared through the white ahead. I knew that it was the cairn and set off for it, the others following in a line. The summit was marked by an icy stone ring around a triangulation pillar. When I suggested that we should content ourselves with this single Munro and turn back, there was no dissenting voice!

White-out conditions returned as we cautiously retraced our steps, sometimes having our upward footsteps as a guide, but often these had been filled with fresh snow. The map and compass provided a bearing and we moved slowly, always aware of the cornice on the left and the risk of coming off the ridge on the wrong side. At the col, the wind was so strong we could barely stand up. We dropped below the lip, got some shelter and were able to think clearly again.

Visibility had improved at this lower altitude and I saw a straggling line of people heading up towards us, most were young boys. I spoke to the adult party leader and warned against going up to the ridge in those conditions. I am pleased that he took my advice as some of the boys were already blue with cold and very tired.

We then decided to cross the glen to gain the line of the track on the north side of the river. As we walked, the clouds broke and sunbeams streamed through, creating strange patterns of light. Patches of brilliance raced along the steep white mountainsides, stopping us in our tracks with wonder. Sgairneach Mhor sent great plumes of spindrift curling into the sky like white smoke on the powerful wind.

12/2/5 Sgairneach Mhor: plumes of spindrift.

Then the light dimmed and the snow drove down the glen towards us. I felt that we were just little specks of life in that winter wilderness.

Sheltering in a small bay in tall heather by the side of the track we had some tea and sandwiches before walking out. All the way back, the light played its tricks, sometimes dark, sometimes brilliant. There were patches of blue in the sky as we got back to the car, weary but exhilarated after our adventure.

Beinn Udlamain. Bynack More

 Deep winter

February

Four days after our hard fight climbing Sgairneach Mhor, we were back in Coire Dhomhain (see previous chapter for map), surprised by the depth of the snow. Huge pillow-shaped drifts lay at intervals along the glen and the path was heavy going, our legs sinking to above the knee time and time again. The soft snow had a different quality to that of our last visit, with bright blue showing in each footprint or hole made by our walking poles.

Red deer were again gathered at the foot of the glen and we watched as they used their hooves to clear patches of snow to get to the plants beneath. We passed a few of these cleared patches and were interested to see that the deer had found grassy areas among the predominant heather.

The glen was beautiful, almost abstract with its monochrome patterns. Ridges running down the steep sides were dark streaks where the wind had blown away the snow to reveal the rock, heather and blaeberry beneath. The gullies between were filled with deep drifts so brilliant white that I had to half shut my eyes. We trudged steadily on, enjoying the experience of walking on virgin snow, wrapped in the silence of these winter mountains.

The GPS was used at the foot of a steep gully and, comfortable with our decision, we began to climb up the side of the stream, heading for a bealach between Beinn Udlamain and A' Mharconaich. The last section was steep and the snow much more solid, with a frozen crust. We considered crampons but our boots were secure with each step. We decided to stop before we reached the exposed ridge. A little ledge cut into the snow made a perfect spot for tea and a snack.

When we reached the top we caught the strong and cold westerly wind. There was a clear view under the cloud of Loch Ericht and its surrounding hills. I thought about the different moods of the Scottish mountains. Five months earlier I had looked over Loch Ericht from the summit of neighbouring Geal Charn on a day so warm that I could have had a nap up there after eating my lunch. Stopping to eat on the ridge on that February day would have been to invite hypothermia.

We turned into the wind and, head down, marched along the crest of the ridge towards the summit. We were soon in cloud again and the wind was stirring up whirling columns of fine snow particles. It was bitterly cold, with ice covering old metal fence posts and horizontal icicles pointing downwind. At one point we knew that we had to veer south and again the GPS was useful as visibility was so poor in the swirling eddies. Out of the spindrift loomed four huge dark shapes moving straight towards us. The shapes turned into hillwalkers, large yes, but of human dimensions. We had been deceived by the strange conditions.

The summit cairn was covered in deep snow in which the four walkers had cut a snow hole to provide some shelter. Given the exposure, however, we decided to turn straight back and take a break later, out of the wind. We retraced our steps back to the bealach and cut a second platform in the pristine snow slope at the top of the gully. Out of the wind it was mild and we enjoyed a late lunch with hot tea.

In good spirits we trudged back down the glen, using the holes made in the snow by our boots on the way up. Back on the track, all was still and silent. A small dark object burst out of a snow bank. Fascinated, I watched as a tiny wren shook the snow from its feathers and cocked up its jaunty tail. Life goes on in the heather beneath the chill white blanket of winter.

wren in Coire Dhomhain 16/2/5.

A thin late afternoon sun appeared as we reached the lower glen. The snow changed to a warm honey colour with deep shadows caused by the low angle of the light. Beinn Udlamain means gloomy mountain, inappropriate for certain on that sparkling day.

Later, in the hostel at Newtonmore, we sat in front of the hot stove and talked to two teachers from Sheffield, up to the Highlands on their half term holiday. They had walked in the Peak District, Wales and the Lake District, but had recently discovered the Scottish mountains. Like many before them, they had initially scorned Munro bagging but, like us, had become drawn into it. We agreed that the discipline ensured that most corners of the Highlands were visited and without the Munro incentive would that be the case?

We left them pouring bottles of Yorkshire beer and set off to the pub for sustenance. A tree at the end of the path was covered with illuminated silver stars and the main street twinkled with festive displays. The pub was in keeping with the rest of the scene, being studded with bright fairy lights. After home-made soup, a large portion of venison casserole and a glass of warm red wine I was at peace with the world.

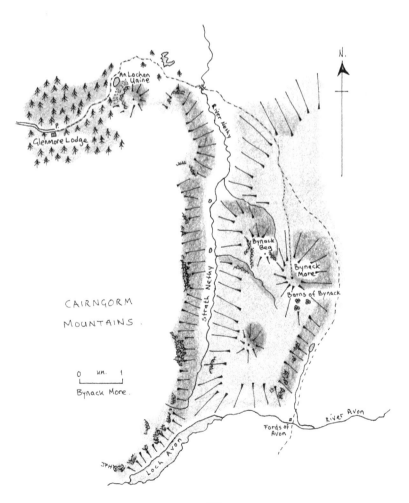

Early next morning I parked at Glenmore Lodge in the Glenmore Forest Park. Dawn revealed high cloud with breaks showing winter blue.

We walked to An Lochan Uaine, The Little Green Loch. This is an oval shaped lochan of an extraordinary dark jade colour. The backdrop is a precipitous slope with a massive scree of angular boulders. Ancient Scots pines cling to the mountainside, rooted among the rocks. Old giants of the Caledonian Forest line the shores. This is an enchanted spot, one of the gateways to the halls of the fairy people. It is in this water that they wash their clothes, the dye giving the green colour.

The path continues through this remnant of Scotland's primeval forest, following the floor of the Ryvoan Pass with its towering walls on either side. Once through the pass the ancient pines begin to thin out and steeply rising moorland dominates. The last sparse scatter of old gnarled pines, limbs broken by the fierce gales of these parts, made me reflect on the forest that had clothed these slopes until the modern age.

As we followed the track south-east through this beautiful but sad landscape we saw a group of black grouse at a lek. They were all cocks, lustrous in the winter light, their bright red wattles little berets shining like jewels in this land of browns and greys. They threatened each other with their fan tails erect, making loud rookooing calls, adding to the wildness of the morning.

Black grouse.

Up we trekked, walking to the side of a path treacherous with ice. A mild wind had thawed much of the snow but there were deep drifts in any fold in the hillside.

As we reached the Cairngorm plateau, we were exposed to more wind and the temperature was notably lower. We walked over that arctic surface of dry powdery snow and icy, frost-shattered stones. The views were on a grand scale, with Ben Macdui to the south-west and the deep-cut Glen Avon to the east. No walks onto the plateau are easy and we felt that we had worked hard by the time Bynack More rose before us. The path

JPH

Bynack More 17/2/5.

led across a bleak tableland of sharp-edged stones lying on drifts of coarse granite sand. Ahead stood the steep-sided triangular prism of Bynack More, thickly iced with snow and studded with substantial granite boulders along its crest.

We scrambled into the shelter of a granite tor at its base. There we stowed our walking poles, fitted crampons and unclipped ice axes.

The snow was frozen hard and crampons were essential. We steadily worked our way to the crest and then threaded upwards between the boulders. Progress was slow because we stopped so often to enjoy the beauty of this mountain in its winter coat.

At the very top the west wind was too cold and strong to be comfortable so we sat behind a colossal boulder which allowed a 180 degree panorama to the north, east and south. We flattened a platform in the snow and sat, weary but happy. Rarely have I enjoyed a lunch as much as on the summit of Bynack More.

We were sad to leave as we retraced our steps back along the crest and down to the tor where we stowed crampons and axes and took up the walking poles for the long trek back to the car.

In Strath Nethy we met an old-timer, straight-backed and spry despite being in his

80s. He had explored these hills and gave us tips for future walks. I wished him farewell and hoped that old age would be as kind to me.

As we approached the Ryvoan Pass the short winter day was nearing its end and the sun was low. There was magic in the light as it illuminated the steep eastern side of the pass. Each of the ancient pines was blood red where struck by the sun and cast an enormous black shadow. The Green Loch held its strange colour but was even more remarkable in this time of red glow and deep shade.

Beinn a' Chreachain
and Beinn Achaladair

A fine spring ridge walk

March

Ray, Morag and I travelled up to the Highlands as passengers in Struan's Landrover on the evening before the Good Friday holiday. I had booked us into the bunkhouse at Bridge of Orchy. This is a conversion of the long, narrow Victorian station building on the platform. We had a drink in the pub then slept like logs in the comfy beds.

Good Friday dawned mild and cloudy, with a fine drizzle. We could not even see the lowest slopes of the mountains but guessed that there was not much snow on them.

Struan drove the short distance to Achallader Farm, just beyond Loch Tulla. The farm is built among the ruins of a castle built by Black Duncan, Campbell of Glen Orchy. The site is a strategic one, guarding a point on the old road which runs along the foot of the Glen Orchy mountains where a high-level route cuts the range by using the bealach between Beinn Achaladair and Beinn an Dothaidh. One overgrown tower still stands, looking out over Rannoch Moor.

The Achaladair Burn was high enough to cover the stepping stones at the ford and I was glad that I had waxed my boots. A good path led north-east along the banks of the Water of Tulla. The air was full of the song of larks above the meadows and a curlew called from the misty mountainside.

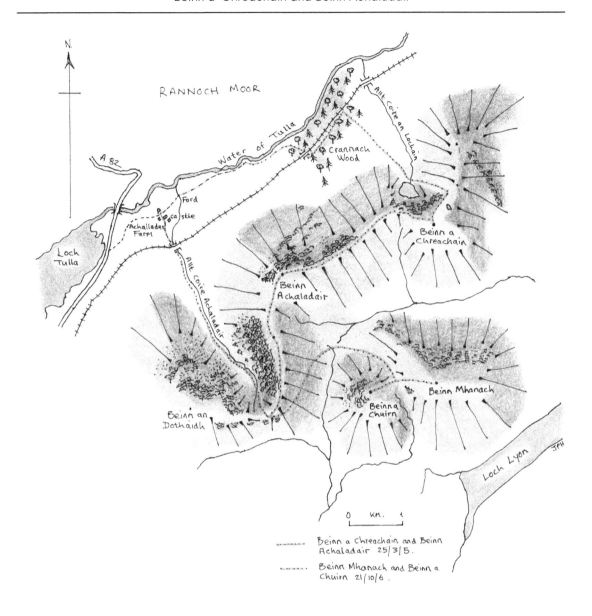

We were soon in Crannach Wood, a remnant of the ancient Caledonian Forest. The wood is open, with a mixture of mature Scots pine, oak, alder, birch, rowan and beech. The deer droppings (and the corpse of a hind on the path) explained why there were no saplings. The wood is an enchanting place, however, with its spring birdsong and long-tailed tits flashing from tree to tree. I hope that a way can be found to keep the deer out and allow it to regenerate.

Long tailed tits
Crannach Wood 25/3/05.

We were nearly through the old wood before we turned south-east and started to climb up towards the corrie which has been eroded in the north side of Beinn a' Chreachain. Up we toiled, the still, humid air making it hard work for our lungs. We passed pools in the peat with glistening frog spawn and frogs hopped from under our boots. I thought about March walks of previous years where conditions were below zero at this altitude and we would be strapping on crampons to complete our climb.

Giant boulders dropped when the last glacier melted provided a good place for tea and elevenses. The boulders sat on the lip of the corrie with its picturesque lochan. There were red deer on the far side, alert to our presence. Looking up, we saw that the cloud was slowly lifting.

Compass bearings were set for the final slog up onto the narrow and rocky north-east ridge of our first Munro. As we walked up it, the cloud finally began to drift up and away, revealing wild mountain country to the south and east and the vast desolation of Rannoch Moor to the north and west. There were deep drifts of snow along the ridge and the cornices were still in place around the rims of each of the corries.

After the cairn on Beinn a' Chreachain we sat on the edge of a snowfield and ate lunch. Ray ate sunflower seeds, a walnut or two and a little dried fruit, apparently good fuel but a bit Protestant for me.

On we walked, enjoying this lovely ridge walk and taking many detours to stand at vantage points on the top of the dramatic north-facing cliffs which plunge down to the Water of Tulla. Views opened up of the Glen Etive mountains far to the west.

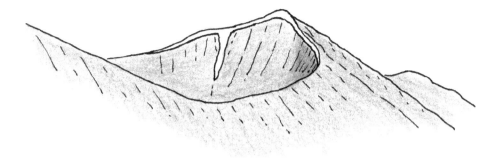

Beinn Achaladair
from the north 25/3/5.

We had considered trying to include Beinn Mhanach in our walk that day, but were all tired by the time we reached the top of Beinn Achaladair, our second Munro. So tired indeed that we stretched out on the flat rocks around the summit cairn, rested our heads on our rucksacks and I fell asleep.

At 1038 metres one does not sleep for long in March without waking with a shiver. We headed off south along the ridge to the bealach at the head of Coire Achaladair and dropped down into this substantial north-facing corrie. The enormous depression before us was a chaotic jumble of boulders of all sizes, mounds of debris and channels of water, looking as if the glacial ice had melted ten years ago rather than ten thousand.

On the lip of this corrie we found flat rocks and sprawled out again for a last cup of tea before the walk out. I lay on my back listening to Struan and Ray bantering and looked around. To the west, massive pinnacles of rock stood in a line, propping up the northeast wall of Beinn an Dothaidh. To the east were Beinn Achaladair's impressive cliffs. I watched patches of sunlight grow and slowly creep across them. The farm lay far below and a miniscule speck of white showed where the Landrover waited. Too soon it was time to go and we trudged back happily along the banks of the Allt Coire Achaladair.

A Cavalier King Charles spaniel from the farm raced alongside the vehicle to see us to the boundary. Struan put on a country tape and we headed for the Clachan Cottage Hotel on the shore of Loch Earn and a much enjoyed dinner.

Cruach Ardrain, Beinn Tulaichean, Beinn a' Chroin and An Caisteal

 A big day out

April

I drove up to the Highlands on a Friday evening after work with Morag, Struan and Ray. We stayed at the campsite at Tyndrum, in one of the little wooden cabins.

The pub was cheery, with a band belting out classics from the 60s and 70s and an interestingly cosmopolitan clientele. Ray brought out Munro books and maps and we discussed possibilities for the next day. Apart from Ray, none of us had walked on the hills south of Crianlarich and as he had not climbed Cruach Ardrain, we decided to do that, taking in Beinn Tulaichean. We would walk back along the ridge which wraps round the east side of Coire Ardrain, climbing Stob Garbh (a Top). The forecast was rain but the route did not seem too demanding and I was not going to allow the weather to dampen my spirits.

We were late in bed and up early, surprised to see the clear blue of the sky and white fair weather clouds. As we expected it to change soon to rain we put on gaiters and packed waterproofs near the top of the rucksacks. By 8.00 a.m. we had begun our walk, the weather was still fair and we were in high spirits. On Grey Height we

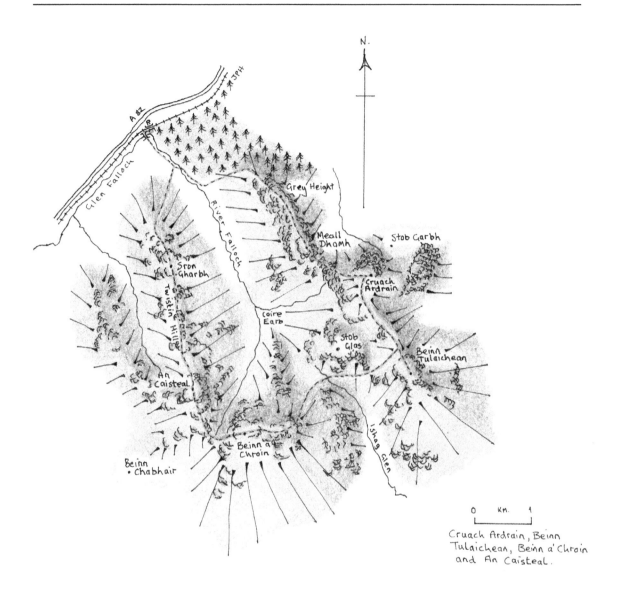

Cruach Ardrain, Beinn Tulaichean, Beinn a' Chroin and An Caisteal.

stopped for a cup of tea and enjoyed the views. Beinn Dorain's distinctive cone rose to the north and in the west the shapely snow-covered peak of Ben Lui touched a patch of white cloud.

By the time we sat on the top of Cruach Ardrain we felt that we had worked hard, but the views in all directions repaid the effort. Due east loomed the massive bulk of Ben More, with its distinctive ridge running south to Stob Binnein. To the south, a ridge ran from where we sat to Beinn Tulaichean, which looked so near that we were surprised that it was classified a Munro. Beyond were Loch Lomond and Ben Lomond and in the west the Arrochar Alps with a glimpse of Loch Fyne. I was grateful that we'd had fair weather and great views all morning and would have been content to finish the walk in the rain.

The weather held, however, as we walked towards Beinn Tulaichean. At the bealach we said farewell to Ray. He had decided to drop down into Coire Earb, climb up to the col between An Caisteal and Beinn a' Chroin, climb Beinn Chabhair (now the only Munro in this range he had not climbed) and return to the car along the road.

Sitting on top of Beinn Tulaichean, we wondered whether we would ever see him again. We ate lunch and rested in the warm sun. As it was not far into the afternoon, Struan suggested that we could change our plans. We could go down into the Ishag Glen and climb up onto Beinn a' Chroin, coming back to the car over An Caisteal. Our tally would then be four Munros. I pointed out that the SMC guidebook had sensibly allocated two days to complete them, but happily agreed to give it a go.

We retraced our steps to the bealach and picked our way around the base of the steep cliffs which plunge down into the glen. After crossing the Ishag Burn we started to climb up onto the impressive ridge along which were our next two Munros.

It was warm down there, with little breeze and the climb was harder than any of us had thought. We stopped on a broad, grassy ledge about half way up to look at three red deer hinds. They were unusually relaxed about us and remained about 20 metres away, studying the three strange creatures who were studying them.

We sat down for a drink and noticed that a group of deer had come up onto the far end of the ledge. They seemed not to have spotted us. I looked with more interest when I saw the first four legs waving in the air. Soon there were more, like a slow, poorly co-ordinated Mexican wave. I stood up cautiously and found that they were stags who had recently cast their antlers and they were rolling in the black mud of a large peat hag.

Red deer wallowing.
Beinn a' Chroin 30/4/5.

The climb up onto Beinn a' Chroin got steeper and steeper. I felt my stamina draining away and wished I'd brought more sweet snacks to give me an energy boost. My legs were like jelly by the time I got to the top, but it was worth all the effort. To the north we could see Glen Coe and the Mamores, with the distinctive profile of Ben Nevis behind. To the south was the last tract of mountain country before the Highland Line. Beyond lay the rolling country of Central Scotland with the Firth of Forth glinting in the east and the salt water of Loch Fyne sparkling to the west. We had tea and a snack, lay back on a patch of warm grass and I was asleep in seconds.

Struan woke me to say that we had a long way to go yet and we were off again. Beinn a' Chroin and An Caisteal are rocky mountains which rise abruptly in a series of crags above their surrounding corries. We made our way carefully down to the col between them and I summoned my remaining strength for the climb up to our fourth and final Munro. Fortunately, the ascent mostly involved scrambling up the rocky crags, which I always find less tiring than a slog up steep grass or heather slopes.

The summit of An Caisteal afforded yet more panoramic views, with relationships between mountains subtly changed by the relatively short distance from our previous viewpoint. I finished the last of my tea, lay back on a flat slab of rock and again fell asleep with my head on my rucksack.

There was no time for more than a catnap, however and I was soon urging my tired legs to take me down Twistin Hill. It was a perfect walk out for a weary body; an easy path along the crest of a bone dry ridge with views down to Glen Falloch and the car, a tiny red dot far below.

Ray was waiting for us and we were soon off to the hotel in Glen Dochart where we knew we would get a warm welcome and a good hot dinner. The meal was interesting in that we were all so tired that we hardly spoke. The atmosphere, however, was one of warm companionship, with no need for lively conversation. We were revived by home-made soup and local venison and normal chatting service was resumed. The inevitable theme on the journey home was, "Where next?"

Abseiling at Bowden Doors

May

At 4.30 p.m. on the May holiday Monday Struan telephoned to ask whether I was up for a bit of abseiling practice to prepare for the Inaccessible Pinnacle in the summer. "Of course," I replied, "when are we going?"

"Is five o'clock ok?" he asked and I was soon in the Landrover with him and two of his pals, both climbers, from Borders Search and Rescue.

We drove around the edge of the Cheviots, through the beautiful rural landscape of north Northumberland and stopped at the towering sandstone crags of Bowden Doors.

Struan introduced me to slings, figure of eight knots, belays and karabiners and we practised on a safe slope at the foot of the cliff.

Then we climbed to the top and had our first practice with me as the guinea pig and Struan as an anchor, feeding out a safety rope. I went to the edge and started, promptly slipping and crashing back into the cliff as our arrest systems had worked. I put my feet on the cliff wall and safely abseiled down.

We were concerned about the initial fall, was it the position of the belay point or my poor technique? I had abseiled before, but always with qualified instructors supervising and this DIY attempt had an entirely different atmosphere.

We moved to the highest section of the cliff, where the descent began with an overhang. The belay was secured, Struan was to control the safety rope and off I went again. The same thing happened at the start, I went over and down abruptly and crashed into the rock. I was then able to abseil perfectly down to the foot of the cliff.

Bowden Doors
2/5/5.

Twice more we tried it and each time I had an inelegant and painful start to my descent.

The light was beginning to go as we sat at the foot of the cliff and analysed the evening. The two climbers had watched my last descent and they felt that I needed to lean out more at the start, keep my back straight and aim for a 90 degree angle.

I drove home with a bruised and sore leg, determined to get my technique right next time.

25/6/05 - 26/6/05

Monadh Mor, Beinn Bhrotain. Mullach Clach a' Bhlair, Sgor Gaoith

Honorary boys

June

On the last Friday evening of June I drove up the A9 for a Jolly Boys adventure with a difference. For the first time in its history an official invitation had gone out to jolly girls who might be interested in joining the boys. The four brave pioneers were Morag, Cath, Geraldine and Katie, an Australian who had worked with us over the past year. It was quite fitting that we were back in Glen Feshie to share the unique experience of Jean Hamilton's hospitality.

All were in good spirits on that Friday night. The women had no adverse effect on the coarse humour and it was the small hours before we retired to our beds, leaving Fionn to sleep in the garden.

The next morning was bright and full of promise. I ate porridge and homemade bread while looking out at the hens and guinea fowl scavenging around the house and trees. An exotic display of greenfinches, chaffinches and bullfinches ate their breakfast on the other side of the window pane. Katie asked what I wanted to get out of my day and I replied that it would be perfect if I was to get a good close-up view of dotterel, a distinctively marked

191

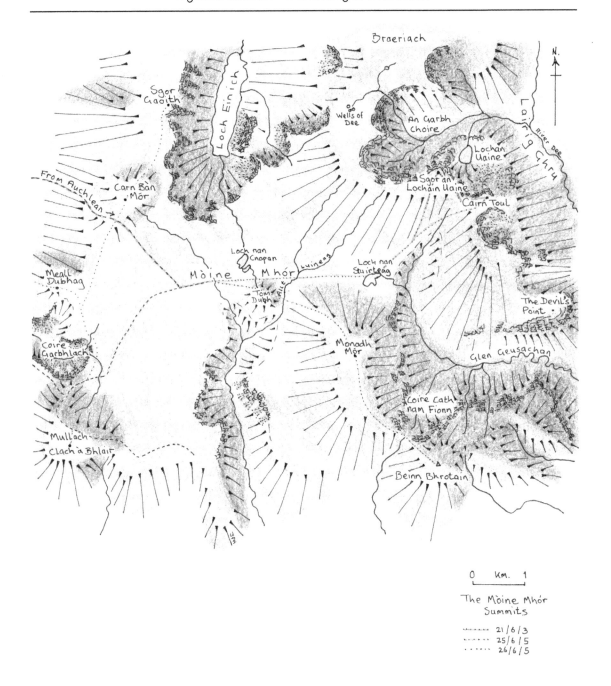

The Mòine Mhòr
Summits

------- 21/6/3
······· 25/6/5
········ 26/6/5

female in particular. I could see from her expression that she thought that I was teasing her.

Shortly after, we were walking from Auchlean up the well-worn path onto the Cairngorm plateau. Blood pumped fast around my body, washing away my headache. The thin straggles of cloud lifted and drifted away to reveal blue sky and an already hot sun.

At the top, most of the party went north-east over Carn Ban Mor to Sgor Gaoith. Morag, Ray and I set off south-east over the Moine Mhor, heading for Monadh Mor far away on the skyline. Our walk was to be almost 28 kilometres and involve a lot of ascent, too much for some like Katie who had not hill walked before.

I had been this way on previous occasions and had found much of the going heavy and wet. That June day, however, the ground was so dry that it crunched with each step.

We saw ptarmigan in early summer plumage, the white confined to the belly and the upper parts mottled olive, grey and brown, perfectly camouflaged apart from the brilliant scarlet eyebrows. The summer feathers also prevent overheating on days like that one, the dense white feathers of winter are designed to let no heat escape.

Ptarmigan, early summer. 25/6/05.

We sat on granite boulders on the side of Tom Dubh to drink tea and eat a snack. My attention was caught by a handsome brown and grey bird with a white stripe over its eye and it dawned on me that I had been granted my wish, it was a dotterel. It posed long enough for me to see the crescent-shaped torc on its breast and admire the rest of its fine colouring.

The air was clear and visibility was excellent. We could see the spectacular cliffs topped by Sgor Gaoith to the north-west, the bare rock plunging into the deep glacial trough occupied by Loch Einich. Looking north and east, we were impressed by the colossal scale of Braeriach, Sgor an Lochain Uaine and Cairn Toul, still with large patches of snow on the upper slopes. Visibility was so sharp that it played tricks with distance, making these Cairngorm giants seem so much closer.

Monadh Mor is an enormous whaleback of a hill and the views from the top on a day like that Saturday are splendid. We sat and ate lunch looking down Glen Geusachan, another of the classic glacial troughs of the Cairngorms. We discussed pronunciation and Morag decided that the G should be silent. The glen is made all the more dramatic by having the Devil's Point towering above the north side of its mouth and the Beinn Bhrotain massif towering above the south side.

In ancient times, warriors who had come to Scotland with Fionn McCool had been pursued up this cliff-lined glen and had turned to fight in the Coire Cath nam Fionn, the corrie of the battle of the Fingalians. Beinn Bhrotain itself is named after Brodan, the black hound that hunted with them.

It was difficult to pack up and leave that marvellous viewpoint but we were soon on our way again and picking our way up the boulder field to the top of Beinn Bhrotain, Scotland's 19th highest peak.

There was a debate on the top about the return route. Ray wanted to drop down to Glen Feshie and walk back along it, Morag and I wanted to stay up high on such a fine day and retrace our steps. Morag and I won the argument and we enjoyed a delightful return journey across the high plateau, with the finest sights in all directions.

When we got back to the hostel, we found a note declaring "gone to pub." It was a jolly crowd that returned and we swapped tales of our walks while watching a red squirrel raiding the bird feeder.

Jean's at
Glen Feshie

Jean's dinner was first class. Tomato, carrot and basil soup with warm, crusty malt bread and butter for a first course. This was followed by free-range chicken and mushroom stuffing, garlic ratatouille, creamy bake with wafer-thin potatoes and a lovely mixed salad with avocado. For pudding we had strawberry flan, fresh strawberries, chilled Greek yoghurt and cream. All washed down with plenty of wine and rounded off with good coffee.

There were the usual toasts and banter, especially around the subject of the first women to be admitted to this once exclusively male territory. Should we rename the events "Dolly Boys"? Or simply make the women honorary boys for the weekend? Katie suggested that all that was needed was a box of badges on which "Boy" was written, these could be issued to all women who wished to attend.

The next morning, after a short but deep sleep, we stoked up on porridge and then splintered into various groups.

I went back to Auchlean with Morag and we were soon striding past the farm, heading up Glen Feshie. Our plan was to go onto the high ground by Coire Garbhlach and then to Mullach Clach a' Bhlair, our third Munro of the weekend.

As we chatted in the glorious sunshine, however, we made the elementary blunder of not consulting the map. We followed what appeared to be a path twisting up the north side of the corrie. It dwindled to nothing and we struggled with a steep climb of 700 metres through heather and over rocks.

When we got to the top of Meall Dubhag we were exhausted. We sat on a granite tor to eat some lunch and looked south across the deep corrie to where we could see the broad track we should have taken winding up onto the plateau. Morag put a positive spin on the experience, saying that one needed such tests of one's hill fitness. I listened but made a mental note to always consult the map before setting out.

The day was perfect after that challenging start. We walked onto Mullach Clach a' Bhlair and were treated to more dotterel. There was a chick on a nest and both the male and female parents tried to distract us from it. The female in particular was very bold, coming close and tempting us away. It was a joy to be so near to such rare birds.

Dotterel
15/6/5.

Leaving them in peace, we settled in the bone-dry mountain grass and lichen for a second lunch. The views, as on the previous day, were splendid.

Refreshed, we set off north, keeping to the highest ground on the edge of the plateau and at the top of the path back down to Auchlean had to decide whether to go back to begin the long drive home or to go on to Sgor Gaoith, the mountain which had so impressed the others. It was the perfect day that tipped the balance and we were soon heading north-east to our fourth and last Munro.

Sgor Gaoith, pronounced skor go-ee, means windy peak, but it did not live up to its name on such a benign day. It has the classic shape of the apex of a triangle and is built of massive blocks of bare granite. Its real character, however, can only be appreciated once at the top and looking down the sheer cliffs into the deep chasm occupied by Loch Einich. An object would fall 600 metres before it crashed to a halt on the shore of the loch, a fact that some had found unnerving the previous day.

We were thrilled by this mountain and we sat on a rock ledge by the summit with our legs dangling over the cliff edge, marvelling at the vista before us. Loch Einich sparkled silver and blue far below and the gigantic cliffs towered up on three sides. Above the cliffs to the east are the deep and wild corries of Braeriach, with not a human being to be seen.

We drank the last of our tea on this high eyrie and then turned our faces to the track and the road home.

Skye: Sgurr na Banachdich; Bruach na Frithe

Mountain rescue!

August

The sun was shining as I drove north with Tom and Morag at the start of our hillwalking trip to Skye. We stopped at Achallader Farm for a picnic. The Cavalier King Charles Spaniel came to join us, along with two hens from the farmyard.

The journey was slow as, in addition to the ubiquitous caravans and motor homes, there were 2CVs on every stretch of road. The world 2CV rally had been held in Kelso the previous week and most of these cool little cars seemed to be fitting in a Highlands tour before returning to the warmer climes of the continent. Those towing a matching mini caravan were struggling with the steeper gradients.

I was much impressed by the elegant sweep from shore to shore of the Skye Bridge and glad that the unpopular tolls had been abolished by the Scottish parliament six months before. I drove slowly west, admiring the dramatic landscapes I had read so much about but never seen.

I had tried before to see Skye. The first time was a family camping trip which was the wettest holiday I have ever experienced. The heavy grey clouds hung low over the roads and rainfall gathered to cascade down the mountainsides in thick brown torrents. We had never seen so much water. We pitched our tent on a sandy campsite among dunes in the far north of the island. I reassured the others that this was a good idea as the sand would absorb the rainwater, allowing it to soak away.

We drove through the unrelenting downpour to Portree to cheer ourselves up with a hot meal. The dampness seemed to insinuate itself into our fish and chips, however, and was certainly dampening our spirits as we drove back to the tent, viewing this watery Armageddon through car windows running with condensation.

Back at the campsite, I adopted a business-like tone, organising an early night with the expectation that such a colossal downpour could not last until morning.

I was awoken early by excited cries from my daughters. "Dad," they shouted, "this is great, we're floating." They were indeed bobbing on their airbeds on the flood water which had invaded the tent.

I splashed to the door to look out on a biblical scene. The entire campsite was a lake which merged seamlessly with the sea beyond. Our flooded tent and car were the only signs of human life. The rain seemed to have become more intense.

We tried to wring the worst of the water from our tent before throwing it into the boot and then climbed, dripping and chilled, into the car. The water was up to the wheel arches. It was an old car and I prayed before turning the ignition key. My prayer was answered as the engine fired and, very slowly, leaving a wake like a boat, we left the campsite, and Skye, to return south to our dry and warm home.

Years later, my eldest daughter's French boyfriend said he would love to see this island he had heard so much about but it remained hidden beneath its curtains of cloud and rain. So it was with a sense of privilege that I enjoyed the beauties of the island on this, my third visit.

Mountains reared up from the sea, each turn in the road revealing higher and more spectacular ranges, until we saw the white hotel at Sligachan with the jagged ridge of the Black Cuillin as a backdrop.

Sligachan did not disappoint. The hotel had a mixed crowd of walkers, climbers, anglers and tourists. As we stood outside naming the high peaks before us we saw that a number of 2CVs had arrived before us.

The hostel was up on the hillside on the other side of the River Sligachan. The brochure had described it as "Himalayan style". The reality was a corrugated iron roof and well-worn timber walls, probably similar to hostels on the trail to Everest Base Camp. Once settled in, however, it turned out to be a great place to stay. It was spacious, with a big communal kitchen and a great sitting room lined with comfy sofas. We soon had a cheery coal fire going.

The others arrived and we went to the hotel bar for a meal. This is a big barn of a place with crowds of fit-looking people wearing Berghaus clothing. There was plenty of choice on the menu and my venison casserole went down well with a glass of red wine.

Back at the hostel, we made friends with the Dutch and Germans who had made the long journey north in their 2CVs. Morag produced a bottle of Laphroaig, a gift from her father, and everyone loved this smoky Islay malt. I sat with my glass, laughing at the tales of the little cars stalling on steep Highland roads and having to go up in reverse gear.

The next morning I was up before the others, delighted to see that the fine weather had held. We did not have the early start I hoped for, however, as Fionn and Tom were rather slow to come round.

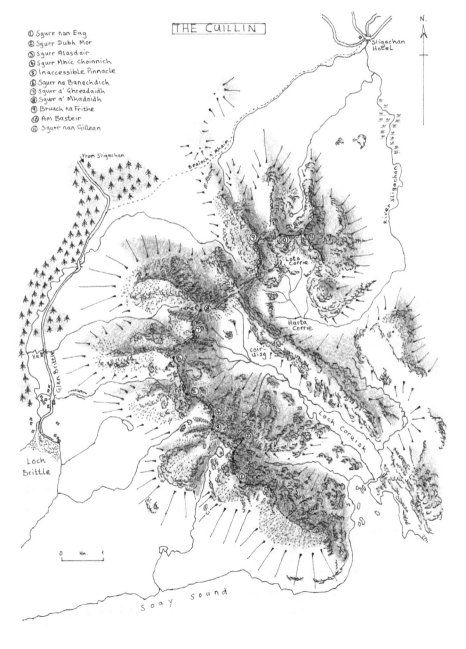

As we drove down Glen Brittle we heard how the barman had allowed Fionn to have a slate for his drinks. He and Tom had then challenged anyone interested to a game of snooker and lost every time. The final indignity was being thrashed by a primary school boy. They were the last to leave, Fionn having an altercation with a member of the hotel staff who tried to prevent him using the fire exit. An hour or so in the children's play area on the zip line had followed before they came back to the hostel, long after everyone else had gone to bed. In the circumstances, it was surprising how fresh they were when we set off at 10 o' clock.

We walked up to the Eas Mor waterfall where the path gives a choice of three ways. We took the middle route and saw it rise steeply before us as it zig zagged up the sharp nose of the arête which leads directly to the Inaccessible Pinnacle, our objective.

It was a perfect day to climb this Munro baggers' nightmare, dry with very little wind. Struan had a rope and the helmets and other climbing items were carried by the rest of us. Always optimistic, I had a good feeling about the forthcoming adventure.

We rapidly gained height and the Cuillin peaks revealed themselves in all their rugged grimness. I had never seen mountains like these, bare and black, thrust straight out of the watercolour beauty of the Hebridean sea. My walking poles were soon tied to my rucksack as I needed my hands for the scramble. The coarse textured gabbro under my fingers gave a great feeling of security as I climbed. At intervals this rough, dark rock was cut by dolerite dykes, these have been less resistant to erosion and made narrow gullies and chimneys. We stopped on a broad ledge for an early lunch and to enjoy the spectacle around us. It was perfect for photographs but they can never capture the quality of such a superb day.

On we went, carefully, concentrating on hand and foot holds. The silence of the mountains was broken only by the occasional cry of a raven. Tom was much fitter now that he was away from the alcohol-fuelled nocturnal life of university and he pulled away from the rest of us. I looked up to see how far ahead he was and noticed two things, the first was the dramatic narrowing of the ridge and the second was the distinctive top of the Inaccessible Pinnacle rising up above the summit of Sgurr Dearg. Tom was a tiny black speck, providing a sense of scale. The Pinnacle was obviously a massive feature.

Our objective loomed nearer and higher as we scrambled up, until we reached the summit and were literally stopped in our tracks by the monster in front of us. A colossal blade of black rock rose from the mountain, leaning to the north. It is another of the many igneous dykes which have been intruded into the gabbro of the Cuillin, this time, however, the dyke has proved more resistant to erosion than the surrounding rock. Big blocks lay around its base where they had fallen. When the others arrived I remarked that we would have to climb it soon before it falls down in a storm.

Four people crawled up the narrow edge of the blade, looking very small and vulnerable. Tom sat at the base and we carefully made our way down to join him. I knew that Struan was going to say that he was not going up before he said it. I felt a stab of disappointment but supressed it. I understood how difficult this was for him and did not want to make it worse. He (quite sensibly) said, that now he had seen it, he felt that he needed more experience as well as more gear to secure the lead climber.

We climbed back up to the summit of Sgurr Dearg and watched the four climbers above us. The leader worked with great skill and confidence, helping the others to descend the steep side of the Pinnacle by rope. An object fell from a pocket and smashed on the rock below, one of them had just lost a camera. I talked to them as they came to join us, the guide was Gerry Ackroyd, a well-known personality in Scottish mountaineering and leader of the Skye Mountain Rescue Team. He gave me his phone number and told me that he lived near where we had parked in Glen Brittle, inviting me to come and see him. Then he was off with his charges, north along the ridge.

The Inaccessible Pinnacle looks daunting on the illustrations in the guide books but no photograph can prepare a hillwalker for the first sight of it. I was thrilled to have got up to see it on such a perfect day, climbing it could wait.

After some lunch, we talked about what we could do next. I had read that the narrow ridge between Sgurr Dearg and Sgurr na Banachdich was a good scramble. If anyone found it too much, they could sit in the sun at the Bealach Coire na Banachdich, the scramblers could return that way and we could go down together into the corrie.

The ridge turned out to be an exciting route, with classic mountain views at every turn. The Cuillin ridge curved round to the north and east, serrated with jagged peaks from which razor-sharp arêtes plunged down into the Coir' Uisg. Indigo Loch Coruisk lay smooth and serene among this multitude of grey and black knife points.

Cath and Dorothy had decided to wait at the bealach and Morag was last to arrive at the highest point of Sgurr na Banachdich, the North Top. She had taken a whole roll of film and was bright eyed with the grandeur of this place. We talked on the summit about what we could do next. Morag and I wanted to continue for a while along the ridge to Sgurr Thormaid. We would go down into Coire a' Ghreadaidh, taking a route from the SMC guidebook which first drops into Coire an Eich. The others wanted to return to Cath and Dorothy and walk out along the Allt Coire na Banachdich.

Tom and Fionn were the last to leave us to go back along the ridge and we said our farewells before turning from the summit down the well-trodden path through the boulders. The gradient was very easy and Morag was 20 metres ahead when she fell. The moment she cried out, I felt my muscles tense and my brain snapped out of its coasting mode. "I'm sorry, I'm sorry," she repeated. I saw the awkward way she lay among the rocks and the possibility of a back injury came into my mind. She asked me to help her up but I replied that I wanted her to lie just as she was for a moment and I would try to call Tom and Fionn before they moved too far down the ridge. My shouts split the silence of the mountains and I was relieved when I heard calls in reply. I turned back to Morag and asked her to move her head, arms, fingers and legs. She said that she thought she had broken an arm and I was able to reassure her that, if it was broken, it was not too serious. I began to feel some relief that there seemed not to be a head or back injury.

Tom and Fionn appeared as I was carefully easing Morag into a more comfortable position. I noticed a deep hole in her left leg, just at the top of her gaiter. I could see what appeared to be bone. She sat up a little to look but quickly lay back again, frightened and fearing the worst. I removed the gaiter and revealed a large hole running 10 centimetres down the leg from below the knee. The sharp rock that had done the damage had acted like a butcher's knife cutting cleanly down the shin. All muscle tissue had been scraped away and I could see tendons as well as the exposed bone. It was clear that she could not get off the mountain without assistance.

I grabbed my phone, there was no signal. I said that I would try higher up on the ridge but Fionn said that he would go down to raise the alarm in case I failed. He would shout to Struan and tell him to go down with the two others.

Tom made Morag more comfortable. She was now white-faced and trembling with shock, her left leg shaking uncontrollably. She vomited. Tom pulled fleeces from the rucksacks to keep her warm. I covered the wound with a sterile pad to keep it clean.

Tom stayed with her while I went back to the summit, hoping for a signal. My prayer was answered right at the top and I called 999. From that moment the emergency services were excellent. The police in Fort William took the details and asked me to remain at the summit with my phone. They asked for a grid reference so I shouted down to Tom who was about 50 metres below. He scrambled up with my map then returned to Morag. The police rang off and I was left standing on the cairn; I lost the signal if I sat down.

I began to worry about the bone being broken in the leg and shouted down to Tom to ask Morag to wiggle her toes. She could do this. Then I remembered something else from a distant first aid course and shouted to Tom to pinch the leg below the wound. She could feel this.

The phone rang and it was the Portree police. I answered their questions and they said that they would try to get a helicopter.

They rang off and again I was left, frustrated to be so far from Morag and Tom. Despite the sunshine, I began to get chilled but did not want to call Tom away from her. I needed someone to run messages between us. At that moment, two young men appeared. They were anxious to help and I asked if they could bring me my mountain jacket to keep me warm.

I had just put this on when the Stornoway coastguard phoned. They wanted the same details plus details of visibility (perfect) and wind (light). They asked us to secure all rucksacks and loose gear because the rotor blades could well whisk these items off the mountain. I asked if it would be best to dress Morag's wound properly and they said that this should be done.

I talked to the young men and told them where they could find sterile swabs, dressing pads and elasticated bandages in my pack and they and Tom dressed the wound. Then they gathered up the rucksacks and gear and weighed them down with rocks. We put out orange survival bags to help guide in the helicopter.

At this point I received another call, this time from the Skye Mountain Rescue Team and I was able to tell them about the helicopter. This was followed by another call from the police, informing me that Fionn had got down safely to raise the alarm. The coastguard phoned again, advising that the helicopter was on its way and that I should go down to be with the casualty.

I scrambled down and we waited, looking anxiously to the north. Morag was pale and shaking. She asked if I would come with her in the helicopter. I talked to the others and the two young men said that they would go down with Tom. Our two helpers then ran up the ridge to wave bright jackets to signal to the helicopter.

We spotted it as a tiny object to the south of the Cuillins and watched as it followed the ridge north. The boys waved their jackets furiously. Tom and I held out an orange survival bag like a banner. The helicopter spotted us, swung east over Coir' Uisg, circled round to cross the ridge and edged towards us from the north.

Our first close-up sight of the helicopter was surreal. It very slowly edged up from below the ridge which marked our northern skyline. First the rotor blades, then the white front of the aircraft, the two pilots staring at us at eye level. It rose gently higher and nearer, white and red and far bigger than I expected.

A figure descended on a rope. He wore flying overalls and a helmet and slowly walked towards us. He was like an astronaut.

The rotor blades began to kick up dust and Tom dropped down to protect Morag's face.

I answered the winchman's shouted questions and he bent to look at Morag's leg. He asked if anyone would accompany her and I said that I would. I asked if he would take our rucksacks and he replied that this must be done immediately. One of the young men ran up with the sacks. The winchman placed a strap around them and I expected them to be whisked up to the helicopter above. He took me by surprise, however, by dropping a strap over my head and quickly tightening it under my arms. Then I shot upwards and was spinning around before I had time to wonder whether I might be scared. Hands reached out from the open door, stopped me spinning and pulled me on board. This second winchman pointed to the rucksacks and then to the rear of the aircraft and I pulled them out of the way.

The helicopter then moved away from the ridge and I caught a glimpse of the 3,000 foot drop down into Coire na Banachdich before Morag appeared, with straps beneath her arms and knees. The winchman beckoned me towards the door and indicated that I should pull her to the rear, up to the seats.

The first winchman was now aboard and he gave us ear protectors as the helicopter banked and headed east. My walking companion was safe, she had stopped shaking and for the first time since she fell I felt myself relax a little. We looked out of the windows to see the Cuillin ridge in sharp relief below. From this viewpoint the mountain range looked even more impressive than it had earlier on this eventful day. Morag, ever the mountaineer, tugged at my sleeve and pointed at the panorama below. Her face was lit up and pain forgotten for the moment.

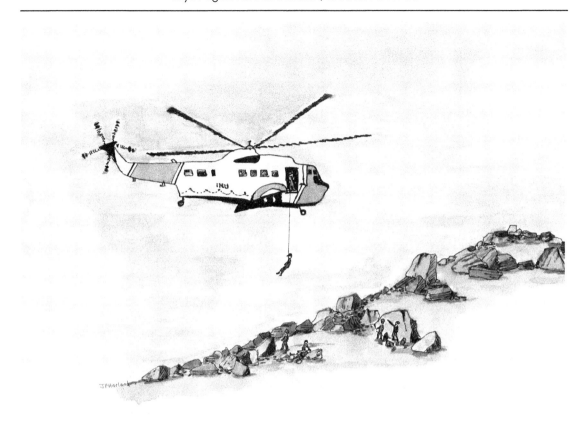

The helicopter landed at Broadford where an ambulance was waiting. I gave the winchman and the rest of the crew my warm thanks.

At the hospital a team was waiting and Morag was taken straight into a casualty room. The dressing was removed and the younger of two nurses held her hands to her mouth and looked faint when she saw the hole. Morag could not bring herself to look. I talked to the doctor while x-rays were taken and she explained how she would repair the wound. Morag had asked if I could be with her so I watched the procedure. The x-rays showed that no bones were broken but that a significant amount of tissue had "disappeared". The tissue at the edge of the hole was pulled together in thin layers and sewn using masses of dissolving stitches. Finally, the skin was pulled together and sewn with 12 nylon stitches. I was amazed by the result, such a large and deep hole had been completely eradicated. It was safe for Morag to look and the stitched wound was impressive, making a perfect upward pointing chevron. With our new companions in the hostel in mind, I named her 1CV.

The hospital staff were excellent, feeding us soup, toast and tea while we waited for Morag's crutches. I offered to take her home the following day but the doctor insisted that she stay for at least two days with her leg kept up before she travelled.

I phoned the hotel and they kindly contacted our party to come to Broadford to pick us up. They suggested that leg of lamb might be a good choice for Morag when we returned to the bar.

The police came, partly to check whether we were properly equipped for the mountains and then we said thank you to the staff and were driven back to Sligachan by Struan. He thoughtfully pointed out that getting a helicopter to take us down was cheating and that we would have to climb Sgurr na Banachdich again if we wished to tick it off as a Munro.

We were soon in the bar. All had got down safely, the two young men having run Tom back to Sligachan. Everyone wanted to hear the story of the mountain rescue. It was a warm and cheery crowd, the perfect antidote to the fear and anxiety of the day. Fionn remarked that Morag had pulled a pretty cheap trick to get out of walking down the mountain like everyone else and wondered whether this would now become routine.

We went back to the hostel where Cath had got a good peat fire burning and laughed and chatted until Morag, exhausted now, was helped to bed.

The following day, Struan drove me to Glen Brittle to retrieve Morag's car. I had informed the police that it was to be left there overnight, with visions of it triggering another mountain rescue call-out in my mind. Tom came with me for company.

I drove the short distance to Gerry Ackroyd's house, where we discussed the previous day's rescue. I asked him about his services as a guide and learned that he would lead small groups up the Inaccessible Pinnacle. This, I decided, was the way to do it. I enjoyed my conversation with Gerry. He described the Cuillin as Britain's only true mountain range. It is no place, he continued, for the inexperienced. None of the Cuillin peaks can be "walked", all must be climbed. Previous scrambling experience and good navigational skills are essential. He ended by advising that it is wise to call off plans to spend a day on the range if the weather is not good.

When we got back, the others had gone to Portree. Tom decided to go fishing so I took Morag to Skye's only distillery at Carbost, where Tallisker is made. She hobbled inside on her crutches. A ring of tulip glasses had been filled with different malts. We lingered over them, both settling for a special edition Tallisker, "double matured and finished in Amoroso sherry casks". The fragrance was warm, peaty, with a hint of the sea and a sherry sweetness which made me think of Christmas. Irresistible. We were surprised at the cost but went ahead with our purchases in recognition of the good outcome to the previous day's drama.

Bottles safely stowed, I drove to Tallisker, curious to see the bay which has lent its name to the whisky. Morag stretched out along the back seat and slept while I walked down the path to the sea. Tall basalt cliffs encircle the cove, with a sea stack off one of the headlands. I stepped over a storm bench of shingle littered with flotsam and jetsam and stood on a stretch of beach, watching the waves froth and bubble as they washed towards me, brilliantly white against the black volcanic sand. I felt spent. On the way back I scooped up a handful of different seaweeds for Morag so that she could smell Tallisker Bay even if she was unable to walk there.

Tom was barbecuing trout on the step of the hostel when we returned. The 2CV set were heading for the bar and shouted for us to join them.

The following morning, the women set off on a motor tour of the island and Struan went fishing so Tom and I decided to go back into the mountains. We walked along the rough path which joins Sligachan to Glen Brittle over the Bealach a' Mhaim. The day was warm and we hoped the cloud would lift from the peaks as the sun heated the air.

We stopped at the bealach for a bite to eat but had to put on our mountain jackets as the wind was freshening from the south-west. It felt like it was going to rain. I had set my mind on one of the Sligachan summits and was not to be daunted. Tom was sceptical, saying, "What's the point if we get soaked to the skin and see nothing?" I have a stubborn streak, however, and we set off up the long spur which runs north-west from Bruach na Frithe, supposedly the easiest of them to climb.

We soon entered the cloud and were on rock again, following the steep path as it twisted upwards. The wind strengthened and the first shower felt as if the giants of Glen Brittle were throwing buckets of water at us. Tom was for turning back.

The ridge narrowed and we had to take great care on exposed sections near the crest, one strong gust and we could have ended up in Fionn Choire, 200 metres below. "It might clear when we're on the top," I said. Tom was for turning back.

The ridge became a knife-edge arête and we started to climb up gullies and chimneys on the west side. I shouted against the wind that we should stop for a snack and a hot drink. I was feeling my energy drain away and, despite the exposure, knew that it was necessary. Tom took some convincing, but ate with me. I then talked him into putting on more warm clothes. I knew that we were now near the top and said so. Tom was for turning back.

We set off again, Tom muttering that he supposed that he would have to stick with the old fool who was clearly incapable of looking after himself. At that point the clouds disappeared from the mountains. The landscape of the Cuillin stretched away from us to the south, the suddenness of its appearance taking our breath away. We stared in silence. I looked back down the ridge and was surprised, it was not how I had pictured it coming up. Tom reminded me that I had promised Morag I would take photographs of Bruach na Frithe. I took the camera from my pack and began by photographing the ridge we had climbed. I then turned to look at the main panorama but all was gone. We were back in the chill of the cloud, our world the wet, dark rock before us. As Gerry had advised, the Cuillin should be saved for fine days. Tom was for turning back.

We edged carefully up the narrow crest until I caught a glimpse of a triangulation pillar perched high above on a black rock. It appeared just in time as Tom was on the point of mutiny. At the top, I shouted against the fierce wind, "Do you not feel a great sense of achievement?"

Tom replied, "Can we go down now?"

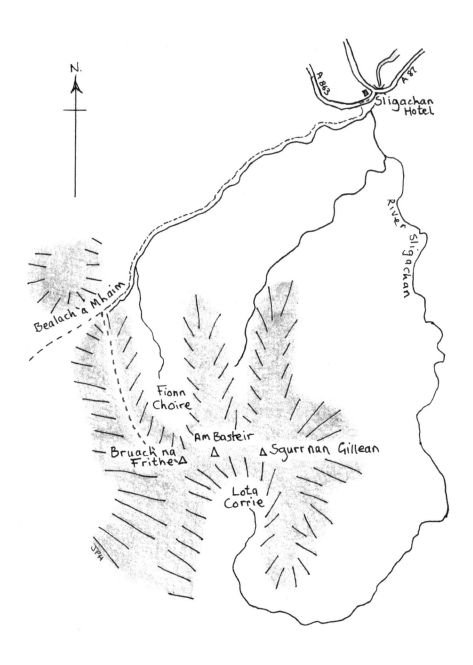

Carefully, we descended the ridge and travelled from one climate to another. Once out of the cloud the wind seemed warm, the fierce showers ceased and the views opened up to the Red Cuillin. Tom asked dryly whether we should have been climbing one of those instead?

Back at Sligachan, we ate soup and tender lamb with dumplings, helped down by a pleasant dry red wine. Cath had lit a cheery fire and the crowd all gathered for our last evening. The 2CV set had already made a good start on a large bottle of Grouse, so I opened my Tallisker. It was the merriest of nights. Tom has the deep, warm and true voice of a folksinger and he sang The Dark Island, The Skye Boat Song, Mairi's Wedding, Caledonia and many other classics, Fionn joining in lustily and the rest of us more harmoniously. Time slipped away, the Dutch and Germans caught up in the deep emotion of the Celtic songs. When the embers were low and both bottles of whisky drunk we went to sleep, some of us where we sat.

A' Bhuidheanach Bheag and Carn na Caim. Meall Chuaich

 First solo Munros

September

I t was a Jolly Boys weekend and the weather forecast was good. I drove up to Weem on Friday evening via Dunblane and Crieff. It was a good choice of route because the road through the Sma' Glen to Aberfeldy was beautiful in the late evening light.

I went first to say hello to Stuart. He had heard about our mountain rescue adventure on Skye and was anxious to hear how Morag was recovering. He told me that the Weem Hotel next door had new owners and was now well worth a visit, so I collected the others and we went there to sample its charms.

Rebecca, our new young colleague from Canada, was looking forward to her first visit to a typical Scottish pub. Her eyes widened as she absorbed the flamenco guitarists, the stamping dancers in their traditional Spanish costume and the jugs of sangria lined up on the bar. The air was redolent with the aroma of paella. Before she could ask, Struan declared that this was **not** a typical Scottish pub and hustled us next door to the lounge so that we could talk and joke without contamination by an alien culture. He was right, of course, and we had a grand evening. It was dislocating when the door opened and we were flooded with the rhythms and sounds of Andalucia.

Back at the hostel, Cath, always cold, lit a roaring log fire in the stove and Fionn produced a bottle of Glengoyne, a Highland malt. He had driven to Perth and back to get this bottle, having been told that Tesco had it on special offer, the detour costing far more than any saving he made. A laughter-filled night followed and when Rebecca asked what one did about sleep I advised her to sleep fast.

Early next morning, I was up at Drumochter with Morag. She was going to try walking on her injured leg for the first time and I had chosen the route for the well-graded track which led to the old quarry on the lip of the plateau.

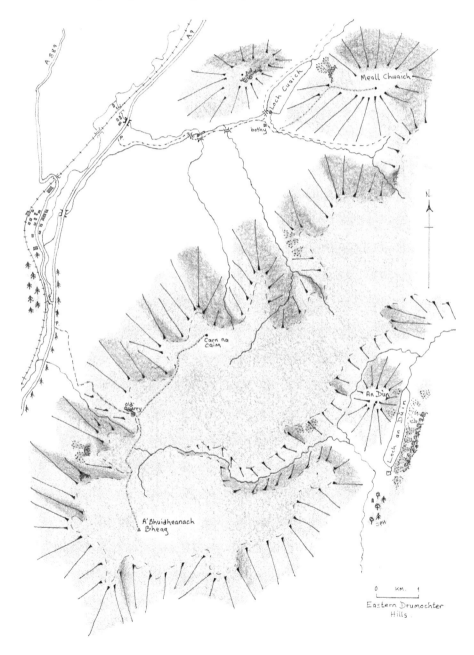

We walked slowly and steadily up to the summit above the quarry at 902 metres. After a cup of tea and a snack she set off back to the car, pleased with her progress.

There was a thin cover of cloud with the sun a pale yellow disc behind. Visibility was excellent but a strong wind blew from the south across this storm-battered upland. I set off into the wind, following a good track which seemed to go in the right direction. I walked faster than my normal pace because I was concerned not to spin things out while Morag waited down at the car.

The path forked and I went straight on, my compass indicating that this was the best choice. Then the path faded to nothing and I walked on over the dry grass. At a spur with a deep gully below I decided to have a hot drink. I used my GPS to get a grid reference and then took a bearing. The Munro summit was further east than I had thought. As I sipped my tea a curlew flew up the gully below me, rising and falling in graceful arcs as it flew against the strong wind. It was the only creature I had seen in this high and lonely place.

Curlew on A' Bhuidheanach Bheag
3/9/5.
JPH

On I went, down to the head of the gully and up the other side, following a path for some of the way. The hill is called A' Bhuidheanach Bheag, the little yellow place. I wondered about the name. The grass was certainly pale yellow on this early autumn weekend, but the scale was anything but little.

The top has a triangulation pillar and is bleak. The best thing was the view. There was a 360 degree panorama which included Lochnagar, the Cairngorms and the Ben Alder mountains.

I was soon off again, with the wind on my back this time, heading for Carn na Caim, the Munro at the north edge of the plateau.

I dropped down into the gully and decided to stop for lunch where there was shelter from the wind. While eating a sandwich I noticed a hare sitting about 15 metres away. The hare was looking at me from one of the large dark eyes positioned on the sides of its head. I waited for it to bolt but it remained, calm and still. At that moment, I realised that I had been tense since leaving Morag. I had been walking fast, concentrating on my route and behaving in a mechanical way. The hare snapped me out of the tension. I lay back against the bank and felt properly relaxed for the first time since I had left home. I watched the clouds racing by and noticed that there were now patches of blue between. The seed heads of the grasses bent and danced in the wind which hissed through the heather. I could have slept.

Instead, I packed up, said goodbye to the hare and started up the track. I was in a completely new frame of mind, relaxed and full of the joys of this wonderful place. I sang as I tramped along, thinking that I rather liked being alone in the mountains.

On I walked along the broad ridge to Carn na Caim. As I neared the Munro I used map and compass again, this time finding that I was, indeed, walking directly to the summit.

The views from the cairn were even better than those from the first one. I was especially interested in Loch Cuaich and Meall Chuaich to the north, my objective for the following day. The name means hill of the quaich or cup and it looked very much like a giant cup placed upside down to drain beside the twinkling blue loch. I began to look forward to my Sunday morning walk.

Coming off the summit, the views to Loch Ericht and the tangle of the Ben Alder mountains, directly ahead, were the best of the lot. At that point I met the first walkers I had seen that day, a young couple. They asked about the top and I told them that that the views were excellent. "Just as well," replied the man, "because those on the way up across to Ben Alder have been so boring." I was lost for words as they said their goodbyes.

Five minutes later they were forgotten as I stopped to look at a rather dark, undersized and weather-beaten rabbit. I was wondering whether it, too, would sit still when it loped away. I followed it to its burrow and was surprised to watch it disappear into the grandest of rabbit holes. It was like the entrance to a megalithic chambered tomb. A large horizontal stone slab was supported by slabs on either side, each tilted at the same angle towards the middle. The hole was oval-shaped and dead centre. A rabbit lord lived there, the stunted one a lookout, running in to report on the human with big boots outside.

The door to the halls of the
Mountain King.
Carn na Caim 3/9/5.

Back at the hostel, Fionn had made a very large pan of soup from an ox tail. We took our bowls outside into the warm, sun-drenched yard and sat there while the others trickled in from their various hills. A buzzard wheeled overhead, ignoring the half-hearted attempts of two crows to mob it. A glass of mellow red wine and two more bowls of Fionn's delicious soup accompanied all the chat about the day's adventures. A heavenly way to see out the last of the light.

After a good dinner of mussels and lamb I returned with the others to Cath's roaring fire. I opened the second bottle of sherry finished Talisker and we were soon a very contented lot of hillwalkers.

Early next morning I walked along the track to Loch Cuaich, the sky a deep blue and the sun already hot. The landscape here is a classic of glacial erosion and deposition. The steep sides of the glen are carved from glacial drift, raw and exposed in large sections as if the last of the ice melted only yesterday. The stream meandering across the flat valley floor is a misfit, too small to have cut such a massive feature. It was easy to picture the stagnant and decaying ice to the north and east, with a raging meltwater torrent rushing down and creating this impressive channel.

Meall Chuaich has great character, isolated from the surrounding hills and rising steeply above the blue loch at its feet. Beauty was everywhere that morning, the azure of sky and water and the white track twisting ahead through the purple heather.

Morag settled on the bank of the Allt Coire Chuaich to doze in the sun while I set off up the steep south-west spur of the mountain, relaxed and happy. All the way up, pairs of yellowhammers rose up from the heather, flashes of yellow bobbing together in the strong wind and calling, "tshripp, tshripp." I climbed quickly and soon the last clumps of heather gave way to dark patches of blaeberry in the dry, tawny deer grass. At the place where the terrain was about to change from hill to mountain, I passed a clear spring which bubbled up beside the path. I stopped to drink and then tackled the boulders which make up the screes around the summit.

On the top were two curious cairns, more like an art installation than the usual jumble of stones. One large cylinder stood next to a tall but thinner cylinder, each of a standard that would not shame a drystone dyker. I know that some hillwalkers hate cairns but I think that these rather suited the top of this particular mountain. As I considered them a solitary snow bunting fluttered up to the top of the smaller cairn. I watched as it flew down to stand at the base of the larger one, its white feathers in sharp contrast to the dark grey stones with their black shadows between.

Then it was a quick descent and lunch with Morag, the tumbling waters of the stream in the background. I could easily have sat longer in that warm and lovely spot but the long road home was calling.

Beinn Chabhair

An unexpected party
and an inaccurate forecast

October

As I was driven up to Tyndrum after work on Friday, I was looking forward to a pleasant autumn walk to Beinn Chabhair. I had checked the weather forecast for Crianlarich for the following day. It was to be a bright day of sunny intervals with a mild southerly breeze, a perfect window in the wet and unsettled weather we were experiencing. This would be Morag's return to the hills after her accident and we promised ourselves a day with a gentle pace.

We threw the gear into the hostel and walked to the pub for a quiet nightcap. Tyndrum seemed particularly lively. The couple who had taken over the café were being married and a pipe band played outside to a cheery crowd. I pushed open the familiar old door to the bar and wondered for a moment whether this, too, had changed hands. The attractive blonde barmaid had a black nose, ears and whiskers and wore a black cat suit, complete with tail. Candles burned on the tables. Bowls of nuts sat on the bar. A large crowd listened to a black singer making a good job of a 70s soul classic. There did not seem to be space for two more but a merry party of middle-aged Liverpudlians waved us inside and we were soon perched on bar stools.

The company could well be described as mixed. There was a wide range of age, shape, size and accent, with a large contingent of students from Eastern Europe (most from the Baltic states as we later discovered). As my eyes got used to the subdued light I realised that the black cat was in the company of a Roman centurion, a dwarf with a pointed red hat and a faun who could have been a relative of Mr Tumnus. I began to spot other characters but the faun was the most impressive, with his bare torso and pale, shaggy beard and legs.

A skinny Liverpudlian with dyed black hair and a home-knitted royal blue tank top stood up abruptly, swung a leg over the back of his chair and pulled me onto the dance floor, shouting, "Come on, let's boogie." His wife and the others followed in a long crocodile, arms pumping the air in time to the music.

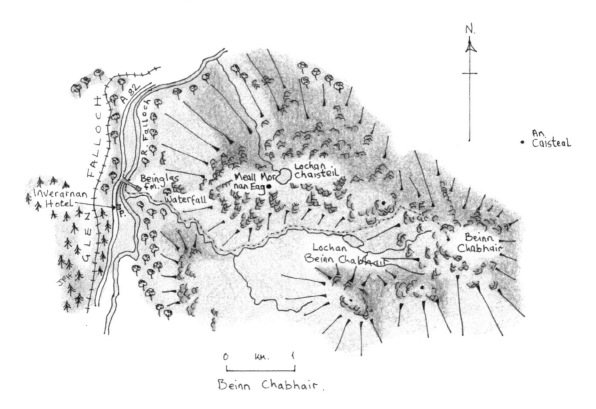

Beinn Chabhair.

We did not have quite the early start intended. It was 9.30 before we reached the Ben Glas waterfall. Glen Falloch was so elegant in its autumn colours that we stopped for a while to absorb it all. The dominant colour was yellow, in a range of pale and subtle shades. Among the yellows were browns, muted oranges and dark, sombre reds. There were blue patches in the sky and I was hopeful that the white cloud which draped the highest hills would lift as the morning passed.

We were rather chilly but the path up the side of the waterfall sorted that. It proved a dramatic ascent up to the hanging valley occupied by the Ben Glas Burn. The burn is a misfit, meandering across the floor of a massive ice-carved valley.

After walking north up a narrow track for a while we struck east, intending to explore the crags and rocky summits of the long ridge which leads east and then south-east up to the cairn on Beinn Chabhair, our objective for the day. Rain had begun to fall, blown in great curtains by a freshening southerly wind. The forecast had not included this particular element.

We sheltered in a gully beneath a steep outcrop of schist, the rock blackened by the rain. Ever optimistic, we were sure that this unexpected rain was no more than a narrow belt which would soon blow over. We ate a second breakfast and warmed our hands on our mugs of steaming tea.

The rain was relentless and the swirling cloud reduced visibility as we struggled on through this wild place of crag and lorry-sized lumps of rock dumped there at the melting of the last ice sheet. Instinct told me that we should be near Lochan a' Chaisteil. We stood beneath an enormous boulder and took stock. My GPS fixed our position near the top of Meall Mor nan Eag, 624 metres. It had taken too long and too much energy to reach that point in those difficult conditions. It was an easy decision to come down off the ridge and follow the path along by the Ben Glas Burn.

Beinn Chabhair
29/10/5.

The rain grew heavier and the wind freshened. We both wondered about that weather forecast as we trudged on, water beginning to run down inside our gaiters.

A clear Munro path leads up onto the ridge from the west end of Lochan Beinn Chabhair. We sat just off the path, looking down on the lochan and ate our lunch. Before eating I changed into my dry waterproof trousers and put on dry socks as the rainwater had wicked down my legs and into my boots. My mistake was to replace my gaiters over the waterproof trousers, but I did not realise this for some time. Dryer and more comfortable, I watched the sheets of rain marking the surface of the lochan and not a creature stirred as far as I could see.

Once fed, we did not linger and were soon toiling through the mud and pools of the saturated path leading up onto the ridge. A grim outcrop, glistening and black in the rain, thrust up into the swirling cloud which obscured the higher parts of the ridge. I stopped at its base and asked Morag whether she wanted to continue. The walk was supposed to be a relatively straightforward return to the mountains for her, the adverse conditions, however, were making it anything but. I was not surprised when she answered, "We've come this far, I'm not about to give up now!"

I doubt whether we would have reached the summit had there not been such a clear path to follow. Even with this, every step was a battle against howling wind, battering hail and sheets of drenching rain. The wind became a serious consideration as we neared the top, threatening to catch us unawares with a great gust and blow us off the ridge. Willpower alone brought us there. We kept very low on the lee of the top, touched the cairn and retreated to the shelter of a large boulder just below. My GPS was still on so I checked that the cairn actually was the right one before we turned back.

It was hard work to get down to the spot where we had lunched looking onto Lochan Beinn Chabhair. We stopped there again to drink a mug of tea and eat something sweet to boost our energy. The walk had taken much longer than we had foreseen and the light was fading fast. Rucksacks were quickly packed again and we were off, striding along the flooded path which follows the Ben Glas Burn. There was an urgency to our walk out. Morag had not packed her head torch and the path down the waterfall was steep and dangerous in the light, never mind in the dark.

One benefit of being soaked to the skin is that you can not get any wetter! We waded through the flooded sections of the path, making excellent time, not even trying to keep the water out of our boots. At times like this, a reader might snuggle more deeply in the armchair, glad that it was not he or she taking such a battering from Highland weather at its worst. Strange then to say that I felt a glow of absolute content at that late stage of the day. I recognised the terrain and knew that the lip of the hanging valley lay not far ahead. I was sure that we would have time to walk down to the glen floor before the light faded away. I knew that Morag had coped with a particularly extreme day and that her confidence must be restored.

The landscape was incredibly beautiful. To our right, three looming black monoliths were perched high up on the ridge, looking down at us like the mysterious figures of Easter Island. The natural woodland which began at the top of the waterfall was striking. Mostly birch, the trunks, black in the rain, provided strong verticals. The delicate yellow leaves seemed to radiate light on this dull, grey day. Thousands of leaves were tossed in sweeping undulations by the strong wind, animating the scene. The waterfall itself was a powerful primal force. We stood and watched it in awe. I found myself stepping back from the edge, frightened of a slip which would slide me into that roaring, foaming, creamy torrent. The wind blew enormous plumes of spray high into the air and drove them back against the flow.

The walk was over. We poured water from our boots and changed into dry clothes. I was wet to my underpants. We stopped on the way home at the Clachan Cottage Hotel in Lochearnhead, taking the table beside the log fire. A pot of tea and a sirloin steak put some warmth and life back into my tired body. We decided that we had learned three lessons: first, not to put gaiters over waterproof trousers[5]; second, to always carry a head torch and last, of course, never to rely on a weather forecast. One can never predict the outcome of these hill days, however, and as we tucked into our dinners we did not know that the headlamps on Morag's car had failed.

Considerably later, as we sat in in the cab of the large breakdown truck, its amber lights flashing, I told the driver that I'd had a great day and it was true.

---

5   Waterproof trousers ride up and water runs down under the gaiters and into one's boots.

Ben Vane

 A raven's warning

January

drove north with Morag on a cold January evening. We were to stay at Tyndrum and climb Ben Vane the next day. The trees were white with hoar frost and the ice broke beneath our feet as we walked to the pub. In the welcome warmth of the bar we toasted the New Year with a glass of Ardbeg, the strong Islay malt. The last time we had been in that place there was a Halloween party and the barmaid was a cat. She wore no costume now but was dressed in black and still had a feline air.

We woke to a still morning of heavy frost. As we left the hostel the car cracked the frozen puddles and I drove on through thick fog. I turned south at Crianlarich and at Inverarnan drove out of the curtain of fog and into another world. The sky was dark blue and the low sun had turned the eastern mountain tops to gold. When we got to the northern end of Loch Lomond, Ben Lomond was generating a small rose pink cloud which curled around the north-east side of its summit.

I parked at the landing at Inveruglas, over the road from the hydro station and we were soon on the way to the Loch Sloy dam. The noise of the road soon disappeared and we had a Highland winter landscape before us. The track was white with frost and all around was frozen hard. The slopes of Ben Vorlich rose steeply to our right and the sharp cone of A' Chrois to our left. Ahead was the impressive Ben Vane, our objective for the day.

Ben Vane, at 915 metres/3002 feet, is the equal lowest of the Munros, but figures can be

misleading. We started at only 13 metres above sea level and the other 902 metres was going to be a considerable climb. The mountain is also steep-sided, with much exposed rock. We were not going to simply walk up those cliffs and crags. Another consideration was the cap of snow and ice which covered the upper reaches, this needed handling with care.

As we walked, the sun rose behind Ben Lomond, its rays bathing the mountainsides around us with pink light. We left the track at the foot of Ben Vane and stepped onto a narrow path that zig zagged up the steep slopes before us. 50 metres along the path was a small tree, its black branches festooned with Christmas baubles. On a high branch there was a present wrapped in gold paper, tied with shiny pink ribbon. I imagine that the Christmas elves would return on Twelfth Night to pack up their silver decorations for another year.

Ben Vane
4/1/6.

We left this last reminder of the festive season behind and climbed the slopes of Ben Vane until we reached a flat rock about half way up where we sat to eat an early lunch. The views were wonderful and the sun had just enough heat to warm our faces a little, so we were in no hurry to leave. The sun's weakness and its low angle explained the thick white freezing fog that filled Glen Arklet and Strath Gartney in the distance. I would like to have telephoned the good folk of those places to suggest that they take a walk up the glen sides. They would soon have broken through the fog and have emerged into a world of blue sky, bright sunshine and burnished winter colours.

The sun was lifting water vapour from the snow and ice caps of the surrounding mountains and each had its own small cloud on top. These clouds were constantly being blown westward by the wind and were constantly being replenished by evaporation and condensation. The clouds would sometimes diminish so that the dark summits would emerge for a few minutes only to be smothered again.

We walked on and the slope steepened. The frozen grasses gave way to rock and the path twisted up around ice-plastered crags. The snow cover started as we entered the cloud. Soon the sun was no more than a pale disc. We stopped to put on warm hats as the temperature, already below zero, dropped sharply. A large raven called crronk, crronk on the rock above us, perhaps warning us of the dangers ahead.

Raven on Ben Vane
4/1/6
JPH

The wind picked up, reducing the temperature yet more. There had been some melting before the cold snap of the previous two days and the result was a slippery film of ice over rock, grass, moss and snow. We began to take extreme care.

Nearer the summit we had to scramble up some outcrops so we stopped in a rock chimney to put away walking poles. Hands and fingers were needed for safety.

We emerged from a second chimney into a little gully with a mainly grass-covered slope before us. This dropped away very steeply into the cloud below. About half way up I remembered my ice axe. I had secure footholds so I removed my rucksack, freed the ice axe and fastened the rucksack again. Morag shouted from below that it was not the most sensible place to be doing that, but I had no choice. I waited until she had done the same then traversed the slope with extreme care, sometimes cutting more secure steps with the axe, testing to see if I could get any purchase were I to slip. It was a tense 15 minutes or so. Morag found it even more difficult, still not fully confident after her fall in the summer. She ended up back-tracking to find a marginally less exposed route.

One more gully and we were surprised to emerge on top of the summit cairn. We were both drained by the tension and concentration of the ascent since entering the cloud. It was as if there were two mountains, one benign beneath the cloud and one hard and dangerous above. Our "note to self" was that, in future, we will take out the ice axes as soon as we reach slopes of ice and snow, not wait until our very lives might depend upon holding one.

The descent was slow as we picked our way with care between the icy crags. Once beneath the clouds, the mood changed completely. The sun was still shining and we could see for miles in the clear air. We had experienced two contrasting walks on Ben Vane.

We stopped as soon as we found a ledge to sit on and enjoyed a second lunch in the sun. A' Chrois was still producing its little cloud, again tinged with pink as the sun fell lower in the sky. It had an almost hypnotic effect on me as I sipped my mug of tea. A raven flew past, its wingspan as great as that of a buzzard. It flew with grace far below our high seat, showing off with aerobatics.

Raven on Ben Vane
4|1|6

As the sun began to sink we slowly walked down. Only the mountain tops were in sunlight by the time we reached the shores of Loch Lomond, the water mirror still and reflecting the faded winter afternoon colours.

We re-entered the freezing fog only a few miles north and it smothered the country until we got back to the Borders. We had chosen a mountain in a rare clear patch.

10/2/06

Beinn a' Bheithir: Sgorr Dhonuill and Sgorr Dhearg

On the mountain of winter and death

February

I t was Morag's turn to drive which meant that I could look out at the moonlit landscape. Glen Coe was particularly spectacular, its black walls towering up to end in snow-capped peaks. Behind, Orion strode across the winter sky.

Our journey ended at the hostel at Inchree on the shores of Loch Linnhe. Before checking in at the pub, we looked across at Beinn a' Bheithir, the mountain ridge we planned to climb the following day. Its snowy peaks were clear against the deep blue of the night sky.

In the pub, we sipped a glass of Ardbeg as we looked at the map and decided on our ascent route, leaving the decision about the descent until we were up there. The Gaelic translates as Bheithir's (pronounced vay-heer's) mountain, Bheithir being the goddess of winter and death. It is a rugged horseshoe ridge with half a dozen peaks, the highest two being Munros. These are Sgorr Dhonuill and Sgorr Dhearg, both over 1000 metres. As the climb starts at sea level, the day was going to be challenging.

We were up in the dark at 6.00 next morning. After breakfast I checked my gear then opened the common room window blinds. The view was of Loch Linnhe with the mountain ridge behind. Everything was covered in thick frost, the dawn sky was completely cloudless and the peaks brilliant white.

The car was soon parked in the forestry car park at South Ballachulish and we strode up the forestry road in high spirits, heading into the huge corrie at the head of Gleann a' Chaolais. As we got nearer, we could see that the rocky corrie walls are very steep and realised that we were in for a hard slog to get up onto the ridge. The cliffs of Sgorr Dhonuill were dark in the morning shadow and draped with frozen waterfalls. It was hot work to climb the corrie backwall. Loose scree moved under each toehold and we had to avoid areas of thick ice. We reached the snowfields of the ridge with relief. The corrie walls had blocked out the sun on the way up, but now we walked into its welcome light. A myriad crystals twinkled with such intensity that it took some minutes for our eyes to adjust. There was little warmth, however, in the low-angled sun.

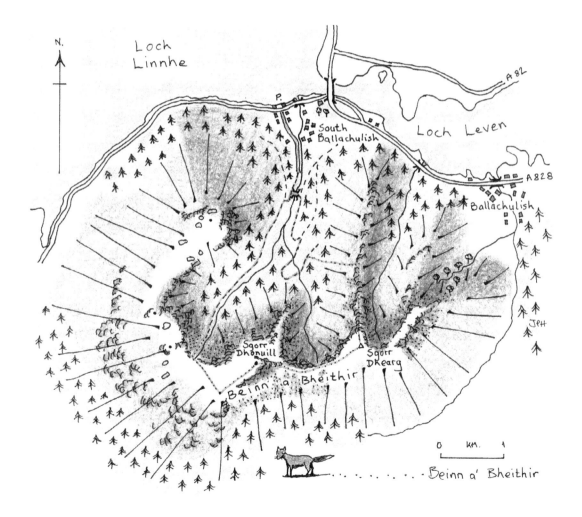

Walking to a top south-west of Sgorr Dhonuill gave us a panoramic view of the whole ridge. Morag took out her camera and said that she was so pleased to have put extra films in her pack, this was a day to get a perfect mountain photograph.

We stopped in the lee of some rocks just under the summit of our first Munro to have some lunch. Morag touched my arm and said in a low voice, "Look up, quick!" It was a golden eagle, no more than eight metres above our heads. Its primary feathers were bent upwards like outspread fingers and the sun turned its tawny colour to gold. We watched as it glided away silently, never once moving its wings, the most appropriate of all creatures for Bheithir's mountain.

Golden Eagle over
Sgorr Dhonuill
10/2/06.

The views from the high perch of Sgorr Dhonuill were wonderful. To the east, my eye was drawn to the graceful curved ridge leading to our next peak. Beyond rose the mountains of Glen Coe, dominated by the massive block of Bidean nam Bian, cut in its upper reaches by deep corries separated by sharp arêtes. Looking through Glen Coe, the distinctive pyramid of Schiehallion stood beyond Rannoch Moor. Sweeping my gaze south and south-west, I watched the sun sparkling on the sea and picked out Ben More, rising above the other mountains of Mull. I turned north to see range after range stretching to Knoydart and Kintail, the highest peaks all snow-capped. The best view of all, however, was north-east to Ben Nevis and the Mamores, snow covered and dramatic above the blue waters of Loch Leven.

I was surprised to see that a fox had recently passed over the summit, his the only tracks in the powdery snow. The steep descent was a tricky business in the icy conditions.

We clambered down rocks and little gullies, very aware of the exposure on this narrow ridge. The drop to the north in particular was considerable. We held ice axes but they would have been of little use should either of us have fallen here. The fox prints showed us the way down, I envied the creature's quadrupedal sure-footedness.

Sgorr Dhearg from
Sgorr Dhonuill.
Beinn a' Bheithir 10/2/6.

At the bealach, we looked back at what had been a tough descent and noticed a pair of eagles, slowly circling around the summit.

We had considered coming off the ridge at this point, taking a route down the northern cliffs into the corrie below. A small stream had frozen, however, turning the rough path into a precipitous chute of shiny ice.

The fox prints led us up the narrow ridge to Sgorr Dhearg, its summit the highest point on Beinn a' Bheithir. Morag was particularly taken with the panorama of Glen Coe and used the viewpoint to take photographs using three different lenses. While she was absorbed in this, I found myself thinking about the fox. I had noticed fox tracks in the snow on the top of another Munro, was this fox a Munro bagger?

We dropped down a few feet to get out of the light but bitterly cold wind and finished our flasks of tea. I wondered how many times I would again be able to sit down like this on top of a mountain in February?

We decided to descend down the keen-edged north ridge of Sgorr Dhearg. It looked intimidating in its upper reaches, but we could always turn back. It turned out to be an ideal way down and opened up yet more beautiful views, particularly back south towards the icy corries of Beinn a' Bheithir.

After about two kilometres, we turned west and scrambled down slopes of grass and heather to the tree line. We then threaded our way among young conifers until we reached a forestry roadway. This led us back up the corrie for a while before it descended to a lower roadway which turned to take us down to a bridge and then on to the route we had used in the morning.

The late afternoon sun was behind the hills as we drove into Glen Coe. We stopped at the bar of the Clachaig Inn and ordered venison steaks with baked apple and redcurrants. Two climbers left their table by the big stove and we were quick to bag it. The logs crackled and sparked and the heat began to toast my chilled body. The company was in a mellow, end-of-day mood, dogs padded about the tables and then came a shout from the bar that our meals were ready.

3/4/06

Na Gruagaichean, Stob Coire a' Chairn, Am Bodach

 Pristine Mamores under April snow

April

A crescent moon shone above Glen Coe. Black buttresses towered up into the night sky, clouds colliding with their uppermost bastions and then tearing themselves free again.

At Inchree, we left our bags in the car and went to the pub to check in. We were welcomed with a cheery "hola" from the olive-skinned barman who was smoking at the door. Inside, a mixture of Latin music and mainstream pop was being pumped out from a Spanish radio station. "Dos cervezas por favor," shouted two customers at the bar. The unexpected has become normal in Highland bars these days.

We ordered Bruichladdich malts to help counter the effects of the long journey. I love the elusive sweetness which reminds me of the aniseed balls of my childhood. The weather forecast for the following day was posted on the wall. It predicted strong and very cold northerly wind, making walking difficult on the tops. The wind would bring fresh accumulations of snow, particularly in the afternoon. Temperatures would be minus four degrees Celsius, but considerably lower when the wind chill was factored in. It looked like it was going to be another tough day.

It was to be an early start so we tore ourselves away from the selection of malts, said "gracias" and "adios" and went to find our bunks.

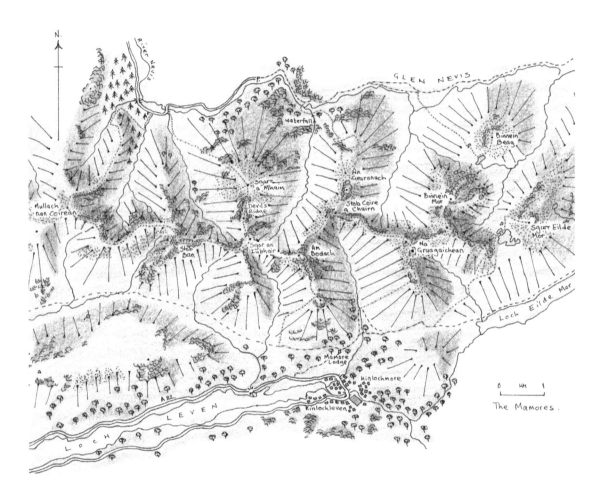

The sun was barely peeping above the Glen Coe mountains as we drove along the north shore of Loch Leven. All was calm in that deep glen, the water like a sheet of mirror glass.

We parked at Mamore Lodge. This old fashioned Highland hotel with its white towers is a well-known landmark. I walked around the front and saw a solitary guest eating breakfast in the genteel dining room. Even at this low altitude, overnight snowfall had deposited a thin blanket of white on the ground. A robin completed the picture as he hopped around our rucksacks.

A broad track led us into the mouth of Coire na Ba and then we started to climb the steep side of Na Gruagaichean's south-east ridge. The snow had obscured any path that might have helped our ascent.

Half way up we stopped for a breather. Coire na Ba has been sculpted on a massive scale. The tall cliffs of Am Bodach, cut by deep, snow-filled gullies separated by vertical spines of black rock, looked positively Alpine. As I remarked on this there was a dull rumble and an avalanche rolled down one of the gullies, throwing up fine clouds of powder snow. It was a scene which belonged more to the Mer de Glace than the heights above Loch Leven.

We were sheltered in the corrie but could see that the wind was strong, blowing billows of spindrift from the ridges and tops, brilliant white against the blue sky. Looking west, I noticed a wall of pale grey rolling towards us along Loch Leven, its front wild with swirling columns of snow. We put on extra clothing and turned our backs to the onslaught.

Onwards and upwards we trudged, the round pellets of snow rattling on my mountain cap. Nearer the crest of the ridge there were large sections of hard frozen snow and I had to kick steps. We descended into a gully before the final steep slope and it was like being in a wind tunnel. The fierce wind picked up the dry grains of snow and blasted great sheets of them against us. My Buffalo jacket was no match for that level of wind chill. It was a bad place to linger so I pushed on up the last slope, again kicking steps.

At the top I looked back down into the corrie. It was wild, with two enormous swirling columns of snow being blown 4000 feet up into the cloud above.

We needed to stop to have a hot drink and top up our energy reserves so I went down the ridge to where a rock step would shelter us from the wind. I put on my outer jacket while I waited for Morag to catch up. There was a deep drift of snow on that south-facing slope, accumulated in the lee of the wind. It was a struggle to get down but worth it. Our platform was secure and sheltered, perched high above Loch Eilde Mor, the big loch of the hind. I spread out my survival bag for a seat and at that moment the snow storm passed and raced off towards Rannoch Moor. We drank tea and ate a second breakfast in glorious spring sunshine. A panorama lay before us, the snow-covered peaks of the eastern Mamores to our left, linked by beautiful curved ridges, the sparkling waters of the loch below and the Aonach Eagach beyond.

Refreshed, we climbed back up and began to walk along the ridge leading to the top of Na Gruagaichean, the Maidens. The snow conditions were difficult. Much was soft, especially on south-facing sections. Any area facing north or east or subject to wind chill was frozen hard. Sometimes the frozen sections were solid, sometimes there was an icy crust with soft snow beneath. I looked ahead and noted the cornice on the east side of this narrow, exposed ridge and determined to avoid stepping on it; it was a sudden drop and a long, long way down!

Climbing higher, the angle of the ridge became even steeper and the hard, icy surface dominated. We stopped at some large boulders, strapped on crampons and unfastened ice axes. Progress was better after that and I certainly felt much more secure.

The sun was still shining as we reached the top of the first of the Maidens. Sharp, snow-covered ridges curved away gracefully to the south, north-west and north-east, the latter two each rising to a peak. From each of these peaks, further ridges curved away and up to yet more summits, the pattern repeated as far as I could see to the west. I was most impressed by this first experience of the Mamores.

Descending the very steep slope from the first Maiden would have been foolhardy without crampons. It faces north, its snow was frozen solid and the surface was a film of ice.

Climbing the equally steep south-facing slope leading to the second Maiden was even more difficult. Here the snow was soft and there was a drift in the narrow col which threatened to swallow us whole.

Na Gruagaichean 3/4/6.
At the bottom of one of
the Maidens.

From the top of this second Maiden, the long, precipitous slope leading down to the bealach far below was frozen solid. As its orientation was northerly, I had expected this. We set off, ice axes ready, muscles tensed, but the crampons again proved invaluable, helping us to reach the bealach without even one scary moment.

I had noticed a wall of grey cloud rolling over the mountains from the north and suggested some lunch before we were hit by the second blizzard of the day. The bealach was not the best of places as it was acting as a wind tunnel for the wind which had now shifted to NNE. We dropped down a little on the south-west side and were relatively well sheltered as we sat gazing across Coire na Ba. We admired Am Bodach as we ate. It looked formidable from this viewpoint, with the last section of the north-east ridge, our route of ascent, appearing impossibly steep.

The first pellets of snow were falling as we shouldered our rucksacks and climbed back to the bealach. We stopped to watch a pair of golden eagles slowly circling the peak we had descended from. What were they looking for up there? Were they the same pair we had seen on Beinn a' Bheithir?

The wind veered back to the north or NNW as the snow shower hit. We wore snow goggles to protect our eyes from the hard pellets and leaned forward into the wind. The snow underfoot was soft again but this was not a good time to take off the crampons.

On the summit of Stob Coire a' Chairn the wind howled and we were battered by curtains of snow coming in on it and swirling clouds of spindrift. I shouted to Morag that this was my hundredth Munro but it was no place to celebrate.

A break between the squalls of snow had shown us the south-west ridge and we began to plod down, wary of the cornice which had built up on the Coire na Ba side. The cold wind and northerly orientation had combined to freeze the snow again and I was pleased I had not removed my crampons.

We had not gone far down the ridge when the falling snow suddenly stopped pelting us, the wind dropped, the clouds broke to fragments and the sun's rays struck the world again. We found a place in the lee of the wind, just down from the crest of the ridge and looking down into the giant corrie again. I ate honey pieces and drank tea, watching vapour rising from the snow. Spindrift was occasionally blown onto us from the ridge below, little icy pellets dropping into my steaming cup.

When we climbed back to the ridge the view north to Ben Nevis, the Carn Mor Dearg Arête and the Grey Corries was superb in that crystal clear air.

The ascent of Am Bodach, the old man, provided the greatest challenge of the walk. It would have been impossible without crampons and ice axe as the snow here was frozen hard. I led the way, calling down to Morag when there were sections to avoid. At one point the icy crust broke and my foot went through to soft snow beneath. The movement dislodged two rocks the size of coconuts and they went hurtling down. I shouted to Morag and she just had time to move to the side. The rocks went crashing down the slope to land in the snow far below.

On top of Am Bodach I was thrilled by the view in front of me. I was looking west along the line of the Mamores, each mountain linked to the next by a graceful ridge, all enhanced by the fresh snow cover. Here the form is sinuous, sensual and I understood the feminine name of the range. I then looked north towards Ben Nevis, east towards Binnein Mor and south towards Glen Coe, each peak looking its very best in its winter coat. Morag arrived and her camera was soon in action. She too turned a full circle, delighted with that sparkling panorama.

It was not easy to leave that mountaintop at such a perfect moment but the conditions had slowed us and we had to drag ourselves away. The sun shone from a cloudless sky as we walked in virgin snow down the south ridge. The walk had provided much spectacle and this last ridge did not disappoint. It is steep and narrow, with near vertical cliffs on a massive scale falling down to the corrie on the east side. The wind had sculpted a fantastic cornice which seemed to defy gravity as it stretched out precariously above those dramatic crags.

The snow was beginning to soften so we stopped to remove our crampons and have the last of our tea. I suggested that we should bring climbing helmets whenever there are particularly steep ascents or scrambling is involved, Morag could have been killed by those falling rocks.

The next snow shower started as we strapped on our rucksacks and began the long descent of the western slope of the ridge. My knees were sore when we joined the track which leads to Mamore Lodge.

A Border collie was waiting for us at the hotel. He kept us company as we changed out of our walking clothes, trying to keep dry in what was, at this lower altitude, sleet rather than snow. The collie was immune to the weather and he happily retrieved the stones I threw for him.

In Kinlochleven we sat in comfy chairs beside an open fire in the Walkers' Bar, waiting for bowls of soup and hot meals. Outside, tall curtains of sleet moved across the black water of Loch Leven.

The North Glen Shiel Ridge: Aonach Meadhoin, Sgurr a' Bhealaich Dheirg and Saileag
The Loch Lochy Munros: Meall na Teanga and Sron a' Choire Ghairbh

The Jolly Boys and the Canadians

June

drove across the Highland Line, through the Trossachs and stopped at the bar of the Clachan Cottage Hotel. We looked out over Loch Earn, which was like a sheet of glass on that lovely summer evening. A plane with floats circled and landed, spoiling the mirror-image of the hills beyond. The image restored itself as we ate, an upside-down castle guarding the glen which leads to Ben Vorlich.

Rannoch Moor seemed more wild and vast than ever. Glen Coe's buttresses of rock disappeared into pink-edged clouds.

The Jolly Boys congregated in the bar of the Invergarry Hotel. A bottle of Caol Ila caught my eye and I tried a glass. It was less powerful than other Islay malts but I liked it the better for that. Natasha, from an Islay family, pronounced it "culeela".

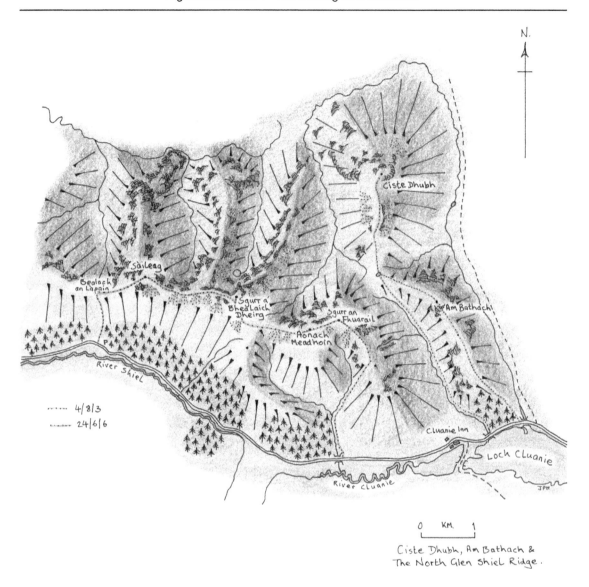

N.

Ciste Dhubh

Sàileag

Bealach
an Lapain

Sgurr a
Bhealaich
Dheirg

Sgurr an
Fhuarail

Am Bathach

Aonach
Meadhoin

River Shiel

P

4/8/3
24/6/6

Cluanie Inn

Loch Cluanie

P

River Cluanie

JPH

0 KM 1

Ciste Dhubh, Am Bathach &
The North Glen Shiel Ridge.

After the traditional late night came the equally traditional bickering over which hills to climb and who might climb them. The old timers were packed and had their boots on when the first of the six Canadian girls appeared in her pyjamas, so there was plenty of time for debate. It was eventually agreed that we would go up onto the North Glen Shiel Ridge or The Three Brothers as it is called by some. Uniquely, all agreed to do this.

I drove to the little parking spot at the foot of the Bealach an Lapain and Struan, who had followed in his car, ran me back to meet up with the others. They had parked near to the bridge over the Allt Coire Tholl Bhruach.

By the time we caught up with the rest they were trying to find a place to cross to the east side of the burn. There had been many days of rain and there was a lot of water. We had to go beyond the forestry to find a safe crossing.

The plan was for Struan to lead a high level circuit around Coire na Cadha, taking in the Top, Sgurr an Fhuarail and the first Munro, Aonach Meadhoin. He would then guide most of the party, including our Canadian guests, down either the Meall a' Charra or the Allt Coire Tholl Bhuach. One of the Canadians had cerebral palsy and all were poorly equipped, so a poor weather option would have been to get up into the corrie and then return to the cars for some sight-seeing.

Morag wanted to test out her leg, still causing problems following her accident the previous summer, so I went ahead with her and we began to climb the steep eastern wall of the corrie. It was cool, breezy and showery.

There is a cairn on top of the southernmost summit of the ridge, marked 864 metres on the Ordnance Survey map. We dropped down a little to the east of it, in the lee of the wind, and spread out survival bags to sit on. As we drank tea the cloud blew away and the sun came through to warm us. I looked across to the Am Bathach ridge and Ciste Dhubh, remembering my son Tom walking this in his socks because his boots were hurting his feet. The late night and warm sun conspired to make me drowsy and I was asleep in seconds. I woke to loud singing and saw that the Jolly Boys had made the ridge and were strung out along the skyline.

We packed up, joined the end of the line and discovered that everyone had struggled to the top. The rain had started again and the Canadian girls were cold and wet but in the highest spirits. It was they who had been singing.

A little scrambling brought us to the top of Sgurr an Fhuarail, where we found a sheltered hollow among the boulders and stopped for an early lunch.

It was too cool and wet to linger and we were soon off along the ridge to the first Munro. Struan is at his very best when leading an inexperienced group and he combined this with close support for the disabled girl.

The cloud clung to the top of Aonach Meadhoin, the prosaically named middle ridge. When asked what this mountain is called, I remembered a pronunciation of oenach vane. We shook the hands of the visitors, congratulating them on climbing their first Munro. There were no views but it was still "awesome" to the girls. Photos were taken of what was the largest group I remember on top of a Munro. Struan then led the bulk of the party down, with the Canadians singing lustily.

I walked on along the ridge with Natasha and Morag for company. The path turned to the north-east and, after a little scrambling, I reached the rocky summit of Sgurr a' Bhealaich Dheirg, the second Munro. As there were no views, I came back to the main ridge and found a sheltered spot to eat a second lunch with my two companions. A patch of blue appeared and seconds later the cloud was shredded by the breeze and streamed off eastwards. A lonely landscape of mountain ridges and deep glaciated valleys was revealed. Looking north we could see the exposed red rock and screes on the west side of Sgurr a' Bhealaich Dheirg. It looked like a large mass of iron-rich felsite had intruded into the ubiquitous grey of the mica schists, hence the name of the mountain, the peak of the red pass.

Warm layers were stowed in rucksacks and we enjoyed a delightful ridge walk under a blue sky to our third Munro. There were great views down into Glen Shiel and across to the South Glen Shiel Ridge. The best views were straight ahead to The Five Sisters, at their most spectacular from this vantage point.

We stopped on the summit of Saileag, pronounced salak and I considered the significance of its name, which means little heel. I opted for the explanation that it was a heel as in the crust of a loaf of bread, the end of the massive Three Brothers ridge. Morag took photographs of The Five Sisters while I sipped my last cup of tea, glad to be on this gem among the mountains of the Highlands.

The walk down to the bealach and then down the path to the floor of Glen Shiel was interesting. My fellow walkers were in no hurry, chatting away as I walked well ahead, enjoying the peace of that beautiful summer day. I began to notice the rich diversity of plant life and stopped to make some sketches. Carnivorous sundews caught my eye, each waiting for its next insect meal. Diminutive orchids peeped out between the blaeberries, little jewels adorning each side of the path.

Sundew

There were pale beige frogs with black Zorro masks. Tiger beetles sparkled like emeralds as they sunned themselves. The highlight, however, was the large dragonflies, their design unchanged over 350 million years. I waited beside a jet black monster with yellow hoops around its abdomen, a big cat among the local insect population, digesting

Bog Myrtle

its last meal in the warm sun. Natasha and Morag caught up and admired this handsome predator, Morag taking a close-up photograph.

I pulled some bog myrtle leaves and we rubbed them on our hair and faces, preparing for the inevitable midge attack on the floor of the glen. Whether it was the bright sun or the pungent aroma of the leaves, we were left well alone, getting to the car without a single bite.

That evening we met up with the other Jolly Boys to swap tales in the Invergarry Hotel, where a meal had been ordered. There is nothing like a day in the mountains to sharpen an appetite and the dinner did not disappoint. I enjoyed Cullen skink with oatcakes then chicken stuffed with haggis and served with grilled aubergines, courgettes, peppers and red onions. A glass of Merlot was a good choice to go with the food and a fresh fruit salad with cream rounded the meal off nicely.

A Jolly crowd walked back to the hostel, full of good food and wine. Most are prone to a nightcap and my contribution was a bottle of Laphroig. Although also from Islay, this is a peatier, smokier malt than a Caol Ila. I enjoyed its deep aroma and full flavour, a perfect end to the day.

The end, however, was premature. Fionn produced his Irish whistle and we were soon singing Flower of Scotland, The Northern Lights, Caledonia and the like. The Canadians declared the singing "awesome". I went to bed at 2.00 a.m. with the party still going strong.

It was a beautiful morning. Ray, Alex, Morag and I set off early down the Great Glen to Kilfinnan, our plan to walk up the Loch Lochy Munros. In the hot sun, dozens of small coppers danced. Once out of the trees, a welcome wind cooled us as we strode up the easy gradient of the Cam Bhealach.

Small Copper

We climbed Meall na Teanga, the hill of the tongue, first. The summit provided a 360 degree panorama of hills, mountains, glens and lochs. I sat on the cairn with my cup of tea, looking across at the immense black bulk of Ben Nevis, still streaked with winter snow. To the west stood range after range of mountains, ending with the distinctive outline of the Cuillin of Skye.

Then it was down to the bealach and up the excellent stalker's path to Sron a' Choire

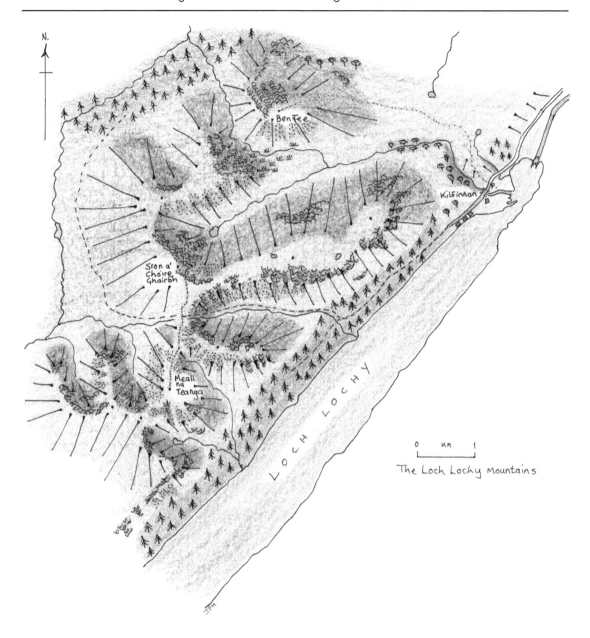

The Loch Lochy Mountains

Ghairbh. We had walked along a tongue and now we were on a nose, the nose of the rough corrie.

The views from the tip of the Sron were similar to those on Meall na Teanga and yet, considering the proximity of these two Munros, strangely different. We picked out the mountains of Glen Shiel in the north and looked along Loch Ness to the north-east. More immediately, impressive cliffs fell down into a large corrie containing a small lochan. The corrie opened onto an ice-carved trough with a small misfit of a stream meandering across its floor. It is post-glacial topography on a grand scale, even grander when it is considered that this is merely a hanging valley above the main glaciated valley of the Great Glen.

We ate lunch on the top, discussing a possible return along the ENE ridge. If it had not been a Sunday with a working week looming, we would have chosen this high route back. Common sense prevailed, however, and we opted to return the way we had come.

Am Faochagach, Cona' Mheall, Meall nan Ceapraichean, Beinn Dearg. A Chailleach. Meall a' Chrasgaidh

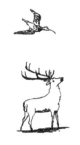

Drought and flood

July had been the hottest on record. I travelled north wearing shorts and a tee shirt. A detour was required to pick up my son, Tom, from his flat in Edinburgh. He was not easy to miss as I rounded the corner of his street, sitting as he was on an enormous pile of bags and rucksacks. Needing a break from the hot and crowded streets of the city, he planned to camp for a month in a little gully on the coast of the Coigach peninsula, looking onto the Summer Isles. As a student he was, of course, of limited means but he had a bag of oats, a bag of rice and his fishing rods. His idea was to be self-sufficient.

It was challenging to pack all that gear into the car but we managed somehow. Tom then remembered that he'd left some things in the close. He reappeared with a guitar which, after some rearrangement, fitted on top of everything and a large plastic sack containing a car wheel. I commented that this was both bulky and heavy and was told that it was necessary for his cooking fire. I pointed out that on my recent camping trip I had cooked successfully every day for his sister and nephew on a fire contained in a ring of stones, a practice continued from my Boy Scout days in the 1960s. Tom responded by explaining the gains made by draughts of air coming through holes in the rim, the consequent increase in temperature and the benefits of a flat surface on which to lay a metal grid. I knew that I was beaten. Once everyone and everything was packed in, I knelt down to see whether the car floor was still above the road surface. By some miracle it was.

As I drove off I asked how his folk singing had gone in the Royal Oak the previous evening. It had gone very well indeed was the reply, so well that he had not finished until 5.00 a.m. I remarked that he must be tired, having had so little sleep. He replied that once he had returned to pack, there was no time for bed.

"I'm so much looking forward to Ullapool," he said sleepily, "the Saigon of the North." These were his last words until we stopped for petrol in Inverness.

At the petrol station, Tom went to stretch his legs and returned straining under the weight of peat blocks. "Great for the fire," he said. I took another nervous glance under the car before pulling gently out onto the road again.

Ullapool was bathed in warm summer sunshine when we arrived. It looked its very best, the brilliant white houses in a long line above the deep blue water of Loch Broom.

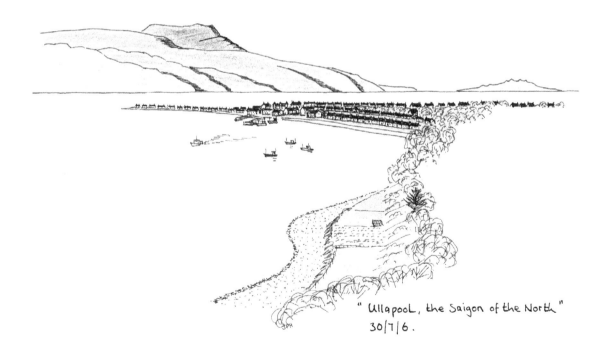

"Ullapool, the Saigon of the North"
30/7/6.

After checking in to the hostel, we strolled down to the pier. I noted with relief that nothing had changed. The smell of fish and chips, the gulls crying overhead, the grey seals waiting for scraps in the harbour. We wandered up to the Ceilidh Place and settled down at a table on the patio, drinking tea and watching the others arriving at our accommodation across the street.

Once we were all gathered we went to the Argyll for our meal. I had grilled tuna with salad which was pleasant but not substantial enough to satisfy if I'd been out walking. The place had recently changed hands and there were only a couple of bottles of malt whisky on the shelf, presumably the least popular. As after dinner drams were required, we tried the Glen Esk, a Highland malt from The Mearns. It was light and sweet.

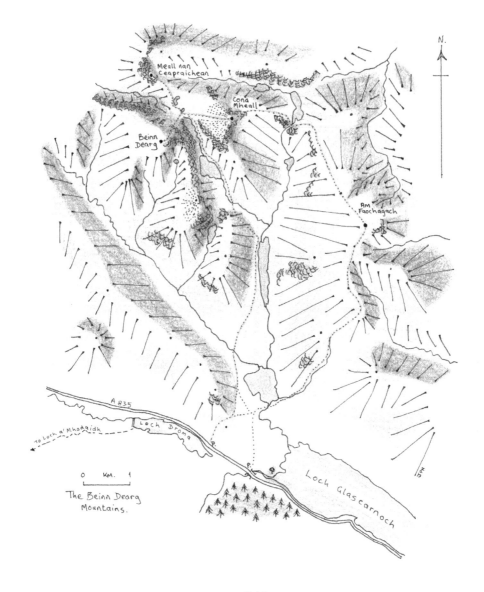

Back at the hostel, we ended the evening drinking tea and listening to Tom and Douglas singing. They had been pleased to discover a twelve string guitar with six strings and soon had it in tune. Tom played his own and we were treated to some great entertainment.

I was up at six the next morning, pleased to see Ullapool bathed in sunlight. There was some delay in getting Tom ("I'm not a mornings person") going, but I was still parked at the eastern end of Loch Droma, on Scotland's watershed, before 9.00a.m.

The guide books had warned about the sodden peat bogs of the Dirrie More and Loch a' Gharbhain area, a place to test the spirit of a hillwalker. Crossing streams like the Abhainn a' Gharbhrain and the Allt a' Gharbhrain is notoriously difficult and potentially dangerous. With this in mind, I had two plans, the first involving an attempt at a river crossing. We would walk to the point where the river flows out of Loch a' Gharbhrain and be prepared to turn away if the water was too high.

Tom (with his fishing rod), Morag and I walked north and then around the spur that marks the end of the Meall Feith Dhiongaig ridge. Luck was on our side. The long, hot, dry spell had dried out the top layer of the peat and walking was relatively easy. Once in sight of Loch a' Gharbhrain, Tom left to walk up to Loch nan Eilean to try for some trout. Morag and I went down to the outflow from the loch. The river was wide and would have been impossible to cross in spate, but we stepped from slippery rock to rock, using our walking poles to help with balance. We reached the far bank with dry feet, grateful for July's drought.

The next stage was to slog up onto the Am Faochagach ridge, 575 metres of ascent. It was consistently boggy underfoot and we realised how tiring the climb would be under normal (wet) conditions. We stopped just under the crest of the ridge where the ground was, at last, dry and stony. We ate a second breakfast while enjoying the panoramic view to the south and west. I had never seen the Fannaich range like that and was pleased to think that I had it all to explore. Further west, the An Teallach ridge was easy to identify, its pinnacles like the teeth in a predator's jawbone. If we were to get a dry, clear, settled day, this is where we would go.

It was an easy walk up to our first Munro, Am Faochagach, which should probably be pronounced foechakoch and means the heathery or berried place. There was little heather near the summit but plenty of blaeberries.

The best thing about this hill was the walk from the cairn down to Loch Prille. On that day the views were superb. Beinn Dearg rose above the cliffs which flanked Choire Ghranda, a deep corrie on a grand scale, its floor occupied by a dark loch. Cona' Mheall, which means adjoining hill, looked equally impressive, particularly the narrow, rocky south ridge which provides an exposed route to the summit. Beyond lay the unmistakeable outlines of the hills of Inverpolly and Assynt. Stac Pollaidh, Cul Beag, Cul Mor and Suilven probably provide the most iconic vista in the Scottish Highlands.

We crossed the fast stream outflowing from Loch Prille just above the point where it plunged down in a spectacular waterfall. This, again, could well be dangerous after heavy rain. Safely on the west bank, we looked south down the classic glaciated valley. Its steep sides are lined with cliffs and crags and where the ice has over-deepened the floor there are two lochs.

A climb up the east ridge of Cona' Mheall followed. This was steep and soon turned into a good scramble. It was, however, relatively easy work on the gritty surface of the Torridonian sandstone slabs.

We spotted two figures on the skyline, the first human beings we had seen since leaving Tom. Once we got to the top we saw that it was Struan and Mark. Mark, also not being a mornings person, had taken rather longer to leave the hostel that day. We perched on a sandstone slab just below the summit and drank tea while they told us about their scary ascent up that same south ridge that we had admired from Am Faochagach.

As we descended west from Cona' Mheall, Struan and Mark followed the path we had taken from our first Munro. We were heading for two tiny lochans on the bealach at the head of Choire Ghranda. The view to the north of the route to Seana Bhraigh brought us to a halt. Our walk in that day had been long enough but it is considerably longer to get to that remote and lonely mountain. The pinnacle of Creag an Duine, its eastern top, stood like a tooth on the horizon.

We stopped at the bealach to look into Choire Ghranda, a deep, wild gorge. North-west of the bealach lies another Munro, Meall nan Ceapraichean, pronounced kapreechan. It looked so near that we succumbed to the temptation to bag it. This turned out to be a good decision because the views west down upper Gleann na Sguaib were splendid. If Morag had not stopped to take photographs we could have touched the summit in 20 minutes or so.

Back at the bealach, the wind had picked up and was blowing from the south-east. The temperature dropped, the cloud swirled over the top of Beinn Dearg and it started to rain. We hoped that it would only be a shower and would clear by the time we got to the top. An old stone dyke, one of the famine dykes, runs up the north-east ridge and provided some shelter.

At the cairn, there was no sign that the cloud was going to lift. The plan had been to walk off by the south ridge and drop down to Loch nan Eilean, picking up Tom. The path runs close to the vertical cliffs of Beinn Dearg and careful navigation would be needed. Morag suggested backtracking to the bealach and descending into Choire Ghranda as a safer way off and this seemed common sense to me. In the shelter of the cairn I used my phone to contact Tom, knowing that I would not get a signal apart from on the mountain top and then we made our way down in the lee of the old wall.

Morag's suggestion had been a good one because we came out from the cloud, the rain stopped and we could see clearly again. My compass could go back into my pocket. As we scrambled down to Loch a' Choire Ghranda we hoped that the cool wind would die down and the sun would return. We were not to know that July's heatwave had ended in that late afternoon of the month's last day.

Tom had sent a text to say that he would try to hitch back to Ullapool and if he was not at the car, we were to return without waiting. This meant that, if not picked up, he could have a long wait in poor weather, so we set ourselves a fast pace. This, however, is rough and wild country and the distances are huge. It was to take us some time to walk out.

Despite our tired legs and knowing that the walk had turned into a marathon, we enjoyed the return journey. Having seen the Beinn Dearg group in perfect conditions from a number of viewpoints, I think that it is at its very best from the floor of secluded Choire Ghranda. Surrounded by towering cliffs, we walked in silence along the east shore of the beautiful loch, surprising groups of red deer hinds and calves. At the corrie lip we took a south-east line from the outfall that tumbles down into the glaciated valley occupied by Loch Coire Lair and found a way along its west banks. We were again grateful for the dry weather as that route would be a heavy slog if the peat was saturated.

The last section down to the old shieling by the Allt a' Gharbhrain, crossing that stream and then rounding the spur to the south, seemed endless. It was with some relief that we got back to the car, after ten and a half hours of walking.

Back in Ullapool, we tracked down the others at an inn. Tom had tried to hitch but no one had been disposed to pick up a bearded young man wearing damp and dirty walking gear, carrying a dripping bag stuffed with brown trout. Having had little sleep the previous evening, he decided to have a nap beside the car in his survival bag. It was this that Dorothy and Cath saw as they drove past, my car and what looked like a body lying beside it. Memories of the previous year's mountain rescue flooded back. They stopped their car and ran to the bag, pulling it back to reveal a startled Tom. Rubbing his eyes he said, "Oh good, you can run me back to the hostel."

Morag, Tom (who had not eaten) and I left the company and went to the Seaforth, passing a group of drunken Spanish sailors on the way. We found a table and had hot food in front of us in minutes. I had seafood soup with mussels and a langoustine swimming in it and a large pan of mussels cooked in a white wine and garlic sauce. My companions tucked into soup and substantial seafood pies. There was little conversation at the start of the meal but the wine and good food soon had us laughing and chatting again. We toasted what had been a great walk and hoped for more to come.

Back at the hostel, Tom and Douglas picked up their guitars and accompanied by Fionn on his Irish whistle, played through the last hours of that big day.

It had rained overnight and the first day of August dawned grey and overcast. All but Morag had plans for the day, none of them involving climbing a Munro. Tom was to take the largest group to Coigach and show them the cliffs and a little cove at Reiff. So Morag and I put on our waterproofs and, ever optimistic, drove up the Loch Broom road, heading for the Fannaichs.

About half way up the loch I had to brake for a fallow deer. She stepped delicately from the trees along the shore, looking as if she was carrying a fawn, crossed the road and melted into the woods. I see roe deer almost daily in my local forest and red deer on most outings to the Highlands, but fallow deer are a rare treat.

Fallow deer
Ullapool 30/7 – 3/8 2006.
JPH

I turned onto the A832 at the Corrieshalloch Gorge and parked above the east end of Loch a' Bhraoin. We walked down the track to the ruined house, looking for clues about its age and history. Crossing the bridge over the outflow from the loch, we decided to take the steep path up the Leitir Fhearna crags.

I had decided to go slowly to compensate for the previous day's marathon, hoping to conserve energy should our last walking day turn out to be fair. Once on the Druim Reidh ridge, however, Morag stepped up the pace. It had been a year since her accident and three walking days in succession would test how her leg had healed. She said that she felt great and certainly had more vigour than I did at that point.

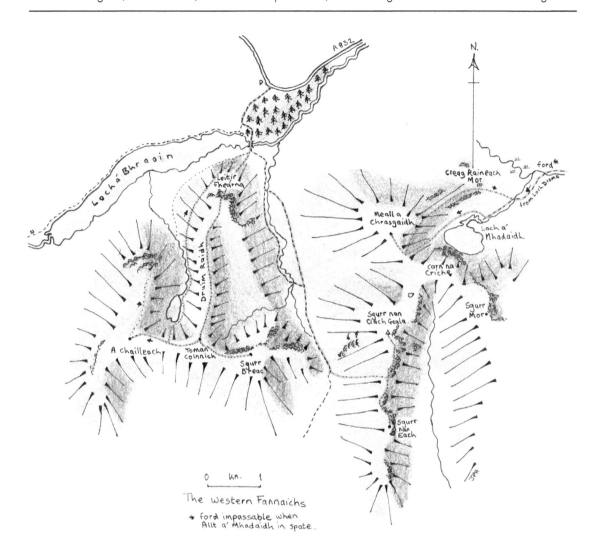

The western Fannaichs
* ford impassable when
Allt a' Mhadaidh in spate.

We stopped for a second breakfast on a rocky outcrop and the thin cloud that had been lying on or just above the ridge blew away, revealing the complex of mountains, corries and ridges that make up the Fannaichs. Over to the west we could see An Teallach, the colour of pale straw in the sunlight. Our break in the cloud did not last long and we were soon on our way, eyes focused on the near at hand rather than the wider views.

The path began to cut across the western slopes of Toman Coinnich, the cloud lifted for a while and we saw the steep cliffs of the corrie, surrounding the pretty Loch Toll an Lochain. We could see A' Chailleach towering above but the cloud came down again like a veil. The last section of that path before we reached the bealach at the head of the corrie needed extreme care. The rocks were slippery and the predominantly grassy slopes were long and steep. One slip and we would have hurtled down the wet grass.

The wind had shifted to the north and was funnelled down the corrie. It was difficult to stand up on the bealach but we decided to go to the top of A' Chailleach despite the conditions, always optimistic that the cloud might clear at the last minute.

The walk up was not as bad as we feared, most being in the lee of the mountain's east ridge. We stopped on the path just below the summit to have some lunch and were well sheltered.

The summit was not a place to linger. Rain was blowing across on the powerful wind, rattling off our jackets. Our plan was to walk off down the north ridge if the wind in our faces did not prove too uncomfortable. We could not see far in the cloud but a clear path led from the cairn. We followed it for a short distance then I noticed the wind drop. Knowing that this should not happen on the north ridge, I sat down with my GPS and map to work out our position. As I suspected, we were walking down the south ridge, about 180 degrees from our intended path. Yet again, I was reminded how easy it is to become disorientated in poor visibility and take the wrong ridge off a mountain.

Back up we went and caught the blast of the wind again on the top. Morag suggested cutting our losses by returning to the bealach and I readily agreed.

We got down quickly and began to follow the same narrow track under the steep flank of Toman Coinnich. We had not gone far before Morag said that she felt unsafe so we returned to the bealach and went down into the corrie. This was a good decision as the wind dropped and we came out from under the cloud. By the shore of the lochan we looked up at A' Chailleach, the old woman and decided that she was in a bad fettle that day.

As so often happens in the Highlands, the hard struggle of the past couple of hours was transformed into the most charming of walks. I could see the sun behind the thin cloud and it looked like it was going to break through. The loch was beautiful and we ambled along its shore. The stream that drained it tumbled in a series of little waterfalls over massive rocks. There were deep pools, perfect for a bathe after climbing on a hot day. Cloud still covered the tops but we could see enough for us to agree that this lovely corrie should be visited again.

Our last cup of tea was at the western end of the Leitir Fhearna crags. Sparse remnants of our ancient woodland survives on these crags, both east and west of the corrie from which we had descended. The deer fencing around these scattered survivors is an investment to encourage natural regeneration before it is too late. As we sat, the sun finally came out, bathing the hillside in a warm glow. We looked down at the loch, noticing old sheep fanks. The sheilings could well have been submerged by a rising water level.

I looked west, beyond the head of the loch to Mullach Coire Mhic Fhearchair and the other peaks of the Letterewe Forest, a wild and remote part of the Highlands and a place I looked forward to exploring.

Close at hand was a profusion of wild flowers. Bees buzzed by and a hawkmoth caterpillar stopped to sunbathe.

We sat a while and then wandered through the lowest trees of the remnant woodland, gnarled and hoary old alders, birch and rowan. I wished them good fortune in reproducing within their new fence.

At the ruined house we met a lone hillwalker who had joined the Paisley Mountaineering Club when he retired. He was hale and hearty and well on his way to completing the Munros. He talked about Skye and said that he was fortunate to have had the services of Gerry Ackroyd as his guide. We told him that we planned to complete the Skye Munros with Gerry next Easter and he said we had made a wise choice. It was comforting to hear this.

Back in Ullapool, Tom surprised us with his brown trout, baked in parcels with lemon and herbs. They were delicious. They were not enough for our main meal though and we were soon in The Arch where Dorothy helped the staff to organise us for dinner. Two large tables were pushed together, glasses of wine were poured and we enjoyed a good meal. I needed something substantial and the hot soup followed by venison pie did the job.

Later, at the hostel, I opened a bottle of Bowmore. The smoky, peaty fragrance seemed in harmony with Tom's sad songs.

It rained heavily during the night and the morning was windy and overcast. Everyone made plans but, yet again, only Morag and I wanted to go into the mountains.

We were soon driving up the Loch Broom road, hoping the weather would lift and we would see a bit of the Fannaichs. I parked at the western end of Loch Droma and we walked across the dam. It was so cold that we stopped at the south end to put on our jackets and hats, the heat wave seemed far away.

We went along the track to the Allt a' Mhadaidh, planning to go up into the corrie and there decide what to do next, depending, as always, on the weather. The huge hydro-electric pipe was full to the brim with water which roared along to Loch Droma under enormous pressure. This should have warned us what to expect as we walked up the valley.

The track ended and we followed a wet path which wound around the peat hags on the north side of the stream. The cloud base up ahead was around 600 metres and a cold wind blew from the north-west but at least there was no rain.

We saw the path go down before us to the stream and climb up the far side. When we got to the crossing place, however, the stream was a roaring river. A huge volume of black water surged past. A step into that would have been the last step a person made.

The only safe course of action was to follow the north bank and look for a crossing place. This was slow going as we found a way around deep flooded pools. It became complicated by a tributary coming in from the north-west. This also was a deep torrent, far too wide to consider jumping. After a considerable detour we found one possible crossing point where there was a massive submerged rock 10 centimetres beneath the water surface. The bank down to the rock was steep and we decided to go further upstream to find something better. Round the next bend though, the tributary had burst its banks and we stood on the edge of a small lake. It was the submerged rock or nothing.

Using the walking poles and taking our time we managed to cross and continued along a sodden path above the northern bank of the main stream. The path came to its end in a bog.

We had seen more frogs than on any walk I remember but now we began to spot black frogs. I guessed that such a variation made them more difficult to see in this landscape of black peat hags.

Peat hag frogs
JPH.

The north-westerly wind blew a fine rain along a line of crags to our right and we sat down to put on our waterproof trousers. I realised that the monochrome day, the endless bog and the slow progress were depressing our spirits so suggested we march to a rocky outcrop to have a hot drink and some food.

Once established on the slippery but flat surface of the rock with steaming cups of tea, things began to look better again. A peat hag formed the near horizon about 10 metres in front of us. I became aware of an animal, moving from right to left. It became elongated, flattened to the ground and turned to look at us. Sure that it was a wild cat, I alerted Morag. Its back became rounded and it bounded across our line of vision, every inch a predator, before disappearing down the far slope. My companion was even more pleased than I was at the sighting, having long wished to see this elusive animal in the wild.

Wild cat
Meall a' chrasgaidh 2/8/6.

Later, at home, I checked what I had seen written about wild cats and smiled when I read that frogs can be a major part of their diet. That's why the peat hag frogs need their black camouflage.

The wild cat arrived at the right time to brighten up our day and next the cloud began to lift, revealing Loch a' Mhadaidh and its huge corrie, walled on the far side with vertical cliffs of black rock. The corrie was full of the sound of water cascading down the cliffs to fill the loch to the brim.

We had left the spongy bog behind and walked over the rough but drier ground on the north side of the loch. At the back wall we decided to climb up beside a little stream to see what conditions were like on the bealach. The stream had formed a gully and we scrambled up to the top.

The bealach was in cloud but was calm, sheltered from the north-west wind by the most northerly of the Fannaich peaks, Meall a' Chrasgaidh, the hill of the crossing. The wide bealach must have been used at one time to cross the main Fannaich ridge.

We decided to climb the hill and set a bearing as we could not find a clear path. At the top we sheltered beneath the cairn and looked at the map. Neither of us liked the idea of going back over the rough ground of the corrie floor and the worst of the bog beyond. Could we find a way along the hill's north-east ridge?

Our descent was on a reverse bearing and, near the lowest point of the col, we picked up a clear path which seemed to run under the crest of the north-east ridge, high above the corrie. We made good time but were careful to stop and check our position with map and GPS. The path did just what we hoped and brought us to the crags of Creag Raineach Mor. Here we set a bearing to walk along the top of the crags and back to our path. We came down out of the cloud, joined our path just where we wanted and made good progress down the valley.

The flood water had subsided a little and the flat rock was only a few centimetres under water at our crossing place. The clouds were beginning to blow away and we got good views up to Beinn Dearg as we strode back to the car.

Dorothy had arranged a table in The Ceilidh Place and by 7.00 p.m. we were tucking into bowls of Cullen skink and chunks of home-made bread. Everyone else had ordered steaks but I chose pan fried monkfish tails with roasted peppers, an interesting salad and new potatoes. I listened to the others as they told the story of their adventures on the limestone above the Knockan Cliffs, of fascinating sink holes down which streams disappeared and attacks by vicious midges. We stayed a while to hear the folk band then ended the day listening to Tom singing all of our favourite songs while we drank the last of the whisky.

The next morning I took him to Badentarbet Pier and stowed his gear under the boat house. Stopping at Ralia on the journey home I read his text, "Base Camp in little cove overlooking Tannera Mor. Have set up ram's skull on pole. Grilling mackerel for lunch."

Ben Lui

At the source of the mighty Tay

September

The Jolly Boys had gathered at Stuart Wagstaff's place in Weem. As I walked through the old door I felt comfortable in this home away from home.

The others were in the lounge of the hotel, so I went to join them. I was weary after the week's work and the drive up to the Highlands but a glass of Lagavulin revived me, its powerful aroma seeming to have a beneficial effect before even taking a mouthful. A well-heeled group, ("Toffs," observed Struan), were being loud in the adjacent dining room. They finished their meal and began to wander into the lounge. A tall, fair chap leaned on the back of Cath's sofa and, in an emphatic voice, said, "You will have to move. We're a wedding party and we need these seats." His wife dragged him off to the bar in the nick of time as Struan was about to hit him.

We kept our seats but the wedding party, occupying the far end of the lounge, were so raucous with their drinking games that it became too much of an effort to speak.

It was much more pleasant in the bunkhouse common room. Over a cup of tea, we decided to come back there after our meal the following day.

Sleep is never abundant on such a hillwalking weekend. It seemed that I had only just nodded off when Fionn and Struan came noisily to bed at 3.00 a.m. Fionn had drunk rather a lot and gave a strident commentary as he attempted to get into his upper bunk. His first two attempts failed and I was glad that there were no sensitive souls in the room as his language was not polite. He tried to balance on a chair and luckily fell the right way, crashing into the bunk and banging his head off the wall in the process. There was instant silence. It crossed my mind that he could be dead but reasoned that it would make little difference if we discovered this in the morning. My conscience was just about to get the better of me when a rattling snore told me all was well.

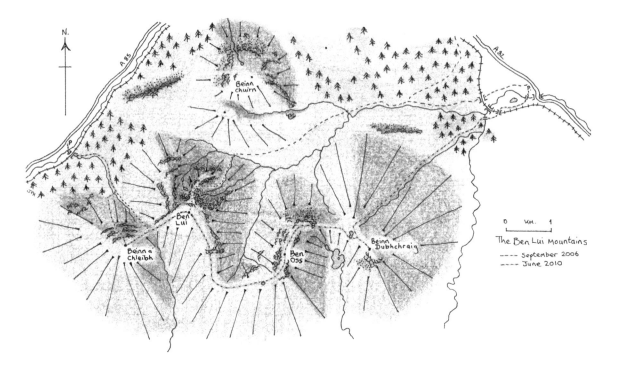

The Ben Lui Mountains
---- September 2006
---- June 2010

The morning dawned grey and damp, but Morag and I were soon on the road to Loch Tay. On a straight section with woodland on each side she slowed down as a buzzard flapped its broad wings to lift off from the roadside. Another buzzard rose beside the first and both went low into the trees to our left. A third, smaller, bird of prey shot out from those trees. It had a rabbit in its talons and it streaked into a close tangle of branches to our right, perhaps judging that the buzzards, with their bigger wingspan, could not follow.

There was no further excitement as we drove west along the shores of Loch Tay but I was reminded that, even on a grey September morning, this is a truly beautiful part of Scotland.

We parked at Dalrigh and within a few steps of the car the rain started. The Inuit have many names for snow, each describing a different type, and I often think that we should have more for Highland rain. This was light and tepid, increasing occasionally for a brief period as the wind rose a little. At times it would reduce to a drizzle and for long periods it stopped completely, giving us hope that it might brighten up.

I was surprised at how quickly we ate up the miles along Glen Cononish, we were soon looking up into the great north-east corrie of Ben Lui. We could see the craggy ends to each of the corrie's arêtes, like a pair of horns, but low cloud obscured the summit.

We left the excellent track and went down to the Allt an Rund. The burn was swollen with the rain and was well above the stepping stones but we crossed safely, our boots and gaiters keeping out the water.

A steep track then followed the stream which tumbled down from the corrie in a series of picturesque waterfalls. Little rowan trees, branches bent under the weight of bright red berries, grew from cracks in the black rock, soaked every few seconds by drifts of spray. As I walked beside this rushing, vibrant young stream I was aware that this is the very start of what grows into the mighty River Tay, which later carries the greatest volume of fresh water of any British river.

The corrie lip marked the base of the cloud so we stopped to have some tea and a bite to eat while we still had a grand view down the length of Glen Cononish to Strath Fillan.

The corrie felt enclosed. Occasionally the cloud thinned and swirled away, revealing very steep encircling walls and massive dark cliffs. The path seemed to vanish. We scouted about and decided that it continued alongside an infant stream which ran down the corrie's back wall. There were certainly boot prints. It was soon evident, however, that we were in an ever-steepening gully, not a safe place, especially in those wet conditions. We back-tracked and on a gentler gradient consulted the map. I knew that a Munro path followed the crest of the more northerly of the corrie's two arêtes, so we climbed north-west to hunt for it.

It was a relief to find it in those poor conditions. We marched up the ridge, setting a brisk pace to make up for time wasted in the gully. Two walkers came down, telling the same story of losing the path in the corrie. They, though, had been more sensible and had taken a bearing to the ridge rather than following a dubious track.

Determined not to make another navigation error, we stopped to eat some lunch. Morag pointed out strange shapes in the mist, one looked like the fuselage of a plane, crashed into the mountainside.

The ridge narrowed and we had to scramble up sections of bare rock. Just before the summit, I met a party of three hillwalkers. The leader was frustrated by the weather. He had guided his group up the north-western corrie and walked up the south-west ridge to the top. He had planned to take in Ben Oss and Beinn Dubhchraig but had got lost and confused on the bealach between Ben Lui and Ben Oss. The group had climbed back up to the summit of Ben Lui and were about to cut their losses and return the way they had come.

I stood and watched them go, waiting for Morag to complete the last section up through crags. At that moment, the cloud on the summit suddenly cleared. The sun shone in an immense deep blue sky and far below a layer of brilliant white cotton wool cloud covered the earth. Holes in that cloud revealed green patches of forest or stretches of sparkling river meandering on the floor of a glen. It was just like being in an aeroplane. Morag had been looking down, concentrating on each foothold and had missed this splendid moment, for when she appeared the cloud rolled back over the summit. I told her about the cloud clearing and the three walkers. As she saw neither, I am sure that she thought the strain of the ascent had done something strange to my brain.

Up we climbed, meeting three young men a few metres below the summit who were also having a tough time finding their way. They had tried to get down twice and both times had been forced to return. There was a hint of desperation about them so we described our ascent and advised them to walk down the same path, watching for a small cairn at the spot where the path onto the north-east ridge branched off. We told them that we would visit the summit cairn and then follow them down.

At the top of Ben Lui we agreed that there would have been little point in walking down the south-west ridge and then up to Beinn a' Chleibh, (something we had discussed as we walked along the glen that morning), as the swirling drifts of cloud spoiled any chance of a good view. I wanted my experience of Ben Lui to be better than this and added it to my list of mountains I would return to on a clear day.

As we turned back to the path a ptarmigan, still in its summer clothes, trotted away into a jumble of rocks. Down we went, watching carefully for the small cairn that marked the point to turn right. Despite our efforts, we missed it and I realised that we were on the north-west rather than the north-east ridge, our second navigation error of the day. This one, however, was easier to fix. After a quick check of the map we took a line due east across the top of the corrie, above two lochans. We followed a well-used path which took us up to the crest of the north-east ridge, right at the cairn we had tried to find.

We were soon on the same path we had followed past the waterfalls and the rowans. We saw the three young men far below. They too had missed the cairn and had come down the north-west ridge.

Ben Lui : walking back along
Glen Cononish. 2/9/6.

The walk back along Glen Cononish was most enjoyable. The rain had stopped, the sky was brightening and the cloud was lifting. The south side of the lower glen has a large section of natural Scots pine forest, protected by deer fencing. The pines, birches, rowans and alders were beautiful in their early autumn colours. A herd of Highland cattle grazed near the track, some red, some black and some beige. Their horns were surprisingly varied, some were huge and at 90 degrees to the head, others were equally impressive but curled rather than straight.

The hotel had set a long table for us all and we relaxed to a sociable and pleasant meal. I ate Weem Skink with crusty bread and a nicely cooked venison steak, washed down with a glass of merlot.

We retired to the bunkhouse after the meal and there I had a glass of Bowmore to round off my day. There was much merriment but my favourite moment was when Eric stood up unexpectedly, gave a crisp salute and sang us his repertoire of Boy's Brigade songs.

The next morning, the rain came down in sheets. I asked Morag if she was up for a walk and her expression gave me the answer. So I finished my breakfast, said my goodbyes and set off on the road home. The mountains were hidden by the weather but I knew they were there, waiting for me to return another day and that made me happy.

Beinn Mhanach and Beinn a' Chuirn

 Mountain spiders

October

S cotland was enduring wet, unsettled weather as a series of depressions passed over. The mountain forecast for Saturday was not promising, with only a 10 per cent chance of a cloud free summit and periods of heavy rain. As I had not had the opportunity to spend a day in the hills since the beginning of September, I was prepared to get wet. Struan and Morag were of the same mind and needed no encouragement to come with me.

I drove north through torrential rain on Friday evening but it was dry after Callander. I hoped that for once we had got it right and were heading to the driest side of the country.

We were staying at Jim's new hostel at Tyndrum. He showed us around and had a right to be proud. Buddhist prayer flags hung from the ceiling, framed maps with route descriptions lined the walls and a montage of sections of the local mountains decorated the cross beams.

The pub had its usual mix of weird and wonderful customers. Most races were represented and the chat was in English at fewer than half of the tables. It was comfortable and cheery and it was after midnight before we left.

I was on the road before I began to notice my surroundings the next morning. The sun was not yet over the mountain tops and the world was hushed and still. The ranges to the east were black silhouettes against vivid pink sky. The trees on the sides of Glen Orchy were coloured yellow, deep red and brown and to the north a dense white mist hung over Loch Tulla.

I parked at Achallader Farm and we walked past the old castle. It was three weeks into October and not long after dawn but it was as mild as a July morning.

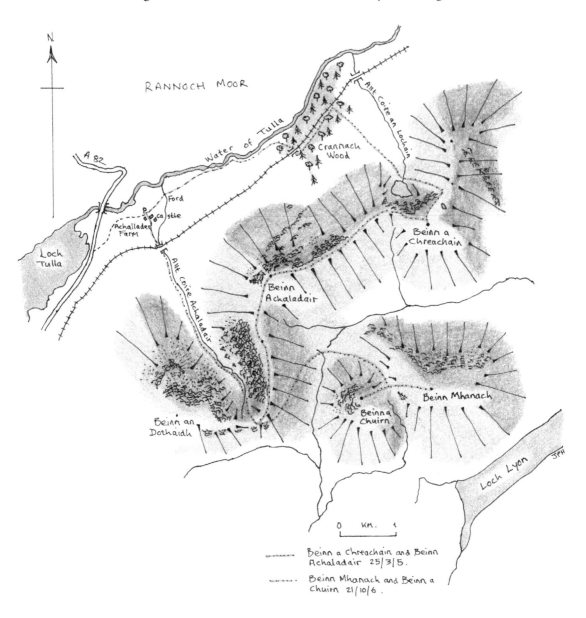

Beinn a Chreachain and Beinn Achaladair 25/3/5.

Beinn Mhanach and Beinn a Chuirn 21/10/6.

We followed the Allt Coire Achaladair up into the high corrie. The scattered birches and rowans along with the bogs and grasses of the steep sides gave us the full palette of autumn colours. The air was filled with the roaring of stags, amplified by the tall cliffs on either side. Twice we saw dominant stags leading their harem of hinds away across the slopes.

A large frog tried to swim to safety in a tiny pool, ending up going in circles. I wondered whether frogs were as active at this date in years past?

The corrie narrowed, with dark crags towering up to Beinn an Dothaidh on the one side and Beinn Achaladair on the other. We had been walking in shadow but the morning sun flooded the high bealach in front with a golden light.

Flat rocks provided a seat just before the highest point. There we enjoyed a hot drink and second breakfast, lingering to absorb the panorama of the Black Mount and the mountains beyond Loch Tulla. Stob a' Choire Odhair and Stob Ghabhar were clear of cloud and we decided that they might well be our next challenge.

We packed up and walked into the sunlight as we crossed over the crest of the bealach. The views on this side were even better. Beinn Dorain rose up to the south-west, separated from Beinn nam Fuaran and Beinn a' Chaisteil by the deep and steep-sided Auch Gleann. Creag Mhor could be seen to the south-east, a massive presence behind Beinn nam Fuaran.

Walkers should look for a small pile of stones on a flat rock as it marks the start of the path that traverses the eastern slopes of Beinn Achaladair. The narrow path leads to the bealach at 354 418, from where it is a straightforward climb up to the wide bealach between Beinn Mhanach and Beinn a' Chuirn. All the way along the side of Beinn Achaladair and up onto Beinn Mhanach's ridge we walked to the accompaniment of the autumn sounds of the rut.

As we strode up to the summit of the Munro, Struan startled a ptarmigan. It was interesting to see that its plumage had turned mostly white in preparation for winter. Strange indeed as we sweated up the slope on that day of summer warmth.

We went beyond the summit cairn to sit on rocks high above Loch Lyon and there we ate our lunch. The view was splendid, with Stuchd an Lochan rising beyond Loch Lyon's dam. Beinn Heasgarnich and Creag Mhor towered above the loch's southern shore. The Ben Lawers range filled the eastern horizon, its high tops free of cloud.

After lunch we walked along the ridge to Beinn a' Chuirn and there looked down into the deep, glacially scoured trough of the Auch Gleann, its steep walls rising to shapely peaks on each side.

We walked back along the track to the Coire Achaladair bealach in sunshine and sat by the pile of stones to have a last cup of tea. Morag had brought large scale maps to help identify surrounding mountains and it was as I put one of these onto the flat surface of the rock that I noticed the spiders. At first I counted only two or three and then I realised that there were dozens, all identical.

spiders on the Coire Achaladair
bealach. 21/10/6 .

They had oval shaped bodies, brown on top, yellow below, the colours separated by a zig zag line. Their movements were curiously slow for spiders. My companions packed up and began walking across the bealach, happy to leave me to study these strange creatures which were, by then, beginning to study me.

The walk back was made a pleasure by the mountain scene to the north and west. We stopped to enjoy it all, noting that cloud was beginning to touch the summits.

We changed out of our walking gear among the farmyard hens and I bumped the car down the track to the main road. At Bridge of Orchy Morag was reminding us of how lucky we'd been, considering the poor weather forecast, when the first raindrops of the day pattered onto the windscreen.

Stob Ghabhar and Stob a' Choire Odhair

 In the deep midwinter

January

The weather had been stormy and wet, many days barely light under the constantly moving ceiling of heavy grey cloud. The forecast, however, was for a window of brightness on January 2nd, which was why I was driving north with Morag on the evening of New Year's Day. I drove through heavy belts of rain, the rain turning to sleet as we got to the Trossachs. When the sleet stopped, the full moon showed that the mountains were capped with fresh snow.

Our gear was dumped at Jim's hostel in Tyndrum and we went to the pub. The atmosphere was as unusual as we had come to expect, a bizarre mixture of loud pop music, clacking billiard balls and people chatting in different languages. Even the English included the varieties spoken in Australia, Yorkshire and North America. I ordered a glass of Bowmore, half price as were all drinks on that New Year's night, put my feet up on a stool and quickly relaxed in the cosmopolitan company.

I was parked at Victoria Bridge as the sky lightened at dawn. Loch Tulla was like a sheet of glass, reflecting the old Scots pine trees which grow around its shores. Four hinds stepped elegantly across the road, not perturbed by our presence. The air was cold and clean, I breathed in deeply.

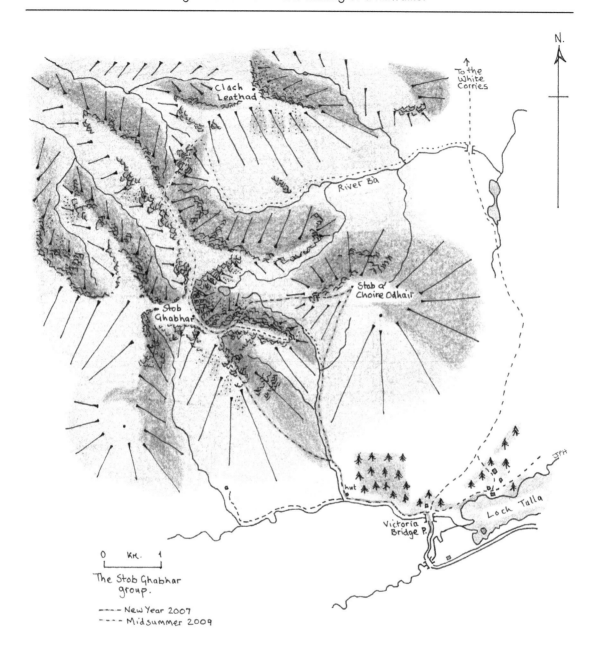

The Stob Ghabhar group.

- - - - New Year 2007
- - - - Midsummer 2009

Turning left, we walked along the track which follows the Linne nam Beathach (Abhainn Shira), passing under a canopy of the ancient pines. The lower branches of the trees, old stumps and even fence posts were bearded with pale grey lichen. I caught sight of something tiny moving along a branch and then saw others. It was a small flock of goldcrests, their orange hats like little sparks in the gloom under the conifers.

2/1/07 Goldcrests
at Loch Tulla.
JPH.

Coming out from under the trees, we stopped to look around. The sun was just high enough to make a gold line along Beinn a' Chreachain, Beinn Achaladair, Beinn an Dothaidh and Beinn Dorain to the east. Small clouds sitting just above the tops were coloured bright pink and the colour was reflected back onto the mountain snowfields. The sky above us and over to the west was dark blue, promising the good day predicted by the BBC weather team.

A solitary stag with impressive antlers looked up from his grazing on the south bank of the river and walked along with us. The track has a steep bank dropping to the left. Just ahead, another pair of antlers rose above the top of this bank and a stag ambled up. He had been feeding and had not noticed our approach. The fine animal crossed only two metres in front of us, showing no signs that he was in a hurry. We stopped to admire him as he climbed the bank on the north side.

2/1/07 Stag crossing track
(on way to Stob Ghabhar).

Beyond the place where the stag had crossed, looking west, the view was an artist's dream. The glen led deep into the snow-capped mountains, a landscape made romantic in the Victorian tradition by two majestic Scots pines in the middle distance.

A little green hut marks the point where a path follows the Allt Toaig, leading to Stob a' Choire Odhair, our first objective. The walking was easy but the sun was so low in the sky that we were soon in the shade of the Beinn Toaig ridge. It was frustrating to see the blue sky above and the brilliant light on the high snowfields. We decided to keep going until we were out of the shadow, our incentive a cup of tea in the sun.

The path crossed a burn with little waterfalls and then zig zagged up the south spur of the mountain. At 500 metres we were walking in soft snow. At 600 metres the snow was deep and walking was heavy work. At 750 metres we were in the sun at last and sat down to have a mug of tea and a snack. I had found the climb hard work and ate honey sandwiches to give myself a quick energy boost. We looked across to Stob Ghabhar, its summit and ridges glinting white. A deep corrie with a massive headwall is carved out of the eastern side, its walls lofty, narrow buttresses, a little lochan on its floor. We did not, however, linger to enjoy such views as there was no shelter from the NNW wind which streamed over the top of the western spur. I had kept on my gloves but my fingers were numb as I packed up my rucksack.

Setting off again, we stopped after only 20 metres as the snow was now frozen to hard ice and crampons were needed. Once they were secured, I swapped my gloves for my mitts, fastened my mountain jacket over my buffalo jacket and put my mountain cap on over my hat. Despite all this clothing, I was still rather cold. The weather forecast had predicted wind-chill temperatures as low as minus 20 degrees Celsius at this altitude. Ice axe in hand, I started walking again, Morag not far behind. This last section was hard going in those conditions, with the Arctic wind in our faces. I began to doubt whether we would be able to climb Stob Ghabhar, the higher of the two mountains.

Luckily, conditions were not as extreme when we reached the summit of Stob a' Choire Odhair. A trick of the topography had directed the icy airstream into us as we toiled up the frozen slopes. The views lifted our spirits and Morag was soon taking photographs in all directions. Rannoch Moor lay below and stretched for many miles to the north-east. It looked wild and desolate, a watery wilderness. On that clear day we could see the distinctive shape of Ben Alder beyond. To the south-east, the small clouds above Beinn Achaladair and its neighbours had kept their pink, making a picture postcard scene. It was to the north and west, however, that the mountains looked most grand. The snow cover and the low angle of the light combined to accentuate the dramatic peaks, sharp curved ridges and cliff-lined corries of the Glen Coe and Glen Etive areas. Dark brown mountains, white snow caps and chocolate clouds, we had climbed up to a land of cappuccino colours.

We could have stayed much longer but I checked the time and it was clear that we had to get moving if we were to climb the monster due west of our viewpoint and get safely down before the early dark of this midwinter day.

Our crampons gave great security as we descended the west ridge. Halfway down, we stopped in the shelter of some big rocks and ate lunch. It was a much less exposed spot than our last, with a wonderful view into the giant corrie. We picked out our route ahead as we ate, down to the bealach, up onto the corrie lip and then turning south to climb the steep and narrow Aonach Eagach ridge. This is a shorter feature than its famous namesake in Glen Coe but was going to test our skills in these conditions. Again, we could have lingered but we were now fighting against the clock.

Crampons were removed for the deep, soft snow of the bealach and corrie floor and we made good progress. At the foot of the Aonach Eagach we tilted our heads back to look up the white wall we had to climb. The lower slopes were not quite as steep and the snow was soft but we soon had to find a boulder to sit on to put on crampons again as the snow was replaced by ice. Near the crest of the ridge I looked down at the little lochan far below, this would not be a good place to slip.

The crest is narrow and rocky, not for the faint hearted in those conditions. At intervals a strong northerly wind picked up spindrift which blew over the top and made billowing clouds which dispersed to the south. Bracing ourselves against the gusts and placing each step with the greatest of care, we made slow progress up the ridge.

The way became easier when the Aonach Eagach merged with the south-east ridge. Ahead, there still seemed a mountain to climb to reach the top of Stob Ghabhar. A graceful cornice curved from where we stood to the summit, precariously overhanging the eastern corrie. The very lip of the cornice was rippled like Mr Whippy ice-cream.

In the west, the sun was sinking towards the tops of the Glen Etive and Glen Orchy peaks. The sky was so beautiful I was frozen to the spot as I marvelled at it. Immediately above the mountain tops it was a deep apricot colour, turning orange higher up where the sun itself was hidden by strange brown clouds. As we looked, two rich golden sunbeams shone from an orange gap in the clouds, striking the north shore of Loch Dochard below. I said, "Wouldn't it be something if they moved across the loch?" and they did just that. Once the sunbeams had turned the loch into a pool of molten gold they held their position for a minute or so before the brown clouds shifted.

The last climb up to the summit of Stob Ghabhar was straightforward. We made the most of our short time there soaking in the splendid views. To the north-west Bidean nam Bian rose majestically above the Glen Coe peaks. Between the two highest tops of Buachaille Etive Mor we could see Ben Nevis and the Mamores looked like a line of frozen white waves.

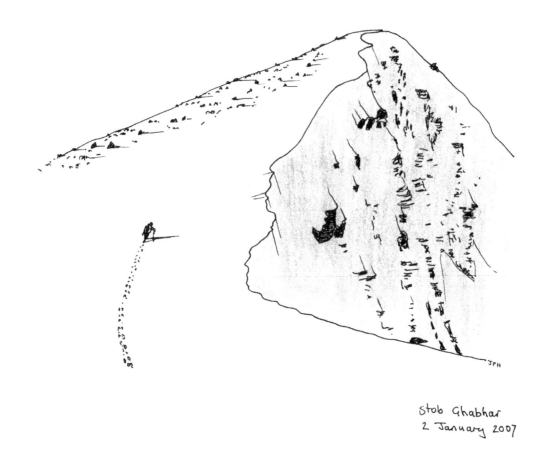

Stob Ghabhar
2 January 2007

The spectacle of the winter light and the long shadows had captivated Morag, who was taking photographs in every direction. I was glad when her film ran out and we started our descent; the light was fading fast.

The walk down the south-east spur was done at a gruelling pace. The first section was on ice, then we removed our crampons for soft snow, then we slithered down slush and mud. A swollen stream was crossed safely below a waterfall and we crossed the Allt Toaig on submerged boulders, using our poles for balance.

By the time we were on the track back to the little green hut the orange full moon in the eastern sky was giving us some much needed light. We got back to the car in darkness and quickly changed out of our hill gear. On the road from Victoria Bridge the headlights caught a large herd of red deer stags and hinds, young and old.

It had been a demanding day, with little time to stop, rest and take in liquid and fuel. My calf muscles were sore, we were both thirsty and in need of some warmth. I pulled off the road to the Suie Hotel in Glen Dochart, hoping for some comfort and sustenance there. An "open" sign was hanging on the door but the lights were off. I called and a surprised owner appeared. "I didn't think we'd have anybody tonight," he said, "where have you been?" We explained. "Oh God!" was his reaction. We asked whether he could provide us with a hot meal and he asked the cook, his wife. "Of course," she replied, "just sit down and make yourselves comfortable."

The lights were switched on, a wood and coal fire was lit in the hearth and we were brought a large pot of tea. Vegetable broth followed and then spaghetti bolognaise. The fire was soon roaring hot, the food was home-made and good and we finished off with another pot of tea. As we sat toasting ourselves we agreed that this was a perfect end to a perfect trip.

The Eildon Hills

The Eildons have played an important part in my life. I could drop off my wife to do some shopping in Galashiels, climb the three hills and return for Jane and her purchases, all in one afternoon.

After the New Year holiday in 2007, work pressures intensified and regular visits to the Eildons became a compensation for Highland expeditions I no longer had time for. Driving towards them from my home in nearby Kelso always filled me with pleasurable anticipation as they appeared, steep-sided and dramatic, mountainous in character despite their modest height.

I parked at Melrose Golf Club, followed the right of way to the footbridges and went through the little gate. With Lilly, my 15 year old Yorkshire terrier, at my heel I climbed steeply to the bealach between the North Hill and the Mid Hill, climbed the North Hill and returned. A little before the lowest point of the bealach we followed a track which branches off to the left, narrowing as it hugs the eastern and southern slopes of the Mid Hill. This track leads to the foot of Wester Hill which we climbed next. We then followed a track on the western side of its rounded summit which led down to the Little Hill. We walked around the base of this craggy outcrop on its east side and so came to the pink screes of the Mid Hill. This is the steepest climb. We would pause at the top to take in the 360 degree panorama over the heart of the Borders. The descent is steep, the sharp screes

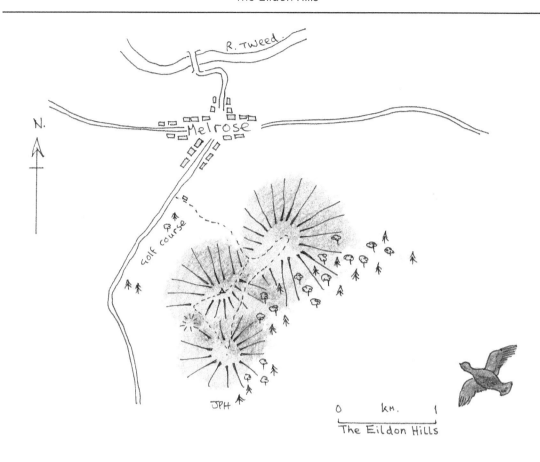

The Eildon Hills

slowing us both down. The final stage is a short walk to the bealach, turn left and steeply down to the start. From car to car this took one hour and ten minutes.

With each visit I began to notice more and think more about the hills. The lowest slopes are mostly clothed in mixed woodland. Higher up there is a middle zone of gorse and scattered hawthorns, a broad, horizontal yellow stripe in the months when the gorse has flowers. Higher again there is a zone of heather and the area around the highest summit is bare rock.

Regular walks helped me connect with the changing seasons. Early in the year I sometimes had the Eildons to myself, especially when the hills were white with snow, dramatic against a charcoal grey sky. In those winter months I was drawn to the beauty of the hawthorn trees. Strong black branches and long black thorns, their blood red berries the only colour on the hillsides. On the higher slopes, I often startled a red grouse which simultaneously startled me as it shot from the heather with a rapid cracking of wingbeats and a loud, raucous alarm call which shattered the stillness of the winter afternoon. I stopped to look at these tough little birds, similar in all but the white plumage to their

The Eildon Hills

northern cousins, the ptarmigan. Strange to be more familiar with the Highland clan than the birds in my own back yard.

With the spring came the sweet smell of the gorse, reminding me of the coconut haystacks my Grandma used to bake. One day, above the bealach, my attention was drawn to a loud noise like someone knocking two pebbles together. It came from a little bird perched on a hawthorn branch, not far from the path. The bird had a dark brown, nearly black, head and face, an orange breast and a white collar. As I walked up through the heather I noticed more of them, filling the air with their sharp calls. Back home, I used my old bird book to identify them as stonechats. It informed me that their breeding habitat is heather and gorse. I was interested to read that they can not survive severe winters and at the time of publication, 1973, they were confined to the west coast of Britain and to Ireland. Perhaps this is another indication that the atmosphere is warming.

I knew that summer had arrived when the hawthorns blossomed. I stopped to look at a branch which grew across the path at eye level. The bark was metallic grey, tapering to red where there was new growth. The leaves were small but distinctively shaped and a subtle olive green. The small white blossom heads were tightly packed and were all on

Stonechat.
Eildon Hills
20/5/07.

the upper side of the branch. The overall effect was a perfect blend of colour and form. I looked more closely at the individual blossoms and saw that they were more than white. Their centres were pale lemon and the outer edges of the petals were blushed with pink.

I had been trying to understand the geology. The three hills and the Little Hill are made of resistant igneous rock. The dark grey crags of Little Hill are of basalt whereas Wester Hill and Mid Hill have outcrops and screes of pink/orange felsite which is evidence of a modest sized intrusion or laccolith. North Hill is littered with strange stones but these are the remains of the walls of an Iron Age fort. These were timber-laced and were set on fire, the heat becoming so intense that the locally quarried building stones began to melt and fuse together. I have seen examples of such vitrified forts in other parts of the country.

Reading at home about the Eildon Hills laccolith gave me more information. The igneous material, (including felsite, riebeckite and trachyte), was intruded into the Silurian and Devonian sedimentary rocks during the Carboniferous period over 300 million years ago when Britain was near the Equator. The country rocks would have been pushed up into a great dome. A volcanic vent was forced through the laccolith and the domed sedimentary rocks at a later stage of the Carboniferous. The volcano has long been eroded away, only the stump of its vent remaining as Little Hill. The sedimentary rocks on top of the great dome have also been worn away, leaving the tough intrusive igneous rocks as the Eildon Hills of today.

When with my Munro climbing friends I have sometimes wished that I could stop more often and for longer. I want to absorb more. Even when taking my time I mostly say at the end of the day that I will have to return to begin to understand a particular mountain. One day is simply not enough. The cloud may have been down or I could have spotted lonely corries or steep-sided ridges to explore. The regular visit to the Eildons gave me a different, deeper experience.

Eildon Hills : geology.

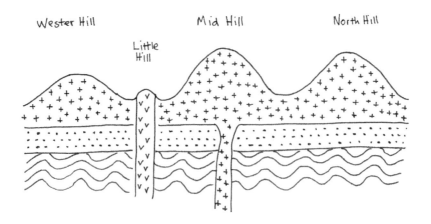

Wester Hill   Mid Hill   North Hill

Little Hill

	Basalt filled volcanic vent
	Felsite and other intrusive igneous rocks (laccolith)
	Old Red Sandstone
	Silurian

Lilly, painted by Mairi, one of my daughters.
(Keen-eyed readers will already have spotted Lilly)

1st to 6th April 2007

The Cuillins

April

The weather was uncharacteristically warm and bright as I drove up to Skye with Morag at the start of the Easter holiday. It matched my mood, lifted by a morning in Edinburgh spent with my handsome third grandson, Joe, only hours old. We stopped in Glen Coe at the foot of Buachaille Etive Mor, just above the mountaineering club hut. I was still smiling as I sipped tea in the spring sunshine.

Loch Harport was a warm red colour when we arrived at The Old Inn where we were to be based for the week. We ate a pleasant meal there that evening, with a comforting glass of red wine, hoping that the good weather had not come too soon for us.

My bedtime reading was about the geology of the Cuillins. A summary of what I learned follows but readers could skip this bit.

In the Tertiary period, which ended two and a half million years ago, Skye was covered by basalt lava flows. A gabbro intrusion pushed up these basalt lavas into a dome, now mostly eroded away, although there are remnants on top of Gars-Bheinn and Glamaig. The rising magma of the intrusion fractured the overlying rock and cone sheets were injected into the fractures.

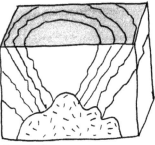
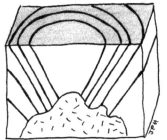

1. Rising magma fractures overlying rock.

2. Cone sheets are injected into the fractures.

The cone sheets are composed of similar basic minerals to the gabbro, being from the same plutonic source.

After the cone sheet activity ceased there was a granite intrusion, now the rock of the Red Cuillin.

At the end of the Tertiary basic dykes of basalt and dolerite were injected to fill cracks and these cut across all structures. These basic dykes are generally less resistant to erosion, forming the gullies and chimneys of the Cuillins. The notched and jagged crest of the ridge is partly due to this. Some, however, are more resistant than the gabbro and they stand out like the Inaccessible Pinnacle, but this is not typical.

The geology, followed by millennia of erosion, especially glacial, has given us the features we see today.

The diagram below shows how this geological story is related to the topography.

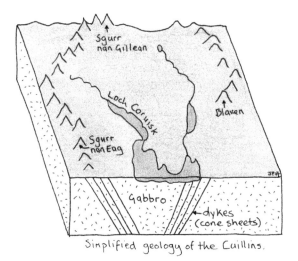

Simplified geology of the Cuillins.

Sgurr a' Mhadaidh, Sgurr a' Ghreadaidh and Sgurr na Banachdich

The Brocken Spectre

At dawn the next day there was not a cloud in the sky. I went out onto the balcony which sits above the sea loch and took a photograph of the sun rising over the mountains.

I had to scrape ice off the car windscreen and then drove slowly down Glen Brittle, stopping at times to watch sunbeams streaming through the peaks, creating fantastically graded bands of light.

Gerry Ackroyd was still in his boxers when we arrived, so we went for a walk on the beach to put some warmth into our muscles.

At 9.30 we had Gerry in the car and five minutes later had picked up Andrea, our Irish companion for the week.

We parked at the Youth Hostel and as we set off a lark sang high above, a small speck in the blue morning sky. Gerry led us up into Coire a' Ghreadaidh and then up to the approach to An Dorus. My jacket was stowed in my rucksack within 15 minutes and I had put on my sun hat. I crossed my fingers that the good weather would hold.

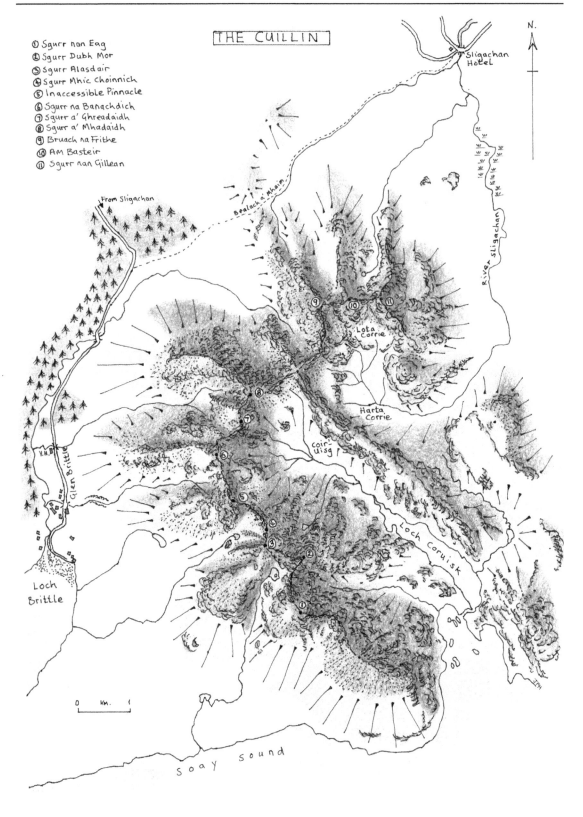

THE CUILLIN

① Sgurr nan Eag
② Sgurr Dubh Mor
③ Sgurr Alasdair
④ Sgurr Mhic Choinnich
⑤ Inaccessible Pinnacle
⑥ Sgurr na Banachdich
⑦ Sgurr a' Ghreadaidh
⑧ Sgurr a' Mhadaidh
⑨ Bruach na Frithe
⑩ Am Basteir
⑪ Sgurr nan Gillean

Sligachan Hotel

N.

From Sligachan

Bealach a' Mhaim

River Sligachan

Lota Corrie

Harta Corrie

Coir-uisg

Y.H.

Glen Brittle

Loch Coruisk

Loch Brittle

Soay Sound

0 KM. 1

(The map on the previous page shows the whole of the Black Cuillin Ridge but I have drawn a sketch map to illustrate each day's route more clearly, starting with this one.)

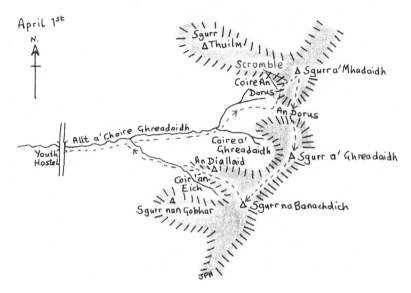

Just before the notch in the Cuillin Ridge below An Dorus, Gerry led us to the north and we began to scramble up the gritty gabbro rock. On a platform below Sgurr a' Mhadaidh we left our rucksacks, put on our climbing helmets and began the steep climb up to our first Munro.

From the top the Cuillin Ridge, bare and jagged, seemed like the old bones of the Earth. We stayed there for a while, enjoying the spectacle and taking photographs before Gerry led us down to the rucksacks and a quick lunch.

Back on the ridge, we were descending to the An Dorus notch when wisps of white cloud drifted up from the corrie. I was thrilled to see my magnified shadow reflected against it, surrounded by a perfect rainbow. This was a Brocken spectre, its circular rainbow named a glory by early Scottish mountaineers.

I had read about this phenomenon but had never experienced it. The Brocken spectre was first described in the Hartz Mountains of Germany, being named after the highest in the area. I spent a while waving my arms, watching the giant shadow do likewise but had to leave this marvel all too soon as Gerry did not slacken his pace for such trivial reasons.

We scrambled up to the next Munro, Sgurr a' Ghreadaidh, the rough gabbro cutting the soft skin of my hands. I stopped to admire a small star-shaped plant firmly attached to a crevice, (whitlow grass I think). I marvelled at how anything could survive in this wilderness of unforgiving rock.

After a short breather, we set off for Sgurr na Banachdich. The fine cloud that had streamed up to provide the screen for my Brocken spectre had drifted away and we were climbing again in hot sunshine.

On the top of Sgurr na Banachdich I left the others to trace the path Morag and I had followed from the summit in the summer of 2005. I stopped at the sharp-bladed rock that had cut into her leg when she had fallen and remembered the trauma of that day. Back with the others, we shared memories of the experience. Gerry was leader of the local mountain rescue team at the time and was one of the people who talked to me by phone as the rescue was co-ordinated. He was interested to hear the details.

The conversation moved away from that bad time and we drank tea in the warm sunshine. I watched Morag as she chatted and laughed, pleased that the ghosts of her accident had been exorcised.

We walked down into Coir' an Eich, tired, silent but happy after a perfect day in these remarkable mountains.

We ate in The Old Inn again, at a table beside the coal fire and enjoyed the company of those who had come to Skye to enjoy its peace and beauty.

2/4/07

Sgurr Mhic Choinnich
and The Inaccessible Pinnacle

"A knife-edged ridge"

April 2nd was another perfect morning. We stretched our legs on the beach and then met Gerry at 9.30 a.m. We walked in silence, enjoying the spring smell of warm grass and a lark singing his joyful song.

Our guide led us past Loch an Fhir-bhallaich and round into Coire Lagan, a massive hushed amphitheatre with the glistening blue water of Loch Coire Lagan on its floor. The ominous rock walls, ribbed with buttresses separated by shadowed gullies, led the eye to a skyline studded with sharp pinnacles like a shark's jaw. Gigantic screes, including The Great Stone Chute, tumble down to the floor in pale coloured fans. Around the little loch are rounded, ice-smoothed humps of black rock, littered with huge boulders dumped as the last of the glaciers melted here.

Gerry led us up the west side of the corrie, along a line where the scree cone left the rock wall. Just below the ridge, we stopped to eat lunch. Morag found a little cave but the rest of us were fine in the warm sun. As I ate, I watched a raven silently circle around the corrie walls, slowly rising to the line of the ridge.

We left our rucksacks and our guide led us up to the ridge and around the rim of the corrie south to Sgurr Mhic Choinnich (pronounced "skoor veech conneech" by Gerry).

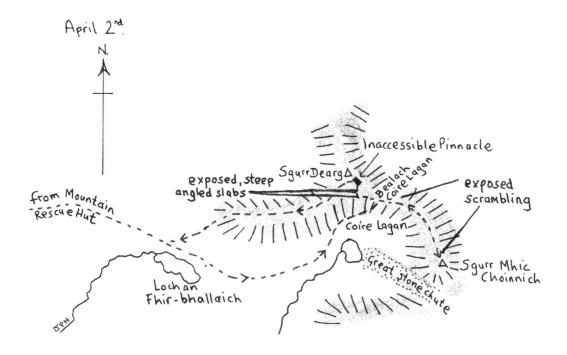

April 2ⁿᵈ

N.

from Mountain Rescue Hut

exposed, steep angled slabs

Sgurr Dearg△

Inaccessible Pinnacle

Bealach Coire Lagan

exposed scrambling

Coire Lagan

Great Stone Chute

Sgurr Mhic Choinnich

Lochan Fhir-bhallaich

JPH

I was soon concentrating on some serious scrambling, my hands searching the coarse gabbro for secure holds. The ridge became a narrow knife edge and I had a constant feeling of exposure. Every move had to be made with care as any mistake would have been fatal. The route included vertical chimneys, overhangs and the narrowest of ledges above precipitous drops. There was no conversation.

The top was narrow and had an unexpected plaque in memory of a climber. I have no wish to offend the family or anyone else but I would rather the plaque had not been there. Our precious areas of wilderness should be left as such.

We made our way back to the rucksacks in the warm sun and then up the east ridge of Sgurr Dearg. This was the most nerve-wracking part of the day. Slowly, we picked our way up steeply angled slabs covered with loose scree of various sizes. There were few secure foot or hand holds.

It was with great relief that I found myself at the foot of The Inaccessible Pinnacle. This Nemesis of so many would-be Munroists was described by W. H. Murray in his classic Mountaineering in Scotland as, "a knife-edged ridge, with an overhanging and infinite drop on one side, and a drop on the other side even steeper and longer." I had wondered whether I would have to battle with nerves at the prospect of the climb but I felt both excited and calm.

Gerry attached a rope to each of the ladies and up they climbed. My job was to use a length of cord to pull the rope back. This I did, then I attached the rope to my harness and it was my turn.

I went up quickly, easily finding secure holds. After 20 metres or so, I switched to the north side of the rock fin, the side which overhangs the massive drop to the corrie below. I stopped to look at this huge leaning blade of rock and suddenly felt small as I clung to its crest.

Starting again, I joined the others on a small section with enough space to stand and cling on. Again my job was to bring up the rear, removing the sling before I climbed. I watched the ladies go before me, retrieved the rope, attached it to my carabiner, removed the sling and began my climb. Most of the climb was straightforward, only one section being challenging. This was where the Pinnacle narrows to a sharp blade and the holds are much smaller. At one point my legs were on either side, edging up to find a toe hold.

On top of the
Inaccessible
Pinnacle.
Easter 2007

Soon, however, I was on the top, feeling exhilarated and it was time for photographs. I had waited a long time for this moment.

I was the first to abseil down and I did so with an assurance that surprised me. I leaned back, spread out my legs and did a professional job. I lay at the foot of the Pinnacle and photographed the ladies as they, in turn, abseiled expertly off the top.

We then went back for the rucksacks, climbed up to Sgurr Dearg, found a sunny spot out of the wind and had a celebratory cup of tea while we waited for Gerry. I ate some honey sandwiches and lay back on the warm rock at peace with the world. A beautiful female snow bunting hopped up close and I gave her a crumb.

Our guide appeared, we packed up the gear and then set off down the west ridge of Sgurr Dearg. We thanked him at Stac Lee for another perfect day.

Back at Carbost, The Old Inn had a chef in place for the season and our meal was splendid. I ate a piping hot bowl of herby home-made broth followed by a large plate of roast beef with potatoes and vegetables. A glass of red wine was taken to aid my ageing digestion.

3/4/07

Sgurr nan Eag, Sgurr Dubh Mor and Sgurr Alasdair

The Great Stone Chute

Miraculously, the day dawned without a single cloud in the dark blue sky. We marvelled at our good fortune as we ate breakfast and made sandwiches for the day ahead.

There was time for a walk on the beach before meeting Gerry. The sparkling water of Loch Brittle was as still as a millpond.

Gerry set off at a cracking pace, heading down to the dunes south of Loch an Fhir-bhallaich and then round into Coir' a' Ghrunnda. We stopped on the first basalt slabs for a drink and to stow our walking poles. Gerry said, "I suppose we should thank The Management for the good weather." I assured him that I had laid it on specially.

We climbed to the corrie over massive rounded outcrops of basalt. The glacier had smoothed and polished the rock. Some of the larger boulders carried within it had made deep scratch marks as they were scraped over the surface and when the ice had finally melted, these boulders had been dropped to litter the corrie lip.

The corrie is huge, lined by towering walls of frost-shattered gabbro. Its floor is occupied by Loch Coir' a' Ghrunnda, bright turquoise and deep Prussian blue in the strong light of that morning. We stopped for lunch by the shore of the loch, awed by the scale of this amphitheatre of rock.

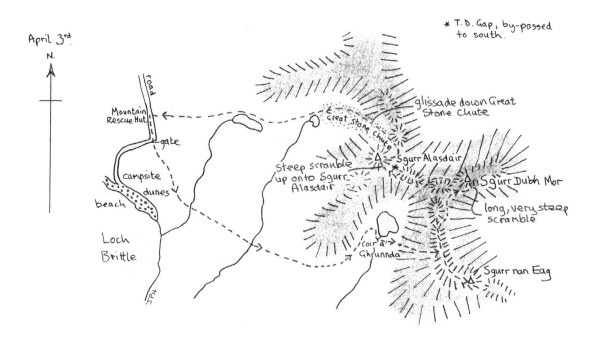

After our brief stop, we were led up the screes on the east wall of the corrie and we left the rucksacks just below the ridge. Following our guide, we scrambled up and through giant blocks of rock, heading south and then south-east to Sgurr nan Eag, our first Munro of the day. We sat on the top in tee shirts, enjoying the superb views in all directions.

The scramble back seemed longer. We collected the sacks and clambered over the crest of the ridge to the very top of the black wall of An Garbh-choire. We had begun to understand Gerry's close relationship with these mountains, a relationship that began at his garden gate. An expression of this was the way that he looked after his paths, kicking away rocks that had rolled onto them and often stooping to pick up a loose rock and hurl it down the mountainside, muttering grumpily as he did so.

We carefully worked our way east until directly below Sgurr Dubh Mor, a near vertical wall of rock between us and the summit. Our guide left us no time to think, however, as he was already climbing this daunting face. He would sense if one of us was in difficulty, look down briefly and give a clear instruction or two to get our feet onto the best holds. Up we went and up and up. After the longest and steepest climb we had done, he announced that we were there.

Looking back at Sgurr nan Eag, I could see that it was like a shapely volcanic peak, complete with small crater. Looking west, we could see the incredible blade of The Inaccessible Pinnacle and then, sweeping north, the whole of the Cuillin Ridge. Gerry named each peak from north to south, showing endless patience when one of us lost the place. It was fascinating to see the peaks from this point, Sgurr na Banachdich in particular looking its best by displaying its triple spires.

As we gingerly climbed down, I noticed the little pink flowers of rose root, another tough plant that seems to survive on vertical slabs of bare rock.

Then we were off again, through the high bealach just west of the summit and then crossing the Bealach Coir' an Lochan to pass the Thearlaich Dubh Gap on its west side. We stopped here, high above the vast, silent Coir' a' Ghrunnda. I drank a mug of tea and ate a chunk of fruitcake to give me some much needed energy.

The next section, the climb up to Sgurr Alasdair, was another long section where our hands were gripping the rough gabbro. Mine, used only to holding a pen or tapping the keys on my laptop, were covered in little cuts, the fingers sore and tender.

Sgurr Alasdair was a fantastic vantage point. We got the clearest of views across to "The Pin", as Gerry called it, down into Coire Lagan and out to the metallic blue of the Hebridean sea. We sat, baking in the sun, chatting and joking about our incompetent political leaders.

Then we climbed down to a dark chasm, the beginning of The Great Stone Chute. I had read about this in many books and it seemed surreal that I was here, ready to go down it.

At the top of the
Great Stone Chute
3/4/7.

I was thrilled by the feeling of rapid descent as I glissaded down the sharp pieces of blue/grey basalt. It was hard on the feet, hard on the knees and even harder on my poor boots. It needed 100% concentration as a trip and stumble could well have resulted in serious damage. In next to no time I was on the corrie floor, photographing the ladies as they clattered down the long, steep cone.

All were bruised and breathless so we sat on the polished rock of the corrie lip for a while to recover. Then it was home at a brisk pace.

At Stac Lee, Gerry announced that the next day was our day off.

We ate that evening in The Old Inn at the table beside the glowing coal fire. The chef's tomato and basil soup and vegetable lasagne were both good and filling. I was tired as I finished my glass of wine but happy.

4/4/07

Glamaig

"Rest day"

The morning was misty, driech and overcast. Andrea needed time to herself so I drove Morag to Portree for provisions, wondering how to spend this day off. On the way back the mist lifted, the clouds rolled away, the blue sky reappeared and the Cuillins were revealed as if by magic. We knew full well that we should be resting but the lure of the mountains in such perfect weather was too much. We parked at Sligachan and decided to have a walk up the Allt Daraich, heading for the bealach between Glamaig and Beinn Dearg Mhor.

The Allt Daraich was a surprise. It winds its way through gorges with fantastic rock formations, spilling from pool to pool in a series of waterfalls. The rock was blue jade coloured in many of the pools and the water crystal clear.

Just under the Bealach na Sgaird is a sheltered stony bowl with the infant river bubbling and chattering across its floor. The sun streamed in and it was as hot as a fine midsummer day. Morag sensibly decided to sunbathe. I, much less sensibly, decided to climb Glamaig. I left my rucksack, took a big drink of water and set off.

I was unprepared for the relentless slog up its steep slopes. It was the most strenuous thing I had done on the trip and the irony of it happening on my rest day was not lost on me. It was with heartfelt relief that I trudged through the snow patch on top and up to the summit cairn. I recommend this vantage point on such a fine, clear day as the views

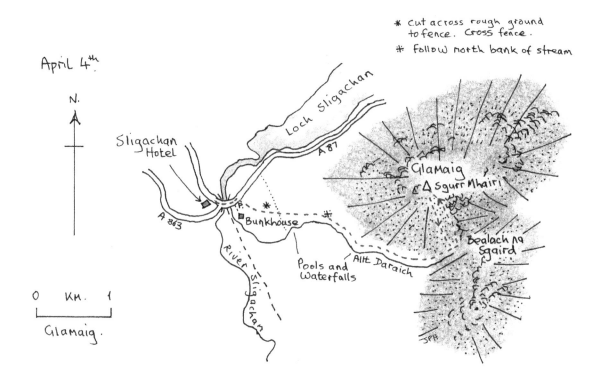

April 4th.

N.

Sligachan Hotel

Loch Sligachan

A 87

Glamaig

Sgurr Mhairi

Bealach na Sgaird

A 863

Bunkhouse

River Sligachan

Pools and Waterfalls

Allt Daraich

✱ cut across rough ground to fence. Cross fence.
✚ follow north bank of stream

0   KM.   1

Glamaig.

were magnificent. I spent a while there naming the surrounding ranges and peaks. Ben Nevis stood tall above all the others, its snow cap gleaming in the sun. Looking down on Sconser's little row of houses was like the view from a plane.

I retraced my steps and stood on the beginning of a scree cone, the bealach far below. I had a twinge of nerves about the steepness of my descent but the scree began to move and I was then unable to think about anything but staying on my feet. This is a longer and steeper scree cone than The Great Stone Chute and I went down at a tremendous pace. When I appeared in Morag's sun trap my knees were like jelly and the soles of my feet were sore. It had taken 70 minutes but would have been much longer without the sudden descent.

It was 4.00 p.m. when we returned to The Old Inn, so much for our day off. I cooked a large meal of pasta which we washed down with a glass of red wine and then I relaxed in the good company of the bunkhouse for the evening.

5/4/07

Bruach na Frithe, Am Basteir and Sgurr nan Gillian

Larks and a sea eagle

We met Gerry at Sligachan and he led us at a brisk pace along the track which leads to Am Basteir. There was a cool breeze and the sun was scattering its light and warmth through holes in the clouds. Larks had sung for us on each of the walks into the mountains and again that morning the air was full of their strident song.

As we climbed over the ice-smoothed rocks of the lip of Coire a' Bhasteir, we looked up to see the cloud lifting from Pinnacle Ridge. The very top of Sgurr nan Gillian was still hidden. We reached the corrie floor and stopped to look at the rock walls, soaring to sharp needles which stabbed into the drifting white cloud.

The path goes in zig zags steeply up the back wall of the corrie, following a long chute of scree. At the top, just under the sheer rock walls of Am Basteir, we left the sacks and made our way up the loose rocks to the Bealach nan Lice.

At the bealach, Gerry led us west along the narrow path around the rim of the Fionn Choire. We then scrambled up to the narrow east ridge of Bruach na Frithe. Stopping at a gap between rock towers, we looked through the window down to the depths of Lota Corrie, which was bathed in bright sunshine. The climb up to the Munro summit was not

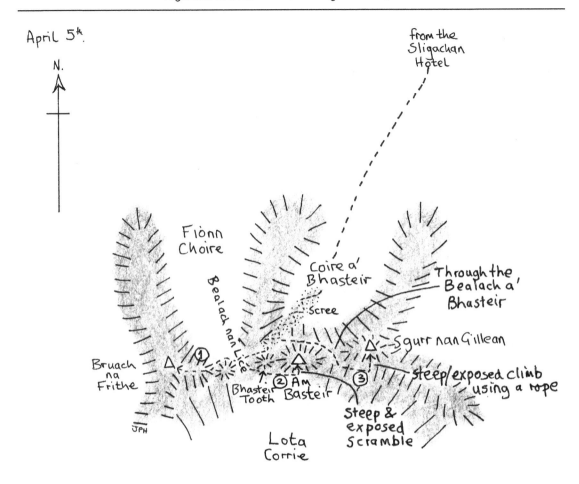

April 5th.

N.

from the
Sligachan
Hotel

Fionn
Choire

Coire a'
Bhasteir

Bealach nan Lice

Scree

Through the
Bealach a'
Bhasteir

Sgurr nan Gillean

Bruach
na
Frithe

① ②Am
Bhasteir Basteir
Tooth

③

steep/exposed climb
using a rope

Steep &
exposed
Scramble

Lota
Corrie

JPH

difficult. Standing by the old triangulation pillar, I joked with Gerry about his failure as a guide in that there were no clear views for us to photograph. He had just replied that this was the responsibility of "The Management" when the thin white cloud drifted away and a panorama of the Cuillin was opened up. I was particularly interested in the views south to Loch Coruisk and east across Glen Sligachan to the mountains of the Red Cuillin. Glen Sligachan is deep, steep-sided and flat floored, a giant trench separating the two Cuillin ranges. The elegant profile of Bla Bheinn dominated all else.

Gerry briskly retraced his steps to the bealach and then dropped to the southern base of the Bhasteir Tooth. I stopped to gaze up at this monolith, soaring up into the wisps of cloud far above and wondered whether I would ever have the confidence and skill to climb its near vertical walls. With this thought still in my mind I watched as Gerry began to climb up a similarly steep face. I had no opportunity to ask questions, so I looked for the first foot and hand holds and followed. An exhilarating climb with one exposed section led to the top of Am Basteir.

Ghostly veils of cloud obscured the view of the Tooth to the west and Sgurr nan Gillean to the east. Looking down into Coire a' Bhasteir and Lota Corrie, we could see the pale yellow glow of the spring sun. We sat for a while to see if the cloud would clear again and it did. We photographed the fantastic black Tooth and the imposing Sgurr nan Gillean before Gerry started to descend, muttering that he needed his lunch.

All lunch stops with him were brief. I had learned to eat and drink quickly, trying to pack in as much energy-producing food as possible before he fastened his sack and stood up, the signal to go again.

We scrambled up to the Bealach a' Bhasteir and were soon climbing up, over and round the outlandish rock formations of the ridge. At the foot of a wall of rock which towered up to the skyline Gerry asked us to leave our packs and put on our climbing harnesses.

Standing at the base of a long, narrow chimney, we watched as two young mountaineers secured their ropes to descend it. Gerry lost his patience, growled, "Come on, we'll be here all day" and shot up the crag face to the right of the chimney. I followed, as did the others, concentrating on each hold. It was not until we had climbed around and above the two young people that I considered the fact that they were using a belay and ropes while we, the amateurs, were not. Our guide, however, was not one to give a client time to think ("too much thinking is bad for you"). He was sorting out the rope and giving instructions as he did so, once only, one just had to take it in first time.

He climbed up to a smooth buttress of rock, edged around it, then up a short chimney, up and over a rock shaped like a steep gabled roof and then onto some giant boulders. Then it was my turn. I clipped the rope to my carabiner and started the climb. I took my time to find solid holds, trying always to make each movement as short as possible and not over stretch. The buttress was the most challenging as there was a slight overhang and as I edged around it I stole a look down to the corrie floor 400 metres below. Secure on the rope, I enjoyed every moment of the climb.

The others came up after me to the narrow perch on top of the boulders. Gerry then left the ropes and began to scramble up the next pitch. As I followed I reflected on the fine line between needing a rope on the last section and climbing without one on this. From above came Gerry's gruff voice, "Too much thinking is bad for you."

We pulled ourselves up and onto the final eroded column of rock and we were on top of Sgurr nan Gillean, the last of our Black Cuillin Munros. The summit of this steep-sided pyramidal peak is narrow and the mountain is taller than its neighbours. The shreds of cloud had blown away and we found ourselves struggling for superlatives as the whole of the Cuillin Ridge stretched from our feet in a great arc to the south.

My attention was drawn back to Am Bhasteir as a bird was steadily flapping its enormous wings just above the sharp summit. It was a sea eagle and we watched this elegant bird as it gained height and then glided along the ridge to Bruach na Frithe. As it circled this peak, Gerry suggested that it was looking for carrion, "Like a climber who has fallen or something like that." We watched as it glided down past the crest of the ridge to Glen Brittle.

5/4/7   Sea Eagle above Am Basteir
JPH

We sat for a while on this mountain top, comfortable in the calm, warm air, watching the pale golden patches of sunlight moving over the corries and lochs far below. Gerry talked about the four months of winter he had just endured, when it had rained nearly every day.

When it was time to go, we climbed down to the ropes and Andrea was the first to attempt the exposed pitch. She found it difficult, perhaps because it was impossible to avoid looking down. Gerry, suddenly tense, shouted instructions for every move, sensing that she had lost her confidence. Sometimes he shouted the same instruction a number of times and Andrea began to get flustered. Safely down, she stood wide-eyed and frozen while Gerry repeatedly shouted for her to release the rope from her carabiner. This was the only moment in that week when one of us showed any nerves, a testament, I am sure, to the qualities of our experienced guide.

Morag went next and I followed, enjoying each move and being rewarded with a brusque, "Well done," at the end.

We removed the climbing harnesses, packed them and the ropes in the rucksacks and set off down the mountain, Andrea laughing now as she recounted what she called her "wobbly". At the top of the scree slope I took out my walking poles, hoping that using them would take some of the strain from my knees.

As we walked over the corrie lip, I looked back at Pinnacle Ridge, soaring up to terminate in a series of gigantic dinosaur's teeth. That, I told myself, was for another day.

The walk back to Sligachan was long but pleasant in the spring sunshine. I had a great feeling of contentment as I followed the gurgling water of the Allt Dearg Beag, admiring each of the sparkling waterfalls and crystal-clear turquoise pools.

Back at Carbost we took our favourite seats by the open fire in the Inn and were told that the chef had sirloin steaks. I ordered mine rare and it was cooked perfectly, just what I needed after five days in the mountains. Back in the bunkhouse, we swapped stories with our fellow walkers. I enjoyed listening to one of them in particular, a white-bearded man, long retired. He had known many climbers, including Bill Murray, author of the wonderful 'Mountaineering in Scotland' and 'Undiscovered Scotland'. I had some sherry finished Talisker and he accepted my offer of a glass or two as a nightcap. I drifted off to sleep with my head full of the exploits of these legendary characters.

6/4/07

Bla Bheinn

Farewell to Gerry

D awn broke on Good Friday with pale pink sky reflected in Loch Harport. Incredibly, it looked like it was going to be another fine day.

We met Gerry at the Glen Brittle road end and followed his car to Sligachan, Broadford and then to the brae leading down to Loch Slapin. The tide was in and barely a ripple stirred the dark blue water. Beyond lay our last challenge of the week, the elegant Bla Bheinn. It was so beautiful that I wanted to stop and take a photograph but Gerry's car was already rounding the head of the loch.

We parked in a forestry car park just beyond the bridge over the Allt na Dunaiche. As we made ready for the day I looked at the map and remarked that Bla Bheinn was more of a range than a single mountain. The southernmost mountain has two summits and it is hard to tell which is the higher. North of this runs a pinnacled ridge with two main peaks and then Garbh-bheinn, a Corbett. The ridge curves to the north-east, drops to a bealach and then climbs again to the final summit, Belig.

The day was already warm in the sun and we needed only tee shirts as we set off, following the track on the north side of the stream.

In the upper reaches of Coire Uaigneich we stopped for a cup of tea and a snack. A raven flew up into the corrie, filling the air with its harsh "craark, craark" call. The brief rest gave us an energy boost and we were soon making good progress up the steepening path to the most northerly of the two summits.

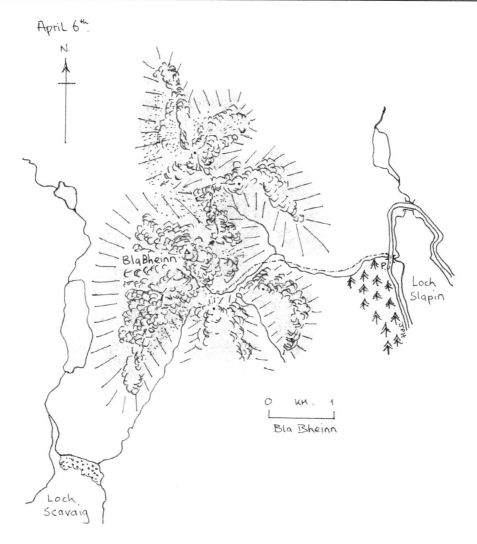

April 6th.

Bla Bheinn

After a few sections of easy scrambling we came to an area with flat rocks just on the brink of a dark chasm which cuts deeply into the mountainside. Gerry announced that it was our lunch stop and promptly set about the business of consuming his sandwiches. We were more interested in the effect that the chasm had on the mountain. A narrow window had been opened in the outcrops along its edge and through it we could see the peaks of the Red Cuillin and the massive trench of Glen Sligachan beyond. The ever-practical Morag brought us down to earth by pointing out that if we didn't eat fairly quickly, Gerry would be packed up and away again. Andrea surprised us by producing chocolate Easter eggs she had brought from Ireland.

Lunch over, we started on the steep path to the summit. The raven had been watching us and flew down to where we had sat to see whether we had left anything.

The top is a broad rocky platform and on such a fine day one of the best viewpoints on Skye. To the north are the steep hills of the Red Cuillin, the west side of Marsco steepened by glacial erosion to give it its distinctive asymmetrical shape. Glen Sligachan, its broad floor a necklace of dark blue lochans, separates the Red Cuillin range from the great curve of the Black Cuillin mountains. I looked at each peak in turn, starting with Sgurr nan Eag in the south and ending with the spire of Sgurr nan Gillian in the north, thankful for a week of fine weather which had given us perfect conditions to explore this iconic range.

We moved to the northern edge of the little summit plateau and looked at the narrow pinnacled ridge which runs from Sgurr nan Each to Clach Glas and then steeply up to where we stood. Gerry said that it was one of the classic scrambling routes of the Cuillins.

I felt a mixture of emotions as we began our descent, sad that this was the last of the week but grateful that all had gone so well. We went down at an easy pace, enjoying the landscape before us with its characteristic mixture of water and mountain. The lower reaches of the Allt na Dunaiche are clothed with birch woods. The bright sun lightened the pale grey trunks which perfectly complemented the fine red branches and twigs. I began to hear the strange, sad cries of curlews. The tide was out now and the birds were feeding on the wide flats of Loch Slapin.

curlews.

Back at the cars we shook hands with Gerry, thanking him for his efforts to ensure that our week was one where we enjoyed his precious Cuillins to the full. He replied that we were not to dare to take the good weather home with us and wished us safe journeys.

That evening, after a hearty meal of herby tomato soup and venison, we sat with the last of the Talisker as the pink faded from the sky.

7/4/07

Home from the hill

Up early the next morning, I ate my breakfast as the sun rose behind the Red Cuillin, suffusing the sky with a warm glow. The light was reflected on the water of the sea loch, which was an unrippled sheet of molten gold. A dog-like head moved slowly across the flat calm water, creating a golden wake. I left my breakfast and went to the balcony where I watched the otter as its curved back rolled into a dive, creating droplets of water like hot metal. Morag came up to the common room and I called her over. The otter reappeared and we watched as it dived for its breakfast.

7/4/7 Otter at dawn on Loch Harport
JPH

Oystercatchers strutted along the shore, stabbing their red beaks into the orange seaweed. Suddenly they took off together, flying over the loch and making their "peep, peep, peep" calls.

Oystercatchers.
JPH.

We loaded the car and started our journey home. Skye was bathed in early morning sunshine and the mountains looked remarkable. Gerry was to have his wish, we were not taking the sunshine home with us.

Loch Alsh was like a mirror, perfectly reflecting the gilded mountains which rose from the far shore. The bright spring light illuminated the most picturesque of landscapes as I drove through Glen Shiel, past Loch Garry, down Glen Mor, under Ben Nevis, through Glen Coe, across Rannoch Moor and through the Trossachs to the Highland Line. I felt privileged to live in this beautiful country.

Home again, I collected my wife, Jane and drove to Edinburgh to see the newest edition to the family again. She had been looking after the other two boys and helping with the baby so was a lot more tired than I was. On the return journey, Jane asked what I had enjoyed most about the Skye trip.

"The good companionship," I replied.

"What about the Inaccessible Pinnacle?"

"A real thrill but not as difficult as I thought it might be."

"Well, you've done the hardest thing, it should be all downhill from here."

I felt sad at the thought that the highlight of my exploration of the Highland mountains was over. As it turned out, I needn't have worried, there were greater challenges and many more wonderful days to come.

And this our life, exempt from public haunt,
Finds tongues in trees, books in the running brooks,
Sermons in stones, and good in everything.
I would not change it.

As You Like It
William Shakespeare

Acknowledgements

Thanks to my wife, Jane, for her patience in coping with the many demands of our large family while I was "away roving those hills again" and for the proofing and critical reading of this book. To my sister, Helen, for her encouragement and corrections. To Dorothy Graham who cast a line from Inverpolly and hooked first Tom then me. To Jim and Jean Muir for befriending the Harlands and providing Rose Cottage as our base in wonderful Coigach and Assynt. To the Jolly Boys for all the fun and adventures.

Three of my walking companions deserve special thanks. Morag for her stoicism and boundless enthusiasm through good days and tough days. Struan for his friendship and time spent teaching me mountaineering skills. And my son Tom who, through his humour and love for the Highlands, turns all walks into great occasions.

I am grateful to the Scottish Mountaineering Club for their excellent guides and the Ordnance Survey for maps the people of the British Isles should be proud of.

Finally, climbing the mountains featured in the book was far easier than writing it. I needed technical support and it was kindly provided by the ever-patient Chris.

Index of mountains and hills featured in Book 1

Munros in bold text